"Few scholars, if any, can communicate with as much clarity and precision as Mark Strauss. His *Acts and Paul's Letters: The Gospel to the Ends of the Earth* serves as a parade example for this. As expected from anything Strauss writes, the book balances concise accessibility with meticulous research, adroitly bridging the gap between the scholarly world and the beginning student or lay reader."

—**Joseph R. Dodson**, The Craig L. Blomberg Chair of New Testament, Denver Seminary

"Mark Strauss has gifted professors and students with a valuable resource on Acts and Paul's letters. Strauss provides lucid discussions of introductory matters such as the authorship and dating of books, while also supplying gospel connections, application for readers, interactive questions, and study resources for more advanced study. His sidebars bring the reader up to speed on important historical and interpretive conundrums such as the speeches in Acts and the interpretation of *pistis Christou*. A perfect book for college and seminary courses!"

—**Miguel Echevarría**, associate professor of New Testament and Greek, Southeastern Baptist Theological Seminary

"Mark Strauss's survey of Acts and the letters of Paul is a very welcome addition to our stock of textbooks. It is well written, rooted in wide research, and succinct. This last descriptor is particularly welcome. In an era of bloat, with books getting longer and longer, it becomes difficult to find textbooks both deep enough and short enough to suit classroom use. This volume admirably qualifies on both counts."

—**Douglas Moo,** professor of New Testament emeritus, Wheaton College

"This is a useful textbook written for undergraduate students who desire an evangelical basis for understanding this portion of the New Testament. One of the strengths of the textbook is its clarity: it helps students understand the New Testament as a unit. Finally, the connections in particular will help students to be better readers of Scripture and to reflect on how Scripture applies to their lives."

—**Osvaldo Padilla**, professor of divinity, Beeson Divinity School, Samford University

"Look no further for a concise yet comprehensive survey of Acts and Paul's letters. This volume provides a clear overview of the context and content of these New Testament books, along with up-to-date discussions on relevant historical backgrounds and modern debates concerning specific books and passages. Both beginning and advanced students will find this guide helpful as they explore the significance of these biblical texts for their own lives."

—**David W. Pao**, dean and professor of New Testament, Trinity Evangelical Divinity School

"The perfect textbook for a basic intro course on the second half of the New Testament (Acts and Paul). I needed a textbook that could be consumed by students in a more compressed time framework. A skilled guide, well-versed in all critical issues, Strauss leads students on a quick tour of these New Testament books, keeping the focus on content. Strauss helps students see the forest while not getting too focused on specific trees."

—**E. Randolph Richards**, research professor of New Testament, Palm Beach Atlantic University

"Strauss has provided an excellent introduction to Acts and the Pauline epistles. This textbook is substantive but also short enough to allow supplemental resources. Its emphasis lies on what the text says, but also connects the book to the Old Testament, the gospel, and our own life. It will serve students for years to come."

—**Patrick Schreiner**, associate professor of New Testament and biblical theology, Midwestern Baptist Theological Seminary

"In this book, Mark Strauss gives the church and Christian students a great gift. This well-organized and clearly written book opens up the book of Acts and Paul's letters for readers. It will be a fine textbook for an introductory university or college course, or an adult Sunday school class. Dr. Strauss knows the biblical material well and illuminates it in engagement with relevant scholarship. He also includes 'life connections' which help readers reflect on the way Scripture speaks to their lives today. Warmly recommended!"

—**Steve Walton**, senior research fellow and professor of New Testament, Trinity College, Bristol, United Kingdom

ACTS AND PAUL'S LETTERS

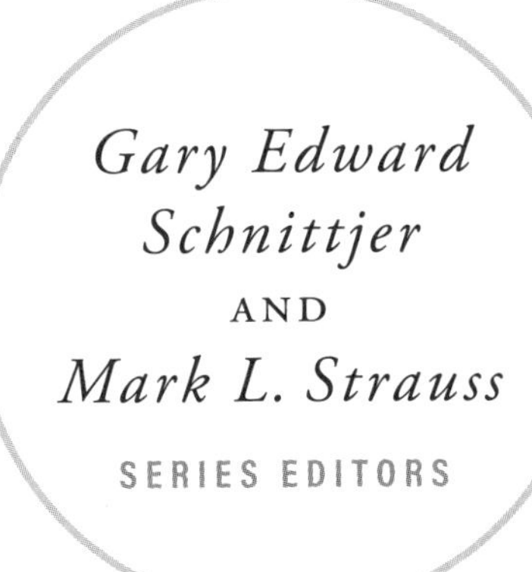

ACTS AND PAUL'S LETTERS

THE GOSPEL TO THE ENDS OF THE EARTH

Mark L. Strauss

Acts and Paul's Letters: The Gospel to the Ends of the Earth

Published by B&H Academic®
Brentwood, Tennessee

ISBN: 978-1-0877-4750-7

Dewey Decimal Classification: 227
Subject Heading: BIBLE. N.T. ACTS--COMMENTARIES \ BIBLE. N.T. EPISTLES--COMMENTARIES \ PAUL, APOSTLE

Cover design by Derek Thornton / Notch Design and Emily Keafer Lambright. Cover images: *Saint Paul Preaching on Mars Hill and Paul Writing His Epistles in Prison*, published 1886. Sourced from benoitb/iStock.

Printed in the United States of America

30 29 28 27 26 25 VP 1 2 3 4 5 6 7 8 9 10

CONTENTS

ABBREVIATIONS

AB	Anchor Bible
ABD	*Anchor Bible Dictionary.* Edited by David Noel Freedman. 6 vols. New York: Doubleday, 1992.
Ant.	*Jewish Antiquities* (Josephus)
ANTC	Abingdon New Testament Commentaries
BDAG	*A Greek-English Lexicon of the New Testament and Other Early Christian Literature.* W. Baur, F. W. Danker, W. F. Arndt, F. W. Gingrich. 3rd ed. Chicago: University of Chicago Press, 2000.
BECNT	Baker Exegetical Commentary on the New Testament
BECS	Brill Exegetical Commentary Series
BJRL	*Bulletin of the John Rylands Library*
BTB	*Biblical Theology Bulletin*
c.	century
ca.	*circa* (approximate date)
CBQ	*Catholic Biblical Quarterly*
CBR	*Currents in Biblical Research*
CEB	Common English Bible
cf.	cross reference
chap(s).	chapter(s)
CNTUOT	*Commentary on the New Testament Use of the Old Testament.* Edited by G. K. Beale and D. A. Carson. Grand Rapids: Baker, 2007.
CSB	Christian Standard Bible

DNTUOT	*Dictionary of the New Testament Use of the Old Testament*. Edited by G. K. Beale, D. A. Carson, Benjamin L. Gladd, and Andrew David Naselli. Grand Rapids: Baker, 2023.
ed.	edition
ed(s).	editor(s)
e.g.	*exempli gratia* (= "for example")
ESV	English Standard Version
et al.	*et alia* (= "and others")
EuroJTh	*European Journal of Theology*
Gk	Greek
HTR	*The Harvard Theological Review*
ICC	International Critical Commentary
idem	Latin for "the same," meaning the same author as the previous reference
i.e.	*id est* (= "that is")
IVPNTC	IVP New Testament Commentary
JSNT	*Journal for the Study of the New Testament*
JSNTSup	Journal for the Study of the New Testament Supplement Series
JTS	*Journal of Theological Studies*
J.W.	*Jewish Wars* (Josephus)
KJV	King James Version
LNTS	Library of New Testament Studies
LXX	The Septuagint, the Greek translation of the Hebrew Scriptures
m.	Mishnah
ms(s)	manuscript(s)
MT	Masoretic Text
n.	note
NA^{28}	*Novum Testamentum Graece*. 28th edition. Edited by B. Aland et al.
NAC	New American Commentary
NCBC	New Cambridge Bible Commentary
NCCS	New Covenant Commentary Series
NET	New English Translation
NIBC	New International Biblical Commentary
NICNT	New International Commentary on the New Testament
NICOT	New International Commentary on the Old Testament
NIGTC	New International Greek Testament Commentary
NIV	New International Version

NIVAC	NIV Application Commentary
NLT	New Living Translation (Second Edition)
NovT	*Novum Testamentum*
NRSV	New Revised Standard Version (1989)
NRSVue	New Revised Standard Version Updated Edition (2021)
NSBT	New Studies in Biblical Theology
NT	New Testament
NTS	*New Testament Studies*
OT	Old Testament
OTP	*Old Testament Pseudepigrapha*. Edited by J. H. Charlesworth. 2 vols. Garden City, NY: Doubleday, 1983.
p., pp.	page, pages
par(s).	parallel(s), referring parallel passages in the Synoptic Gospels
PNTC	Pillar New Testament Commentary
SBLDS	Society of Biblical Literature Dissertation Series
SGBC	The Story of God Bible Commentary
SJT	*Scottish Journal of Theology*
SP	Sacra Pagina
TDNT	*Theological Dictionary of the New Testament*. Edited by G. Kittel and G. Friedrich. Translated by G. W. Bromiley. 10 vols. Grand Rapids: Eerdmans, 1964–76.
TNTC	Tyndale New Testament Commentaries
tr.	translated by
TTCS	Teach the Text Commentary Series
TynBul	*Tyndale Bulletin*
v., vv.	verse, verses
vs.	versus
vol(s).	volume(s)
WBC	Word Biblical Commentary
WTJ	*Westminster Theological Journal*
ZIBBC	*Zondervan Illustrated Bible Backgrounds Commentary*. Edited by Clinton E. Arnold. 4 vols. Grand Rapids: Zondervan, 2002.
ZECNT	Zondervan Exegetical Commentary on the New Testament

A NOTE TO PROFESSORS FROM THE EDITORS

The textbooks in the Scripture Connections series feature somewhat shorter page counts than many traditional survey texts. Professors in traditional courses can use these textbooks to provide room in their courses for other targeted readings.

Professors teaching courses in more concise formats can assign the entire textbook. In sum, the short page count is meant to offer maximal flexibility in course design. Professors who adopt this book as a required text are welcome to access its supplemental professor's materials at no cost. Please go to https://bhacademic.bhpublishinggroup.com/requests/.

Gary Edward Schnittjer, editor of Old Testament
Mark L. Strauss, editor of New Testament

1

Introduction

This textbook covers some of the most exciting and momentous events in human history. The book of Acts recounts the birth of the church of Jesus Christ and its remarkable spread throughout the Mediterranean world. For Christian believers, this period marks the arrival of God's final salvation, the transition from the Old Testament age of promise to the New Testament age of fulfillment. Next to Jesus Christ, the apostle Paul was the most influential figure of the early Christian movement and its greatest theologian, and so his letters provide an interpretive commentary on the events that unfold in Acts.

Yet before even starting a book on Acts and the letters of Paul, I feel like I need to apologize for its format. By beginning with Acts, we are starting in the middle of a story! This is because the Gospel of Luke and the book of Acts are widely regarded as *two volumes of a single work*, commonly referred to as "Luke-Acts."[1] Together they form a literary and theological masterpiece, telling the good news of Jesus's life, death, resurrection, and ascension and continuing with the proclamation of Jesus's message by his followers from Jerusalem to the ends of the earth. Various themes that are

[1] See especially the pioneering work of H. J. Cadbury, *The Making of Luke-Acts* (New York: MacMillan, 1927). For recent discussion see Darrell L. Bock, *A Theology of Luke-Acts* (Grand Rapids: Zondervan, 2012), 55–61. For a dissenting perspective, see Mikeal C. Parsons and Richard I. Pervo, *Rethinking the Unity of Luke and Acts* (Minneapolis: Fortress, 1993).

introduced in the Gospel of Luke do not reach their narrative conclusion until the book of Acts.[2] Skipping the Gospel and starting with Acts is like picking up a great novel and reading from the middle onwards.[3]

From another perspective, however, reading Acts with the letters of Paul makes perfect sense. Acts provides the historical setting for these letters. It recounts Paul's dramatic conversion on the road to Damascus (Acts 9) and his subsequent missionary journeys (Acts 13–28), during which most of his letters were written. Acts thus serves as a companion volume for the letters of Paul.

The solution to this quandary is to read Acts as both history and theology.[4] On the one hand, the book provides important historical data concerning the growth of the early Christian movement and the life and letters of Paul. On the other hand, together with Luke's Gospel, Acts is *narrative theology*, using elements such as plot, characters, and settings to guide readers toward a better understanding of Jesus and the Christian movement. In this chapter we will provide an introduction to Luke-Acts and an introduction to the life and letters of the apostle Paul.

Introduction to Luke-Acts

Author

It is widely acknowledged today that the same author wrote both the Gospel of Luke and the book of Acts. At the beginning of Acts, the author refers to "the first narrative" that he wrote (1:1)—a clear reference to the Gospel (Luke 1:1–4). Both volumes begin with an address to Theophilus (Luke 1:3; Acts 1:1). Most significantly, both share common vocabulary, literary style, and theological themes.

A variety of early church sources identify this author as Luke, a physician and missionary associate of the apostle Paul.[5] There is also internal evidence that the

---

[2] See, for example, the promise of the enthronement of the Messiah (Luke 1:32–35), fulfilled in Acts 2:30–36, and the promise of the salvation of the Gentiles (Luke 2:32; Acts 13:47), fulfilled in Acts 13–28.

[3] Whether Luke considered Acts to be a "sequel" to the Gospel or the second half of a single work (Luke-Acts), it seems clear that he viewed Acts as the continuation of the story that began in the Gospel.

[4] See I. H. Marshall, *Luke: Historian and Theologian*, 3rd ed. (Exeter: Paternoster, 1993).

[5] Second-century sources include Justin Martyr (*Dialogue with Trypho* 103.9; *ca.* 160 CE); Irenaeus (*Against Heresies* 3.1.1; 3.14.1; *ca.* 175–195); and the Muratorian Fragment, an early list of New Testament books (ca. 170–80). Our earliest extant manuscript of Luke's Gospel, 𝔓[75] (*ca.* 200–225), includes the title "The Gospel According to Luke." See Martin

author traveled with Paul. Several times in Acts, the author refers to Paul and his associates in the first-person plural "we" (16:10–17; 20:5–16; 21:1–18; 27:1–28:16). These "we" sections indicate that the author was with Paul during various parts of his missionary journeys and that he accompanied Paul to Rome following the apostle's arrest. From the Pauline letters, we know that Luke was both a traveling companion of Paul and was with him in Rome (Col 4:7–17; Phlm 23, 24; 2 Tim 4:11). Though Paul had many associates, when this internal evidence is placed beside the strong and unanimous external evidence, there seems no reason to doubt Luke was the author.

We know very little about Luke from the New Testament. Paul calls him "the dearly loved physician" (Col 4:14) and his "coworker" (Phlm 24), indicating that he was a member of the medical profession as well as Paul's missionary associate.[6] Some ancient traditions claim Luke was from Antioch, in Syria.[7] Another possibility is that he was from Philippi, in Macedonia (the Macedonian man in Paul's vision of Acts 16:9?), since the first "we" section begins in Acts 16:8–10 as Paul is about to cross from Troas to Macedonia. The "we" section then resumes several years later in Philippi (20:5–6).

Luke was likely a Gentile (a non-Jew). In Col 4:10–14 Paul first names his Jewish coworkers ("these alone of the circumcised") and then his Gentile ones, identifying Luke with the latter. This may help to explain Luke's keen interest in showing that the good news of salvation promised to Israel was all along intended for all people everywhere.[8]

Recipient(s)

Both the Gospel of Luke and the book of Acts are addressed to a certain "Theophilus" (Luke 1:3; Acts 1:1). The name means "lover of God," suggesting to some that it is a general address to all Christians. Yet Luke's address to him as "most excellent" suggests Luke is writing to an individual, and one of high social standing. One creative suggestion is that he was the government official overseeing Paul's trial in Rome. Yet this cannot explain the length of Luke-Acts. If Luke wrote primarily to defend Paul, why would

---

Hengel, "The Titles of the Gospels," in *Studies in the Gospel of Mark* (Philadelphia: Fortress, 1985), 64–84, 66.

[6] On the nature of ancient physicians and medicine, see Laura M. Zucconi, *Ancient Medicine: From Mesopotamia to Rome* (Grand Rapids: Eerdmans, 2019).

[7] Eusebius, *Ecclesiastical History* 3.4.6–7. The Anti-Marcionite Prologue to Luke (second to fourth c.) begins, "Luke is a Syrian of Antioch, a doctor by profession." See R. G. Heard, "The Old Gospel Prologues," *JTS* 6, no. 1 (1955): 1–16; quote from 7.

[8] See Stephen G. Wilson, *The Gentiles and the Gentile Mission in Luke-Acts* (Cambridge: University, 1973).

he include so much extraneous material related to Jesus and the early church?[9] Others have suggested that Theophilus was a recent convert needing instruction or that he was a curious and inquiring unbeliever. Either of these could fit Luke's statement that he is writing so that Theophilus would know "the certainty of the things about which you have been instructed" (Luke 1:4). Whether a recent convert or an interested inquirer, the formal style suggests the dedication to a patron who is sponsoring the work (see Ancient Connections 1.1: Comparing Prologues). In any case, while the book is addressed (or dedicated) to Theophilus, it is no doubt intended for a wider audience. The nature of this audience will be discussed under the message and purpose of Luke-Acts below.

Date

The dates of both Luke and Acts are uncertain. The earliest possible date for Acts is around 62 CE, since the book ends with Paul in prison in Rome about this time. Advocates for an early date claim that if Paul had been martyred or released, Luke would certainly have reported this. But this is not conclusive. Luke may have had theological reasons for ending his story with Paul's arrival in Rome. Reaching the capital of the Gentile world confirms that the gospel is advancing relentlessly towards its goal of "the ends of the earth" (Acts 1:8). Two main arguments have been made for a date in the 70s or 80s. First is Luke's greater detail than Mark concerning the destruction of Jerusalem in 70 CE, suggesting the Gospel was written after this event (cf. Luke 17:31; 19:43–44; 21:20–24). But this is not decisive unless we discount the possibility of predictive prophecy. In any case, Luke's description of the siege is still quite general and could have been written by anyone familiar with ancient warfare.[10] A more convincing argument for a later date of Acts is Luke's probable use of Mark as a source for his Gospel.[11] If Mark were written shortly before or shortly after the events of 70 CE, as most scholars affirm,[12] Luke and Acts must have come later,

[9] As C. K. Barrett famously put it: "No Roman official would ever have filtered out so much of what to him would be theological and ecclesiastical rubbish in order to reach so tiny a grain of relevant apology." Barrett, *Luke the Historian in Recent Study* (London: Epworth, 1961), 63.

[10] C. H. Dodd claimed Luke 21 was modeled after the fall of Jerusalem in the sixth century BCE. "The Fall of Jerusalem and the 'Abomination of Desolation,'" in C. H. Dodd, ed., *More New Testament Studies* (Manchester: Manchester University Press, 1968), 69–83.

[11] For a convincing defense of Markan priority, see Robert H. Stein, *Studying the Synoptic Gospels: Origin and Interpretation*, 2nd ed. (Grand Rapids: Baker, 2001), 49–96.

[12] See Mark L. Strauss, *Mark*, ZECNT (Grand Rapids: Zondervan, 2014), 37–39. This is especially based on the narrative aside, "let the reader understand," in Mark 13:14, an apparent allusion to the siege of Jerusalem.

sometime from the 70s to the 90s. If Mark were written in the mid-50s, however, a date for Acts in the 60s remains a possibility. Fortunately, a firm conclusion on date does not affect the central message of the text.

ANCIENT CONNECTIONS 1.1: COMPARING PROLOGUES

In the prologues to his two-volume apologetic work, *Against Apion*, the Jewish historian Josephus (late first c. CE) has some interesting parallels to the prologues of Luke and Acts, including reference to his previous work, a dedication to an individual of high social status, and a claim to be defending the antiquity and legitimacy of his religious tradition.

Josephus, *Against Apion* 1.1[13]	Josephus, *Against Apion* 2.1	Luke 1:1–4 (NIV)	Acts 1:1–2 (NIV)
In my history of our *Antiquities*, most excellent Epaphroditus, I have, I think, made sufficiently clear to any who may peruse that work the extreme antiquity of our Jewish race, the purity of the original stock, and the manner in which it established itself in the country which we occupy today.	In the first volume of this work, my most esteemed Epaphroditus, I demonstrated the antiquity of our race, corroborating my statements by the writings of Phoenicians, Chaldaeans, and Egyptians, besides citing as witnesses numerous Greek historians . . . I shall now proceed to refute the rest of the authors who have attacked us.	Many have undertaken to draw up an account of the things that have been fulfilled among us, just as they were handed down to us by those who from the first were eyewitnesses and servants of the word. With this in mind, since I myself have carefully investigated everything from the beginning, I too decided to write an orderly account for you, most excellent Theophilus, so that you may know the certainty of the things you have been taught.	In my former book, Theophilus, I wrote about all that Jesus began to do and to teach until the day he was taken up to heaven, after giving instructions through the Holy Spirit to the apostles he had chosen.

[13] Quotations from H. St. J. Thackeray, *Josephus: The Life; Against Apion*, Loeb Classical Library (Cambridge, MA: Harvard University Press, 1926), 163, 293.

Message

As noted above, Luke's Gospel prologue says he is writing "so that you [Theophilus] may know the certainty of the things about which you have been instructed" (Luke 1:4). Luke's purpose is therefore *to confirm the truth of the gospel message*. Luke does this especially by identifying his narrative as the continuation of a larger story that began in the Hebrew Scriptures.

This metanarrative (overarching story) of Scripture begins in Genesis with the creation of the heavens and the earth by the one true God (Gen 1–2). As the pinnacle of that creation, God made human beings in his own image to be caretakers of his creation and to live in loving relationship with their creator (Gen 1:26–2:25). But rather than honoring God, they turned away and rejected his authority (Gen 3). They became fallen creatures, sinful, and alienated from him. But in his love, God was not finished with his people. He launched a plan to rescue his creation and bring human beings back into a right relationship with himself. He did this through a series of promises made in the context of covenant relationships. He made a covenant with Abraham, promising to raise up from him a great nation, through whom all nations in the world would be blessed (Gen 12:1–3). He delivered that nation, Israel, from bondage in Egypt and made a covenant with them through Moses at Mount Sinai. They would be his people, and he would be their God (Exod 19:3–6). Later, God raised up David to be their king and promised David that one of his descendants would reign forever on his throne (2 Sam 7:12–16). The Hebrew prophets expanded on this theme, predicting that God would one day raise up a king from David's line, who would establish an eternal kingdom and would reign in justice and righteousness over a renewed creation (Isa 9:1–7; 11:1–10; Jer 23:5–6; Ezek 34:23–24). During the latter part of the Second Temple period (ca. 200 BCE–70 CE) this figure came to be known as the "Messiah" (*Mashiach*, Hebrew for "Anointed One"), translated into Greek as *christos*, the "Christ."

Luke picks up the story at the dawn of this promised salvation. The age of promise is becoming the age of fulfillment. Throughout his two-volume work, he seeks to show that God's great plan of salvation has come to fulfillment in the birth, life, death, resurrection, and ascension of Jesus the Messiah and in the growth and expansion of his church, the new covenant people of God.

The Gospel of Luke

Luke begins his Gospel with an account of the birth of the Messiah (Luke 1:5–2:52). The characters in the story are faithful Jews, longing for God's promised salvation

(Luke 1:6, 28; 2:25, 36–37). The angel Gabriel announces to a virgin named Mary that her son will be the promised king from David's line who "will reign over the house of Jacob forever" (Luke 1:33). Mary sings a song of praise in response, saying that God "has helped his servant Israel, remembering his mercy to Abraham and his descendants forever" (1:54–55). At the birth of John the Baptist, John's father Zechariah prophesies that, in Jesus, God "has raised up a horn of salvation in the house of his servant David, just as he spoke by the mouth of his holy prophets." He has "remembered his holy covenant—the oath that he swore to our father Abraham" (1:69–73). The angels announce to the shepherds, "Today in the city of David a Savior was born for you, who is the Messiah, the Lord" (2:11). An elderly prophet named Simeon predicts that Jesus will be not just "glory to your people Israel," but also "a light for revelation to the Gentiles" (2:32; cf. Isa 49:6). As promised to Abraham and affirmed by the prophet Isaiah, God's salvation is not just for the Jews; it is for all people everywhere. Luke is intent to show that this is not a new story or a new religion. It is the continuation of Israel's story and the fulfillment of God's promises in the Hebrew Scriptures.

But there are some surprising twists in the story. Simeon also predicts that "this child is destined to cause the fall and rise of many in Israel and to be a sign that will be opposed" (Luke 2:34–35). The coming of the Messiah will provoke division and opposition within Israel. Sure enough, while Jesus's teaching and miracles confirm he is indeed the Messiah, he faces opposition from his own people. This opposition is previewed in his first public appearance in the Gospel, a sermon in his hometown synagogue at Nazareth (Luke 4:16–30). Jesus reads from Isa 61:1–2 and announces that the Spirit of God has "anointed" him to bring good news to the poor and freedom to the oppressed. While the townspeople are at first thrilled—thinking they are the poor and oppressed—Jesus illustrates his sermon by telling stories of God's love for Gentiles! The people of Nazareth are outraged and attempt to murder him by throwing him off a cliff.

This episode turns out to be a preview of the Gospel story. When Jesus eventually comes to Jerusalem at Passover, he is betrayed by one of his own disciples, arrested by the authorities, tried before the Roman governor, and executed by crucifixion (Luke 19–23). The claim that he is the Messiah from David's line seems to be negated. But in the greatest plot twist of all time, defeat turns to victory as Jesus rises from the dead and appears to his disciples (Luke 24). Before ascending to heaven, he teaches them that all along it was God's plan, predicted in Scripture, that "the Messiah will suffer and rise from the dead the third day, and repentance for forgiveness of sins will be proclaimed in his name to all the nations, beginning at Jerusalem" (Luke 24:46–47).

The Book of Acts

If the Gospel of Luke concerns the fulfillment of God's promised salvation through the life, death, and resurrection of the Messiah, the book of Acts concerns the continuation of Jesus's work as the message of salvation goes out to the whole world. In Acts 1, following his resurrection and before ascending to heaven, Jesus tells his disciples that they will receive power from the Holy Spirit to be his witnesses "in Jerusalem, and in all Judea and Samaria, and to the ends of the earth" (Acts 1:8). The rest of Acts is essentially an account of how the church, in the power of the Spirit, accomplishes this task. The central theme throughout is the *unstoppable progress of the gospel.* No matter what obstacles the church faces, the gospel advances, confirming that the Jesus movement is indeed the work of God. This expansion of the gospel is both geographical and ethnic. It expands outward from *Jerusalem* to the *ends of the earth* and from its *Jewish* roots to the *Gentile* world.

Luke's purpose in writing this two-volume work may therefore be identified as apologetic and legitimizing. Apologetic means defending the message of the church against those who are attacking it. Legitimizing means confirmation for Jesus's followers that they are the true heirs of God's promises to Israel.[14] The church of Luke's day is under attack. Its Jewish opponents are claiming that Jesus cannot be the Messiah since he suffered and died as a criminal and the promised kingdom did not arrive. How could Jesus be the fulfillment of God's promises to Israel if many Jews were rejecting the gospel and the church was increasingly becoming a Gentile entity? Gentile opponents claimed the church was a threat to the *Pax Romana*, the stability and prosperity brought by the Roman empire.

Luke answers these challenges through his narrative theology: (1) The suffering of the Messiah was all along predicted in Scripture and was part of God's plan. (2) The kingdom has been inaugurated, since Jesus the Messiah has assumed his messianic reign at the right hand of God. (3) This is confirmed by the pouring out of the Spirit on the day of Pentecost, which is also in fulfillment of Scripture. (4) The rejection of the gospel message by many in Israel is part of that nation's long history as a stubborn and resistant people. (5) The entrance of the Gentiles into the church was all along part of God's plan and was also predicted in Scripture. (6) Paul, the apostle to the Gentiles, is not a renegade Jew nor an insurrectionist. He is absolutely faithful to his Jewish heritage and a law-abiding Roman citizen, fulfilling God's plan to take

---

14 See Mark L. Strauss, "The Purpose of Luke-Acts: Reaching a Consensus," in *New Testament Theology in Light of the Church's Mission: Essays in Honor of I. Howard Marshall*, eds. Ray Van Neste and Jon Laansma (Eugene, OR: Cascade, 2011), 135–50.

the message of salvation to the ends of the earth. We will see these and related themes in the next chapter, as we go through an interpretive overview of the book of Acts.

Introduction to the Life and Letters of the Apostle Paul

The main character of the second half of the book of Acts is Saul of Tarsus, known more commonly as Paul the apostle. In addition to his leading role in Acts, thirteen letters in the New Testament are attributed to Paul. In this section we will introduce his life and letters.

Paul's Background

We have two main sources for biographical information about Paul, his own letters and Luke's account of his ministry in Acts. Some scholars have doubted the latter's reliability and built a biography based solely on Paul's undisputed letters.[15] This is unnecessarily skeptical, however, especially in light of the author's close connection with Paul (indicated by the "we" sections of Acts) and the evidence that Luke was a generally reliable historian.[16] While all historical sources must be read critically and with caution, information about Paul found only in Acts (such as his Roman citizenship and his tutelage by Gamaliel) may be assumed to be true unless there is good evidence to the contrary.

So what do we know about Paul? (1) First, *he was a faithful Jew*. In his letter to the church in Philippi, Paul defends his own Jewish credentials against those of his opponents, describing himself as "circumcised on the eighth day, of the people of Israel, of the tribe of Benjamin, a Hebrew of Hebrews" (Phil 3:5 NIV; cf. 2 Cor 11:22). While all of these point to his authentic Jewish identity, they appear to run from general to specific. Paul's circumcision identifies him as obedient to God's covenant with Abraham (Gen 17:11). "Of the people of Israel" identifies him as one of God's chosen people through the covenant established at Mt. Sinai (Exod 19:5). His specific tribal identity as a Benjamite (cf. Rom 11:1) is impressive since many first century Jews could not trace their tribal ancestry. A "Hebrew of Hebrews" (NIV) probably means a Hebrew born of Hebrew parents. Hebrew may here be contrasted with "Hellenist"

[15] For the disputed and undisputed letters, see "Pseudepigraphy and the Letters of Paul," later in this chapter.

[16] See especially Colin J. Hemer, *The Book of Acts in the Setting of Hellenistic History*, ed. Conrad H. Gempf (Winona Lake, IN: Eisenbrauns, 1990).

(see Acts 6:1; 9:29), the former meaning someone whose family spoke Aramaic and used the Hebrew Scriptures in synagogue worship. Hellenists were Greek-speaking Jews from the diaspora who used the Septuagint in their synagogues.

(2) *He was a Pharisee, zealous for the law.* The Pharisees were a sect or party within Judaism whose most distinctive characteristic was their strict adherence to the law of Moses, both the written law and the oral traditions passed down from their ancestors (see Ancient Connections 1.2: Who Were the Pharisees?). Paul identifies himself as a Pharisee and connects this to his faithfulness to the law (". . . regarding the law, a Pharisee . . . regarding the righteousness that is in the law, blameless," Phil 3:5–6; cf. Acts 23:6; 26:5). Paul further claims to have graduated at the top of his class: "I advanced in Judaism beyond many contemporaries among my people, because I was extremely zealous for the traditions of my ancestors" (Gal 1:14). Paul is similarly quoted in Acts as saying he was educated in Jerusalem as a disciple of Gamaliel (Acts 21:39; 22:3), one of the leading Pharisees of his day (cf. Acts 5:34–40; see Ancient Connections 2.1: Rabbi Gamaliel).

ANCIENT CONNECTIONS 1.2: WHO WERE THE PHARISEES?

The Pharisees likely arose as a party in the second century BCE, during the period of Jewish independence known as the Hasmonean Dynasty (167–63 BCE). The Hasmoneans were the descendants of the Jewish priestly family that had led the Maccabean revolt against the Syrian king Antiochus Epiphanes IV (167–164 BCE).[17] While the revolt was launched in opposition to the forced Hellenization of the Jews, the later Hasmonean rulers ironically tended to adopt Hellenistic ways common to the aristocratic classes. They were subsequently opposed by conservative groups like the Pharisees and the Essenes.[18] The chief rivals to the Pharisees were the Sadducees, who likely arose from the aristocratic supporters of the Hasmoneans.

---

[17] Hasmon was likely an ancestor of the priest Mattathias, who together with his five sons launched the revolt (1 Macc 2). The revolt gets its name from the nickname *Maccabeus* (Aramaic for "hammer") given to Mattathias's son Judas (1 Macc 3:1), apparently because of his prowess in battle.

[18] The word "Pharisee" probably originally meant "separatist" and represented their opposition to the ruling dynasty.

(3) *He was a passionate persecutor of the church.* Paul's zeal for the law and for his ancestral faith caused him to defend it at all costs. In Gal 1:13 he writes, "For you have heard about my former way of life in Judaism: I intensely persecuted God's church and tried to destroy it" (cf. 1 Cor 15:9; Phil 3:6). From Paul's perspective, Jesus was a false messiah and his followers were dangerous heretics. Especially alarming was how quickly this sect was growing in Jerusalem and beyond. In Acts 7:58–8:1, Saul is presented as a supportive observer of those who executed Stephen, the first Christian martyr. Saul then launched his own campaign against the followers of Jesus (Acts 8:3; 9:1–2).

(4) *He was familiar with Gentiles and Gentile ways.* Although a thoroughly orthodox Jew, Paul was born in Tarsus, the capital of the Roman province of Cilicia (modern southeastern Turkey) and a major center of trade and culture. It is unclear how Paul's family came to Tarsus, but the early church father Jerome claims they were taken there following the Roman destruction of their hometown of Gischala in Galilee.[19] Whether resettled there as refugees or sold as slaves, they must have recovered a measure of wealth and status in time. Paul seems proud of his Cilician heritage, referring to himself as a "citizen of an important city" (Acts 21:39; cf. 22:3). He no doubt grew up speaking Greek as well as Hebrew and Aramaic and was exposed to Greek culture and Gentile ways. While there is no evidence Paul had a classical Greek education, his letters demonstrate a proficiency in the common (*koinē*) Greek of his day. He occasionally quotes Greek poets and philosophers.[20]

(5) *He was a Roman citizen.* Even more surprising, several times in Acts Paul identifies himself as a Roman citizen (Acts 16:37; 22:25–29; cf. 25:9–12). Roman citizenship was a privileged status not available to everyone. It was either inherited or conferred as an honor for exceptional service to Rome. Paul claims he was born a citizen (Acts 22:27), but it is not known how his father or grandfather attained it.[21] Citizenship could not technically be purchased, but bribery was sometimes used to "buy" it (likely the case in Acts 22:28). With citizenship came a variety of privileges

---

[19] Jerome, *Commentary on Philemon* vv. 23–24; *De Viris Illustribus* 5.

[20] For example, in 1 Cor 15:33 Paul quotes Menander (*Thais* 218; fourth c. BCE): "Bad company corrupts good morals." In Titus 1:12–13, Paul quotes a Cretan writer, usually identified either as Epimenides (sixth c. BCE) or Callimachus (*Hymn to Zeus* 8; third c. BCE): "Cretans are always liars, evil brutes, lazy gluttons." Finally, in Acts 17:28, Luke quotes Paul again quoting Epimenides, "For in him we live and move and have our being," and Aratus (*Phaenomena* 5; third c. BCE): "We are also his offspring."

[21] F. F. Bruce, *Paul: Apostle of the Heart Set Free* (Grand Rapids: Eerdmans, 1977), 37n3, mentions a suggestion made to him that a family of tentmakers like Saul's could have provided invaluable service to the Roman legions.

and protections under Roman law, including exemption from flogging, the right to a fair trial, no summary execution, and the right to a final appeal to Caesar.[22]

Paul never mentions his citizenship in his letters, but this is not surprising. He appeals to it in Acts only with secular authorities and only to be exonerated from or to escape unjust beatings (16:37; 22:25–29) or to avoid being sent into a dangerous situation (25:9–12). When writing to Christians, such status was of little importance. It is our heavenly citizenship that counts (Phil 3:20). Worldly status like Roman citizenship was valuable only as a means to an end: to more effectively proclaim the gospel (cf. 1 Cor 9:19–23).

ANCIENT CONNECTIONS 1.3: SAUL OR PAUL? WHAT'S IN A NAME?

As a "Hebrew born of Hebrews," Paul would have been given a Jewish name at birth, which was "Saul." This was the name of the first king of Israel, who, like Paul, was from the tribe of Benjamin (1 Sam 9:1–2; Acts 13:21; Rom 11:1; Phil 3:5). Roman citizens typically had three names, a first name (*praenomen*), an ancestral name (*nomen*), and a family name (*cognomen*), by which they would be commonly referred. *Paulus* (Latin for "small") was Paul's *cognomen*. It may have been chosen because of its verbal similarity to "Saul."[23] We don't know his first name or his middle (ancestral) name. If we knew the latter, we might be able to discern more about his family background, since citizens often took the *nomen* of the founder of their clan or the benefactor who granted them citizenship.

Luke's switch from "Saul" to "Paul" begins in Acts 13:9 ("But Saul—also called Paul . . .") and continues for the rest of Acts. Paul may have begun using his Roman name when his ministry focus turned toward the Gentiles.

The Damascus Road Christophany

The most significant and transformative event in Paul's life was his encounter with the resurrected Jesus on the road to Damascus. The details of this encounter will be surveyed in the next chapter in the context of Luke's narrative theology. Here we discuss its significance for Paul and his theology.

---

[22] Bruce, *Paul*, 37–39.

[23] Bruce, 38.

This event turned Paul's life upside down and radically changed his perspective. From the church's greatest opponent and persecutor, he became its greatest advocate. Paul's theological understanding was transformed. If Jesus was indeed the Messiah, then Paul's persecution of Christians had actually been in opposition to the work of God. If his identity as a "blameless" Jew obedient to law (Phil 3:6) had not brought him salvation, then salvation must come through allegiance to something other than his Jewish identity or allegiance to the law, namely, through faith in Jesus the Messiah. If Torah observance was not the means of salvation, then the sacrificial system set out in the law could not provide forgiveness of sins. This opened the way for understanding Jesus's death as a sacrifice for sins (Rom 3:21). While Saul had previously viewed Christ's crucifixion as evidence that he was cursed by God (Deut 21:23), he now came to believe Christ took the curse of *our* sins upon himself as a sacrifice of atonement (Gal 3:13–14).[24]

Paul's Commission: Apostle to the Gentiles

Paul repeatedly asserts that his commission from God was specifically to preach to the Gentiles,[25] and he connects this calling to his Damascus-road experience (Gal 1:16; Acts 9:15; 22:21; 26:17). Yet this does not mean he avoided preaching to the Jews. In fact, according to Acts, whenever Paul entered a city, he would go first to the synagogue and preach there (Acts 13:14; 14:1; 17:2, 10, 17; 18:4, 19; 19:8). In part this was expediency. The Jews were the recipients of God's covenant promises and so were able to understand and respond to Paul's message of the arrival of salvation through Jesus the Messiah. Furthermore, present in the synagogues were many "God-fearers," Gentiles who had come to believe in the one true God of Israel but had not yet become full proselytes to Judaism.[26] These God-fearers were among the most receptive to the apostle's message.

But Paul's proclamation "first to the Jew" (Rom 1:16) was more than a matter of convenience. It related to Israel's role as "a kingdom of priests and my holy nation" (Exod 19:6). Israel was meant to mediate God's presence and to reveal his glory to the world, to be "a light to the nations" (Isa 42:6; cf. 49:6). In preaching the good news

---

[24] For the claim that Paul's theology arose primarily from his Damascus-road experience, see Seyoon Kim, *The Origin of Paul's Gospel* (Eerdmans, 1982).

[25] Rom 1:5, 13–16; 11:13; 15:16; Gal 1:16; 2:2, 7–10; Eph 3:1, 6, 8; 1 Tim 2:7; 2 Tim 4:17; Acts 9:15; 22:21; 26:17.

[26] For evidence in the first century of Gentile "God-fearers," see Irina Levinskaya, *The Book of Acts in Its Diaspora Setting* (Grand Rapids: Eerdmans, 1996).

first to the Jews, Paul was fulfilling his obligation to call the righteous remnant of Israel to fulfill their role as the people of God.

Israel's role as God's mediator to the Gentiles was not a new idea. More than 700 years earlier, the prophet Isaiah had predicted that "in the last days" the nations would stream to Jerusalem to know and worship God (Isa 2:2–4). The Messiah from the line of David would reign in righteousness and justice (Isa 9:1–7; 11:1–5, 10). There would be a return to paradise, when "The wolf will dwell with the lamb, and the leopard will lie down with the goat. . . . They will not harm or destroy each other . . . for the land will be as full of the knowledge of the LORD as the sea is filled with water" (Isa 11:6–9). For Isaiah, as for Paul, the coming of the Messiah, the salvation of the Gentiles, and the restoration of creation were all essential components of God's plan of salvation.

Paul's Letters in the Context of First-Century Letter Writing

We know a great deal about Paul's theology because of the letters he wrote.[27] But why did Paul write letters? The answer is related to the nature of his ministry, which was an itinerant one. Paul would enter a city or town and preach the gospel there, calling people to faith in Jesus and gathering those who responded together as an "assembly" or "congregation" (the meaning of *ekklēsia* = "church"). They would generally meet together in homes. Paul would stay until persecution forced him to leave or until leaders could be appointed and the church could stand on its own. He would then move on, trusting God's Spirit to guide the leadership. Paul would maintain contact with the church through his disciples and/or through letters, which were meant to be a substitute for his presence. In this regard we should think of Paul's letters as community correspondence rather than private letters. They were meant to be read aloud when the church gathered in community, as though Paul was present and speaking. This context is evident in passages like Col 4:16, where Paul writes, "After this letter has been read at your gathering, have it read also in the church of the Laodiceans; and see that you also read the letter from Laodicea." This public nature of the letters is true even of those addressed primarily to individuals (1 and 2 Timothy; Titus; Philemon), which would likely also be read aloud in the church.

---

[27] See Stanley K Stowers, *Letter Writing in Greco-Roman Antiquity* (Philadelphia: Westminster, 1986); E. Randolph Richards, *Paul and First Century Letter Writing* (Downers Grove, IL: InterVarsity, 2004); Jeffrey A. D. Weima, *Paul the Ancient Letter Writer: An Introduction to Epistolary Analysis* (Grand Rapids: Baker, 2016).

This community nature of the letters applies not only to their reception but also to their composition. Paul often names his companions as cowriters, identifying his letter as from "Paul, Silas and Timothy" (1 Thess 1:1), "Paul . . . and our brother Sosthenes" (1 Cor 1:1), "Paul and Timothy . . ." (Phil 1:1), and so on. While Paul is clearly the primary author, these others were likely present with him helping to craft and edit the letter.[28]

Because of the technical expertise involved, most people did not themselves write but used secretaries to draft their letters. Wealthy people often had slaves who were trained for this. Anyone, however, could hire a secretary in the marketplace. A secretary's role might vary depending on the circumstances. They might be the primary author, composing the letter with a few general instructions from the client. Or, at the opposite extreme, they might serve essentially as a stenographer, writing verbatim the words that were dictated. We know that Paul commonly used secretaries because of comments in his letters. At the end of Romans, the secretary suddenly appears, identifying himself in a list of greetings: "I, Tertius, who wrote this letter, greet you in the Lord" (Rom 16:22). At the end of Galatians, Paul notes the change in handwriting style as he "signs" the letter by writing its conclusion: "Look at what large letters I use as I write to you in my own handwriting" (Gal 6:11).

Sending a letter was also more complicated than it is today. While Rome had an imperial postal service, it was only for government correspondence. Private citizens either needed to send the letter with someone already traveling to the destination or else to commission someone specifically for this task. Tychicus is likely the one carrying the letter to the Colossians, since Paul says, "Tychicus . . . will tell you all the news about me. I have sent him to you for this very purpose" (Col 4:7–8). Phoebe, a deacon from the church of Cenchreae, appears to be the one carrying Paul's letter to the Romans (Rom 16:1–2). Paul commends her as a great benefactor for him and the church and encourages the church to give her any support they can.

The format of Greco-Roman letters is quite consistent, and Paul's letters follow a common format:

Author, with self-identification and/or titles. For example, "Paul, a servant of Christ Jesus, called as an apostle and set apart for the gospel of God" (Rom 1:1). Paul tends to emphasize his authority as an apostle in letters to churches where this authority was being challenged (Gal 1:1; 1 Cor 1:1; 2 Cor 1:1) and in churches he had not yet

[28] This plurality of authors/editors might also help to explain some of the stylistic differences among Paul's letters. See the discussion of pseudepigraphy later in this chapter.

visited (e.g., Rom 1:1; Col 1:1), but he omits the title in letters to churches with which he is particularly close (e.g., Phil 1:1; 1 Thess 1:1; 2 Thess 1:1; cf. Phlm 1).

Recipients. For example, "To the church of God at Corinth . . ." (1 Cor 1:2). "To Philemon our dear friend and coworker . . ." (Phlm 1).

Greetings. "Grace to you and peace" is Paul's typical greeting. "Grace" (*charis*), meaning God's gift of salvation, is Paul's Christianized version of the standard Greek greeting *chairein* meaning "greetings," "hello," or more literally "joy to you" (see Acts 15:23; 23:26; Jas 1:1). "Peace" (*eirēnē*) is the Greek equivalent of the Hebrew *shalom*, which also served as a common greeting among Jews. So while "grace and peace" is Paul's common way to say "hello," this two-fold greeting carries theological significance: God's gift of grace (*charis*) through Jesus Christ brings the peace (*eirēnē*) that reconciles us to God.

Thanksgiving and/or prayer. Greco-Roman letters often include wishes for good health or prayers to a god for the recipient. Paul commonly includes a prayer or thanksgiving for the recipients, often introducing themes that will become important in the letter.

Body of the Letter. By Greco-Roman standards, Paul's letters are extraordinarily long. A typical personal letter at the time was less than 100 words long. Paul's shortest letter (Philemon) is 335 words, and his longest (Romans) is 7,114 words. This dwarfs even the great letter writers of antiquity. Cicero's (106–43 BCE) average letter is only 295 words, and his longest is 2,530 words. Seneca's (ca. 4 BCE–65 CE) longest letter is 4,134 words, and his letters average about 995 words.[29]

Conclusion. Paul's conclusion often includes final instructions, greetings to common friends, and final benedictions.

Pseudepigraphy and the Letters of Paul

While thirteen letters in the NT are attributed to Paul, scholars are divided as to whether all were written by him. Pseudepigraphy or pseudonymity was quite common in the Greco-Roman world. There are examples from Greek, Roman, Jewish, and early Christian literature. Jewish pseudepigraphic works appear in a variety of genres, including apocalyptic literature (e.g., 1 Enoch, 2 Baruch, 4 Ezra, Apocalypse of Adam), testaments or "last words" of great figures (e.g., Testament of the Twelve Patriarchs, Testament of Moses), poetry and wisdom (e.g., Psalms of Solomon,

[29] Statistics from David B. Capes, Rodney Reeves, and E. Randolph Richards, *Rediscovering Paul: An Introduction to His World, Letters and Theology* (Downers Grove, IL: IVP Academic, 2017), 113.

Wisdom of Solomon), and letters (e.g., Letter of Aristeas, Letter of Jeremiah). Early Christian pseudepigrapha include apocalypses (e.g., Apocalypse of Peter, Apocalypse of Paul), infancy narratives (e.g., Protoevangelium of James, Infancy Gospel of Thomas), gospels (e.g., Gospel of Peter, Gospel of Thomas), acts (e.g., Acts of Paul), and letters (e.g., 3 Corinthians).

While everyone acknowledges the reality of pseudepigraphy, debate rages over whether the New Testament contains any pseudepigraphic works. Of the thirteen letters attributed to Paul, seven are almost universally regarded as authentic. These include Romans, 1 Corinthians, 2 Corinthians, Galatians, Philippians, 1 Thessalonians, and Philemon. Six are "disputed," including (from least to most disputed) Colossians, 2 Thessalonians, Ephesians, and the Pastoral Epistles (1 Timothy, 2 Timothy, Titus). These are sometimes called "Deutero-Pauline," meaning written by a disciple of Paul or in the second generation after Paul.

Undisputed Letters		Sometimes Disputed	Widely Disputed
Romans	Philippians	Colossians	1 and 2 Timothy
1 Corinthians	1 Thessalonians	2 Thessalonians	Titus
2 Corinthians	Philemon	Ephesians	
Galatians			

Some scholars claim that pseudepigraphy was an accepted literary genre in the early church. A disciple might write to honor the legacy of a mentor or to apply their teaching to a new situation. Readers would know that the work was pseudonymous but still view it as authoritative and even inspired by God. Richard Bauckham writes of 2 Peter, "The pseudepigraphal device is therefore not a fraudulent means of claiming apostolic authority, but embodies a claim to be a faithful mediator of the apostolic message."[30] Others, however, reject the claim that pseudepigraphy was considered legitimate, pointing to examples where works were rejected when it was discovered that they were pseudonymous. The Muratorian Canon rejects the Epistle to the Alexandrians and the Epistle to the Laodiceans, since both were "forged in Paul's name" (Mur. Can. 64–65). Similarly, according to Tertullian, the elder from Asia Minor who wrote The Acts of Paul and Thecla was deposed from ministry, even though he claimed to have written out of his love for the apostle (Tertullian, *de Baptismo* 17).[31]

---

[30] Richard J. Bauckham, *Jude, 2 Peter,* WBC (Grand Rapids: Zondervan, 1983), 161–62.

[31] D. A. Carson and Douglas J. Moo, *An Introduction to the New Testament*, 2nd ed. (Grand Rapids: Zondervan, 2005), 342–44.

In our introductions to the disputed letters, we will (very briefly) summarize the evidence for and against Pauline authorship. The conclusion reached in each case is that it is *reasonable* to affirm that Paul was the author. We should acknowledge, however, that while this conclusion is based on an analysis of the evidence, it is also influenced by belief in the divine inspiration of Scripture and an authoritative canon. These beliefs, in turn, are affirmed through the testimony of the Holy Spirit, both individually and corporately in the church. It would be disingenuous to claim that our conclusions on historicity come solely from an "objective" analysis of the data. All of us approach the Bible with certain presuppositions concerning its nature and authority, and these presuppositions inevitably affect the conclusions we reach.

SIDEBAR 1.1: A CHRONOLOGY OF PAUL'S LIFE AND LETTERS

(dates are approximate)

Events	Date	References
Jesus born in Bethlehem; raised in Nazareth Saul born in Tarsus of Cilicia; educated in Jerusalem	6–4 BCE 1–10? CE	Luke 1–2 Matthew 1–2 Acts 21:39; 22:3
Jesus's public ministry, death, and resurrection	27–30 or 30–33	Matthew 3 28; Mark 1–16; Luke 3–24; John 1–21
Martyrdom of Stephen in Jerusalem; Saul persecutes the church	32–35	Gal 1:13–14; Acts 7:58–8:3; 22:4–5; 26:9–11
Saul encounters the resurrected Jesus on the road to Damascus	32–35	Gal 1:15–16; Acts 9:1–19; 22:6–21; 26:12–18
Saul's time in Damascus and Arabia	35–38	Gal 1:17
Saul visits Jerusalem and meets Peter and James	35–38	Gal 1:18–19; Acts 9:26–29
Saul's ministry in and around Syria and Cilicia	37–45	Gal 1:21; Acts 9:30–31
Execution of James; Peter's escape from jail; death of Herod Agrippa I	44	Acts 12:1–19 Acts 12:19b–24
Barnabas brings Saul to serve with him in Antioch	43–47	Acts 11:25–26

Events	Date	References
Barnabas and Saul's visit to Jerusalem with famine aid	43–47	Acts 11:27–30; Gal 2:1–10?
Paul's "First" Missionary Journey to Cyprus and Galatia; churches started in Pisidian Antioch, Iconium, Lystra, and Derbe	46–48	Acts 13–14
Paul writes **Galatians**, probably from Antioch, Syria	48–50	
Jerusalem Council	48–50	Acts 15; Gal 2:1–10?
Paul's "Second" Missionary Journey Paul and Silas revisit the Galatian churches; Timothy joins them in Lystra Churches started in Macedonia (Philippi, Thessalonica, Berea) and Achaia (Corinth) Paul meets Priscilla and Aquila in Corinth	48–52	Acts 15:36–18:22
Paul writes **1 & 2 Thessalonians,** probably from Corinth	51–52	
Proconsul Gallio dismisses case brought against Paul by Corinthian Jewish group	51–52	Acts 18:12–17
Paul Returns to Jerusalem, then Antioch in Syria	52	
Paul's "Third" Missionary Journey; three years in Ephesus	52–57	Acts 18:23–21:16
Paul writes **1 Corinthians** from Ephesus	55–56	
Paul writes **2 Corinthians** from Macedonia	56–57	
Paul writes **Romans** from Corinth	57–58	
Paul's return to Jerusalem with support from his Gentile churches	57–58	Acts 20:1–21:17
Paul's arrest in Jerusalem; appearance before the Sanhedrin	57–58	Acts 21:27–23:11
Paul's incarceration in Caesarea for two years; appearances before Felix, Festus, and Herod Agrippa II and Bernice	57–59	Acts 23:12–26:32

Events	Date	References
Paul's voyage to Rome under guard; shipwreck in Malta	59–60	Acts 27:1–28:16
House arrest in Rome	60–62	Acts 28:17–31
Paul writes the prison letters from Rome: **Ephesians, Philippians, Colossians, Philemon** (possibly from Caesarea [57–59] or from Ephesus [51–54])	60–62	
After Acts:		
Release from house arrest and subsequent travels; perhaps an outreach to Spain	62–67	Phil 1:25 Rom 15:23, 28
Paul writes **1 Timothy** to Timothy in Ephesus, probably from Macedonia	62–65	1 Tim 1:3
Paul writes to **Titus** in Crete, perhaps from Nicopolis	62–65	Titus 1:5; 3:12
Paul arrested (probably in Troas); final imprisonment in Rome	64–67	2 Tim 4:6–8, 13
Paul writes **2 Timothy** from the Mamertine prison in Rome	64–67	
Paul's execution in Rome	64–67	

Notice that in this chart the letters of Paul are identified chronologically in the context of Paul's ministry. This is the order we will follow when surveying the letters of Paul (chaps. 3–12).

Interactive Questions

1. Why do scholars use the designation "Luke-Acts"?

2. From what two perspectives should the book of Acts be read?

3. What is the evidence that Luke wrote this two-volume work? What are the "we" sections of Acts?

4. Who might Theophilus have been? What are some options?

5. What is Luke's stated purpose in the Gospel prologue? How does Luke fulfill this purpose?

6. How does the birth narrative in Luke's Gospel develop the theme of God's promises about to be fulfilled?

7. What are the key aspects of Paul's background that prepared him for his ministry as an apostle of Jesus Christ?

8. How did the Damascus-road Christophany change Paul's perspective?

9. What was Paul's commission? What patterns did he follow to fulfill this commission?

10. How do Paul's letters compare with other Greco-Roman letters of his day?

Study Resources

Luke–Acts

Bartholomew, Craig G., Joel B. Green, and Anthony C. Thiselton, eds. *Reading Luke: Interpretation, Reflection, Formation.* Grand Rapids: Zondervan, 2006.

Beers, Holly. *The Followers of Jesus as the 'Servant': Luke's Isaianic Model for the Disciples in Luke-Acts.* LNTS. New York: T & T Clark, 2015.

Bock, Darrell L. *A Theology of Luke-Acts: God's Promised Program for All Nations.* Edited by Andreas J. Köstenberger. Biblical Theology of the New Testament. Grand Rapids: Zondervan, 2012.

Conzelmann, Hans. *The Theology of St. Luke.* London: Faber, 1961.

Green, Joel, ed. *Methods for Luke.* Cambridge: Cambridge University Press, 2010.

Harris, Sarah. *The Davidic Shepherd King in the Lukan Narrative.* LNTS. New York: T&T Clark, 2015.

Keck, Leander E., and J. Louis Martyn, eds. *Studies in Luke-Acts: Essays Presented in Honor of Paul Schubert.* Nashville: Abingdon, 1966.

Kee, Howard Clark. *Good News to the Ends of the Earth: The Theology of Acts.* Philadelphia: Trinity Press International, 1990.

Marshall, I. Howard. *Luke: Historian and Theologian.* 3rd ed. Exeter: Paternoster, 1993.

———, and David Peterson, eds. *Witness to the Gospel: The Theology of Acts.* Grand Rapids: Eerdmans, 1998.

Porter, Stanley E., and Ron C. Fay, eds. *Luke–Acts in Modern Interpretation.* Grand Rapids: Kregel, 2022.

Strauss, Mark L. *The Davidic Messiah in Luke-Acts. The Promise and Its Fulfillment in Lukan Christology.* JSNTSup 110. Sheffield, UK: Sheffield Academic Press, 1995.

Tannehill, Robert. *The Narrative Unity of Luke-Acts.* 2 vols. Minneapolis: Fortress, 1986–1990.

Paul the Apostle

Barrett. C. K. *Paul: An Introduction to His Thought.* Louisville, KY: Westminster John Knox, 1994.

Bruce, F. F. *Paul: Apostle of the Heart Set Free.* Grand Rapids: Eerdmans, 1977.

Capes, David B., Rodney Reeves, and E. Randolph Richards. *Rediscovering Paul: An Introduction to His World, Letters and Theology.* 2nd ed. Downers Grove, IL: IVP Academic, 2017.

Dunn, J. D. G. *The Theology of Paul the Apostle.* Grand Rapids: Eerdmans, 1998.

Gorman, Michael J. *Apostle of the Crucified Lord: A Theological Introduction to Paul and His Letters.* Grand Rapids: Eerdmans, 2004.

Gupta, Nijay K., Erin M. Heim, and Scot McKnight. *The State of Pauline Studies. A Survey of Recent Research.* Grand Rapids: Baker, 2024.

Hawthorne, Gerald F., Ralph P. Martin, and Daniel G. Reid, eds. *Dictionary of Paul and His Letters: A Compendium of Contemporary Scholarship.* Downers Grove, IL: InterVarsity, 1993.

Longenecker, Bruce W., and Todd D. Still. *Thinking through Paul: A Survey of His Life, Letters, and Theology.* Grand Rapids: Zondervan, 2014.

McKnight, Scot, gen. ed., *Dictionary of Paul and His Letters. A Compendium of Contemporary Scholarship.* 2nd ed. Downers Grove, IL: InterVarsity, 2023.

Moo, Douglas J. *A Theology of Paul and His Letters: The Gift of the New Realm in Christ.* BTNT. Grand Rapids: Zondervan, 2021.

Schreiner, Thomas R. *Paul, Apostle of God's Glory in Christ: A Pauline Theology.* Downers Grove, IL: InterVarsity, 2001.

Wright, N. T. *Paul and the Faithfulness of God.* 2 vols. Minneapolis: Fortress, 2013.

———. *Paul: A Biography.* New York: HarperOne, 2018.

2

The Book of Acts

But you will receive power when the Holy Spirit has come on you,
and you will be my witnesses in Jerusalem, in all Judea and Samaria,
and to the ends of the earth.

—Acts 1:8

Outline

I. Introduction (1:1–26)
   A. Jesus Commissions the Apostles and Ascends to Heaven (1:1–11)
   B. Matthias Chosen to Replace Judas (1:12–26)
II. The Gospel to Jerusalem (2:1–8:1a)
   A. The Coming of the Spirit at Pentecost (2:1–41)
   B. Characteristics of the Growing Church (2:42–47)
   C. The Healing of a Crippled Man and the Beginning of Persecution (3:1–4:31)
   D. The Community of Sharing and the Purity of the Church (4:32–5:11)
   E. More Signs & Wonders and More Persecution; Gamaliel's Counsel (5:12–42)
   F. The Problem of the Hellenistic Widows and the Choice of the Seven (6:1–7)
   G. The Ministry and Martyrdom of Stephen (6:8–8:1a)

III. The Witness of the Gospel to Judea, Samaria, and Beyond (8:1b–12:25)
   A. The Persecution and Scattering of the Church (8:1b–3)
   B. Philip's Ministry to Samaria (8:4–25)
   C. Philip's Ministry to an Ethiopian Eunuch (8:26–40)
   D. Saul Encounters the Risen Lord (9:1–31)
   E. Peter's Ministry in Lydda and Joppa (9:32–43)
   F. The Conversion of Gentiles: Cornelius and His Household (10:1–11:18)
   G. Gentile Outreach in the Church at Antioch (11:19–30)
   H. The Jerusalem Church Persecuted by Herod Agrippa I (12:1–25)
IV. The Gospel to the Ends of the Earth: The Journeys of Paul (13:1–28:31)
   A. First Journey: The Gospel to Cyprus and Galatia (13:1–14:28)
   B. The Jerusalem Council (15:1–35)
   C. Second Journey: The Gospel to Macedonia and Achaia (15:36–18:22)
   D. Third Journey: The Gospel to Asia Minor (18:23; 19:1–21:16)
   E. Fourth Journey: Paul's Arrest, Imprisonment, and Journey to Rome (21:17–28:31)

Interpretive Overview

In the last chapter, we discussed introductory issues related to Luke and Acts, including author, date, and purpose in writing. We suggested that Luke wrote his two-volume work to confirm the truth of the gospel message by demonstrating the continuity between God's promises to Israel and the fulfillment of those promises through the coming of Jesus the Messiah and in the growth and expansion of his church. In this chapter we will provide an interpretive overview of Acts, tracing the theme of the unstoppable progress of the gospel from its Jewish roots in Jerusalem outward to the ends of the earth.

Introduction (1:1–26)

Jesus Commissions the Apostles and Ascends to Heaven (1:1–11)

Luke begins by linking this volume to his "first narrative" (the Gospel of Luke), which was about "all that Jesus began to do and teach until the day he was taken up" (1:1–2). Acts is the continuation of God's saving actions through Jesus the Messiah. "Taken up" refers to the ascension, which Luke briefly described at the end of the Gospel

(Luke 24:50–53) but now recounts in greater detail. We learn here that the event occurred not immediately after the resurrection (as might be presumed from Luke 24:50), but forty days later, and that during this period Jesus gave further proof of his resurrection (v. 3), taught the disciples concerning the kingdom of God (vv. 3, 6–7), and prepared them for the coming of the Holy Spirit (vv. 4–5, 8).

Jesus's teaching about the kingdom of God clarifies the mission of the church in Acts. The disciples express traditional Jewish expectations by asking, "Lord, are you restoring the kingdom to Israel at this time?" (1:6). The kingdom for them meant the restoration of Israel's political sovereignty. Jesus redirects them toward their present mission. They are not to be concerned with the timetable the Father has set. Their task is to bear witness to the message of salvation: "But you will receive power when the Holy Spirit has come on you, and you will be my witnesses in Jerusalem, in all Judea and Samaria, and to the ends of the earth" (v. 8). This verse may be viewed as both the central *theme* and the *outline* of Acts. Thematically, it points to the agents, their agency, and their agenda. As Jesus's agents, the disciples' role is to be "witnesses," testifying to his mission and message. Their agency will come from the Holy Spirit, who will empower and guide them, and their agenda will be to cross cultural and geographical boundaries to take the message of salvation to the ends of the earth.

The book may be outlined to reflect this outward expansion, from Jerusalem (chaps. 1–7), to Judea and Samaria (chaps. 8–12), to the ends of the earth (chaps. 13–28). Though the book ends in Rome—more like the "center" of the Gentile world than its end—for Luke the story is not over but ongoing, and Rome is an appropriate launching point for the gospel's continued growth.

Following this commission, Jesus is "taken up" to heaven and two angels appear, assuring the disciples that Jesus will return just as he departed (1:9–11). The ascension has special theological significance for Luke.[1] It indicates Jesus's vindication as Messiah and his enthronement as Lord and Messiah at the right hand of God, from

---

[1] See the key narrative turning point at Luke 9:51, where being "taken up" is shorthand for the salvation Jesus will accomplish in Jerusalem through his death, resurrection, and ascension. On the importance of the ascension for Luke, see David K. Bryant and David W. Pao, eds., *Ascent into Heaven in Luke–Acts: New Explorations of Luke's Narrative Hinge* (Minneapolis: Fortress, 2016).

where he pours out the eschatological Spirit.[2] While the ascension and the pouring out of the Spirit inaugurate the kingdom, the return of the Son of Man will be its consummation.[3] Luke notes that the ascension took place on the Mount of Olives (1:12), the hill overlooking Jerusalem from the east. This is appropriate since the prophet Zechariah identified the Mount of Olives as the place of Yahweh's return in the final eschatological conflict (Zech 14:4).

Following the ascension, the disciples return to Jerusalem, where they "were continually united in prayer" (1:14). Just as Jesus's prayer life was a major theme in Luke's Gospel,[4] so the prayers of the church in Acts indicate their complete dependence on God.[5] Luke provides a list of the eleven remaining apostles (1:13), setting the stage for the replacement of Judas that follows.

Matthias Chosen to Replace Judas (1:12–26)

Peter takes the lead in organizing the replacement of Judas, who died a gruesome death after betraying Jesus (1:18–19).[6] Why was a successor necessary? Peter refers to the fulfillment of Ps 69:25 and 109:8, "Let his dwelling become desolate; let no one live in it; and let someone else take his position" (Acts 1:20). But the number also carries symbolic significance, representing the twelve tribes of Israel and so the restored people of God (see Luke 22:28–30). The two qualifications are (1) to have been present for the whole of Jesus's ministry (from Jesus's baptism to his ascension) and (2) to be a witness of Jesus's resurrection (1:22). This is because the Twelve will serve as guardians of the Jesus tradition, giving testimony of his life, death, and resurrection (cf. "the apostles' teaching"; 2:42). Two nominations are made for Judas's position, Joseph Barsabbas and Matthias. Lots are cast and Matthias is chosen.[7]

---

[2] See Luke 1:32–33; 22:69; Acts 2:16–21, 24–36; 5:31; 7:55. Prophecies cited as fulfilled include Joel 2:28–32; Pss 16:8–11; 110:1–2.

[3] Dan 7:13–14; Luke 9:26; 12:8, 40; 17:24–30; 18:8; 21:27, 36.

[4] Luke refers to Jesus's prayers nine times in his Gospel (3:21; 5:16; 6:12; 9:18, 28–29; 11:1; 22:41; 23:34, 46). Jesus repeatedly exhorts his disciples to pray (6:28; 10:2; 11:1–2, 9–13; 22:40), tells parables about prayer (11:5–8; 18:1–8, 9–14), and prays for Peter (22:31, 32). Most of these passages are unique to Luke.

[5] Acts 1:14, 24; 2:42; 3:1; 4:24–31; 7:59–60; 9:11; 10:4, 9, 31; 12:5, 12; 13:3; 14:23; 16:13, 16, 25; 20:36; 21:5.

[6] For a comparison of Luke's account here with Matthew's report of Judas's suicide, see Craig S. Keener, *Acts*, NCBC (Cambridge: Cambridge University Press, 2020), 116–19.

[7] Casting lots, something like throwing dice, was a common method of discerning God's will in ancient Israel (see 1 Chr 24:5, 31; 25:8; 26:13–16). Proverbs 16:33 says, "The lot is cast into the lap, but its every decision is from the LORD."

The Gospel to Jerusalem (2:1–8:1a)

The Coming of the Spirit at Pentecost (2:1–41)

Jesus's pouring out of the Spirit on the Day of Pentecost marks the promised end-time coming of the Holy Spirit.[8] While the water-baptism of John was preparation for the kingdom (Luke 3:3; Acts 13:24; 19:4), Jesus's Spirit-baptism marks its inauguration and the beginning of the "last days" (see 2:17). The miracle of tongues is also a reversal of the events at the Tower of Babel (Gen 11:1–9). While Babel divided people into diverse nations and languages, the Spirit now unites those from many nations to form one new people of God.

The event begins with a noise like a "violent rushing wind" (indicating the presence of the Holy Spirit) and "tongues like flames of fire" resting on each believer (2:2–3). The disciples are filled with the Holy Spirit and begin speaking in "different tongues," presumably languages they had never learned. Jews from throughout the Roman world visiting Jerusalem for the festival are astonished. Some accuse the disciples of being drunk. Peter again takes the lead, refuting the claim of drunkenness and identifying the event as the eschatological outpouring of the Spirit predicted by the prophet Joel (Acts 2:16–21, citing Joel 2:28–32).

Peter's argument in his sermon runs as follows: (1) Jesus's miracles confirm that he was sent from God (2:22). (2) Though godless people put Jesus to death, this was all part of God's plan (2:23). (3) This was confirmed when God raised Jesus from the dead (2:24), fulfilling the prophecy of David in Ps 16:8–11: "You will not abandon me in Hades or allow your holy one to see decay" (2:25–28). (4) This prophecy could not refer to David since David died, and his tomb remains undisturbed (2:29–31). So, David must have been speaking of the resurrection of the Messiah (2:30–31). (5) Having been raised from the dead, Jesus is now exalted at God's right hand, as predicted of the Messiah in Ps 110:1 (2:33–35). (6) Peter's conclusion: "Therefore let all the house of Israel know with certainty that God has made this Jesus, whom you crucified, both Lord and Messiah" (2:36). The outpouring of the Spirit confirmed in the miracle of tongues proves that Jesus, the crucified one, is the Messiah, now exalted as Lord at God's right hand.

---

[8] Pentecost was one of the three great pilgrim festivals (along with Passover and the Feast of Tabernacles). It occurred seven weeks (fifty days) after Passover. The eschatological outpouring of the Spirit is predicted in the Old Testament not only in Joel 2:28–32 but also in Isa 32:15; 44:4; Jer 31:33–34; Ezek 36:26–27; 39:29.

The crowd is convicted by Peter's words and cries out, "What should we do?" Peter calls for repentance and baptism in the name of Jesus for the forgiveness of sins and reception of the Spirit (2:37–40). Throughout Acts, salvation comes through faith in Jesus for the forgiveness of sins and is accompanied by baptism and the reception of the Spirit. Over 3,000 people respond to Peter's message and are baptized (2:41).

SIDEBAR 2.1: THE SPEECHES IN ACTS

A key feature of the book of Acts is the many speeches by key characters, including Peter, Stephen, Paul, and James. There has been much discussion concerning the nature of these speeches. To what extent do they represent the actual words that were spoken on these particular occasions and to what extent are they free creations of the author of Acts?[9] Mediating positions are that they were composed by Luke but represent the gist of what was said on that occasion or that they represent the kinds of things that the speaker would likely have said on such occasions. Support for Lukan compositions is the fact that the speeches share common literary style and fit well with Luke's theological themes. Yet this could just bear witness to Luke's skills as an editor, integrating his sources seamlessly into his narrative. Support for the historicity of the speeches is the fact that their themes and theology fit well with the historical speakers. For example, the only reference to the doctrine of justification in Luke-Acts comes in a speech by the apostle Paul (Acts 13:39).[10]

Insight into Luke's approach may be found in the Greek historian Thucydides (fifth c. BCE), who described how he handled speeches in the preface to his history of the Peloponnesian War:

[9] See Martin Dibelius, "The Speeches in Acts and Ancient Historiography," in *Studies in the Acts of the Apostles*, ed. Heinrich Greeven, trans. Mary Ling (London: SCM, 1956), 138–85; F. F. Bruce, *The Speeches in the Acts of the Apostles* (London: Tyndale, 1942); Marion L. Soards, *The Speeches in Acts: Their Content, Context, and Concerns* (Louisville, KY: Westminster John Knox, 1994); Osvaldo Padilla, "The Speeches in Acts: Historicity, Theology, and Genre," in *Issues in Luke-Acts: Selected Essays*, ed. S. A. Adams and M. Pahl (Piscataway, NJ: Gorgias, 2012), 171–93; Janusz Kucicki, *The Function of the Speeches in the Acts of the Apostles* (Leiden: Brill, 2018).

[10] For parallels between the letter of James and James's words in Acts 15, see Scot McKnight, *James*, NICNT (Grand Rapids: Eerdmans, 2011), 24–25. For Pauline parallels in Paul's speech to the Ephesian elders in Acts 20, see Ben Witherington, *The Acts of the Apostles: A Socio-Rhetorical Commentary* (Grand Rapids: Eerdmans, 1997), 610.

> With reference to the speeches in this history, some were delivered before the war began, others while it was going on; some I heard myself, others I got from various quarters; it was in all cases difficult to carry them word for word in one's memory, so my habit has been to make the speakers say what was in my opinion demanded of them by the various occasions, of course, adhering as closely as possible to the general sense of what they really said.[11]

Luke may have been present on some occasions as he traveled with Paul; he could have received summaries from others who were present; or, he could have summarized the kinds of things that were said on such occasions.

Characteristics of the Growing Church (2:42–47)

Luke follows the Pentecost account with the first of several summaries concerning the church and its explosive growth:[12] (1) The *apostles' teaching* refers to their role as authoritative guardians of the story of Jesus. (2) *Fellowship* (*koinōnia*) is not merely socializing, but rather "partnership" (Phil 1:5) in the common goal of proclaiming and living out the gospel. (3) *Breaking bread* (2:42, 46–47) likely refers to a common meal (known as the *agapē*, or "love," feast) shared when the church gathered, during which the Lord's Supper was observed (cf. 1 Cor 11:20–22; Jude 12). (4) *Prayer* is constant dependence on and seeking direction from God. It is a prominent theme throughout both Luke and Acts (see comments on 1:14; 4:23–31). (5) *Wonders and signs* (2:43) represent the continuation of the miracles that characterized Jesus's ministry in Luke's Gospel (see Acts 1:1). These miracles not only confirm Jesus's identity as sent from God (2:22), but also symbolize the renewal of creation that comes with the inauguration of the kingdom (see Luke 9:2, 11; 10:9; 11:20). (6) *Holding all things in common* (2:44–45; cf. 4:32–35) was not the mandatory relinquishment of private property (see 5:4), but rather generosity that flowed from the church's identity as a family supporting its own. (7) *Praising God* (2:47a) is a major theme throughout Luke and Acts.[13] It is the church's natural response to the recognition that all these things come by God's

---

[11] Thucydides, *The Peloponnesian War* 1.22.1, trans. Richard Crawley (New York: Dutton, 1910).

[12] Cf. Acts 1:14; 2:42–27; 4:32–37; 5:12; 6:7; 9:31; 16:5; 19:20.

[13] Luke 2:20; 5:25–26; 7:16; 13:13; 17:15, 18; 18:43; 19:37; 24:53; Acts 2:47; 3:8–9; 4:21; 11:18; 13:48; 16:25; 21:20.

grace. (8) *Explosive growth*: It is "the Lord" (not human strategies) who "every day . . . added to their number those who were being saved" (2:47b). The overall picture is one of unity directed both inwardly in mutual love and support, and outwardly in boldly proclaiming the good news of salvation.

The Healing of a Crippled Man and the Beginning of Persecution (3:1–4:31)

The events in 3:1–4:31 illustrate the "wonders and signs" that characterize the growing church (2:43) and mark the beginning of escalating conflict between the disciples and the Jewish leadership in Jerusalem. The incident occurs as Peter and John are going up to the temple for the time of prayer. The temple was the center of Israel's worship and community life, and references to Jesus's followers praying, teaching, and worshiping in the temple confirm that the church did not view itself as a new religion, but as the fulfillment of God's promises to Israel (2:46; 3:1; 5:20, 25, 42; 21:26).

When a disabled beggar asks Peter and John for money, Peter responds that he has no silver or gold but will share with him what he does have: "In the name of Jesus Christ of Nazareth, get up and walk!" (3:6). The man is healed immediately, and a crowd gathers, giving Peter an opportunity to deliver another speech (3:12–26). Its main theme, like that of Pentecost, is that God's covenant promises have come to fulfillment in Jesus the Messiah. Although the people of Jerusalem rejected Jesus, God raised him from the dead and is now giving them a second chance to respond. The speech is notable for the variety of messianic titles applied to Jesus: Messiah (3:18), servant (3:13, 26), holy and righteous one (3:14), source of life (3:14), and prophet like Moses (3:22; an allusion to Deut 18:15).

The gathered crowd attracts the attention of the temple authorities, who arrest Peter and John and hold them overnight. Such opposition, however, does nothing to slow the church's explosive growth, and a short Lukan summary (4:4) notes the church has now grown to about 5,000 "men" (= family units?). The next day Peter and John are brought before the Sanhedrin, the Jewish high court, and questioned about their authority to do these things. Peter boldly states that the power to heal came from Jesus Christ of Nazareth, "whom you crucified and whom God raised from the dead" (4:10). The Sanhedrin is shocked by the audacity of these "uneducated and untrained" men but is unable to retaliate since the healed man is standing in front of them and the people are all praising God. They let Peter and John go with a warning to stop speaking about Jesus. Peter and John remain defiant, however, claiming they must obey God rather than any human authority.

When Peter and John return to their people and report what happened, the church turns to God in prayer (4:23–31). Though the church has no political power or influence, the prayer is an acknowledgement of the creator God's sovereign power and saving work through the Messiah (4:24–28) and a request for greater boldness and power (4:29–30). Drawing on imagery from Psalm 2, an enthronement psalm for the Davidic king, the prayer identifies those who crucified Jesus (Herod, Pilate, the Gentiles, and the people of Israel) as the kings, rulers, nations and people who in Ps 2:2 rebel "against the Lord and his anointed one" (NIV). God responds to the prayer both physically, as the ground is shaken, and spiritually, as the disciples are filled with the Holy Spirit to speak the Word of God more boldly (4:31).

The Community of Sharing and the Purity of the Church (4:32–5:11)

Luke provides another summary in 4:32–35,[14] this one focusing on the unity and sharing attitude of the community (cf. 2:44–45). This generous spirit is illustrated with the example of Joseph, a Levite from Cyprus, whose nickname among the apostles was Barnabas, meaning "son of encouragement."[15] Barnabas sells some land and gives the money to the apostles for distribution to the poor (4:36–37).

Barnabas's generosity and the public honor that came from it are evidently what prompted Ananias and Sapphira, a husband and wife, to make a similar contribution. These two, however, keep back part of the money for themselves. Their sin was not withholding part of the sale, but rather hypocrisy and deceit, lying to the church and to the Holy Spirit (5:3–4). Ananias and Sapphira are individually confronted by Peter and each drops dead, and "great fear came on the whole church and on all who heard these things" (5:11). Why such harsh judgment? Luke's point seems to be the extreme importance of purity for God's people during this critical point in salvation history.[16]

---

[14] Cf. Acts 2:42–47; 4:4; 4:32–37; 5:12–16; 6:7; 9:31.

[15] "Encourager" is an apt description of Barnabas's conciliatory role throughout Acts. The etymology of the word, however, is not clear. *Bar* means "son" in Aramaic, but scholars puzzle over the meaning of *nabas*.

[16] For similarly severe acts of judgment to preserve God's holiness, see Lev 10:1–5 and Josh 7:16–26.

More Signs & Wonders and More Persecution; Gamaliel's Counsel (5:12–42)

Another summary follows in 5:12–16, this one emphasizing the signs and wonders performed by the apostles (cf. 2:43). Paradoxically, Luke says, "No one else dared to join them" (5:13) but "believers were added to the Lord in increasing numbers" (5:14). The gospel both repels and compels. It is terrifying in the cost of commitment but irresistible for those seeking truth.

Perhaps no episode in Acts illustrates its main theme better than the next one. The growing popularity of the apostles provokes jealously from the high priest and the Sadducees, who arrest them. God supernaturally intervenes and an angel releases them, telling them to return to preaching in the temple. In an almost farcical scene, the full Sanhedrin solemnly assembles for the hearing and calls for the prisoners to be brought in. While the guards and gates are still in place, the prisoners have disappeared! An awkward pause follows, until a messenger arrives and reports that the disciples are again preaching in the temple. When they are again brought in, the high priest accuses them of disobeying his orders to stop preaching and accusing the Sanhedrin of murder for the death of Jesus (5:28). Peter again replies as spokesperson. To the first charge he says, "We must obey God rather than people" (5:29). To the second, he essentially says, "That's right, you killed your own Messiah, but God raised him from the dead and exalted him as ruler and Savior." The council is enraged at this accusation and threatens to put the apostles to death, until a Pharisee named Gamaliel intervenes. In a short speech, Gamaliel points to various troublemakers of the past, like Theudas and Judah the Galilean, whose actions eventually came to nothing (see Ancient Connections 2.1 and 2.2). Gamaliel concludes, "So in the present case, I tell you, stay away from these men and leave them alone. For if this plan or this work is of human origin, it will fail; but if it is of God, you will not be able to overthrow them. You may even be found fighting against God" (5:38–39).

Though Gamaliel himself does not believe the gospel, he inadvertently prophesies that *if this movement is from God, it will be unstoppable*. And this is exactly what happens throughout Acts. Despite persecution, imprisonment, beatings, stonings, demonic opposition, storms, shipwreck, and snakebite, the gospel moves relentlessly forward. This is confirmation that the Jesus movement is God's promised salvation for Israel and for the world.

ANCIENT CONNECTIONS 2.1: RABBI GAMALIEL

Gamaliel, who appears here as an esteemed member of the Sanhedrin (Acts 5:34), is identified later in Acts as Paul's teacher and mentor (Acts 21:39; 22:3). Gamaliel is also well-known in Jewish tradition as one of the most influential Pharisees of his day. The Mishnah speaks of his great piety: "When Rabban Gamaliel the elder died, the glory of Torah ceased, and purity and abstinence died" (m. Sotah 9.15). He was the grandson of the great rabbi Hillel, founder of one of two influential schools within Judaism (the other was the School of Shammai) and grandfather of Gamaliel II, who became president (*Nasi*) of the Sanhedrin after 90 CE.[17]

The Sanhedrin follows Gamaliel's counsel and chooses not to execute the apostles, instead releasing them with a flogging and a command to stop speaking about Jesus. The apostles leave not in anger or bitterness but rejoicing that they have been considered worthy to suffer for Jesus's name (5:41). And they keep on preaching (5:42).

ANCIENT CONNECTIONS 2.2: JUDAS THE GALILEAN AND OTHER REVOLUTIONARIES

The book of Acts refers to several revolutionaries who took up arms against the Roman authorities, including Theudas (5:36), Judas the Galilean (5:37), and a certain Egyptian who led 4,000 men known as the "Assassins" into the wilderness (21:38). From the Gospels we could add Barabbas, the murderer and insurrectionist released in place of Jesus (Luke 23:18–19) and the two "criminals" executed beside Jesus (Luke 23:32–43). The Jewish historian Josephus refers to a number of insurrectionists and identifies them as a fourth "philosophy" within Judaism (in addition to the Pharisees, Sadducees, and Essenes). They held theological beliefs similar to the Pharisees but would accept no one but God as their king and so actively sought to overthrow the Romans.[18] Josephus

---

[17] For more, see Bruce Chilton, "Gamaliel," in *ABD* 2:904–6.

[18] Josephus, *J.W.* 2.8.1 §118; *J.W.* 2.13.3 §§254–56; 2.13.5 §§261–63; *Ant.* 18.1.6 §23; 18.1.1 §§5–7; 20.5.1 §§97–98; 20.8.6 §§167–72; 20.8.10 §185. For more on these rebels see

identifies Judas the Galilean, who led a tax revolt against Romans in 6–7 CE, as the founder of this sect.[19] He also refers to the Egyptian mentioned in Acts 20:38, calling him a "false prophet" who led his followers from the wilderness and claimed the walls of Jerusalem would fall at his command. Instead, the Roman governor Felix (52–59 CE) arrived and defeated the rebels, although their leader escaped.[20] Josephus also refers to a certain Theudas, who claimed that at his command the Jordan River would part, and the people would walk through on dry land. The Romans sent troops who beheaded Theudas and dispersed the rebels.[21] Whether this is the same Theudas mentioned in Acts 5:36 is unclear, since Josephus dates him much later, during the governorship of Fadus (44–46 CE).

The Problem of the Hellenistic Widows and the Choice of the Seven (6:1–7)

While the church stays strong through external persecution, an internal conflict arises in chapter 6 that threatens to undermine its unity. The "Hellenistic Jews" (6:1) were Greek-speaking Jews who had relocated to Israel after living abroad. The "Hebraic Jews" were native-born, Aramaic-speaking Jews. As is often the case, immigrants have fewer connections and less influence than the established community. With the rapid growth of the church, widows from the immigrant community were being neglected in the daily distribution of food aid.

The Twelve convene a meeting to resolve the issue. Recognizing they cannot neglect their role as authoritative teachers of the Jesus tradition, they instruct the church to choose seven qualified individuals to take charge of this ministry. The seven chosen—Stephen, Philip, Prochorus, Nicanor, Timon, Parmenas, and Nicolaus—all have Greek names, perhaps suggesting that they came from the immigrant community. Stephen and Philip head the list, since their stories will be told in the episodes

---

David Rhoads, "Zealots," in *ABD* 6:1043–54; Martin Hengel, *The Zealots* (Edinburgh: T&T Clark, 1989).

19 Josephus, *J.W.* 2.8.1 §118; *Ant.* 18.1.6 §23

20 Josephus, *J.W.* 2.13.5 §§261–63; *Ant.* 20.8.6 §§167–72. Josephus puts the number of his followers at 30,000 instead of Luke's 4,000. Luke's number may be more accurate since Josephus is known to exaggerate at times.

21 Josephus, *Ant.* 20.5.1 §§97–98.

that follow. Stephen is singled out for special attention as "a man full of faith and the Holy Spirit" (6:5), setting the stage for his ministry and martyrdom.

Before moving on to the story of Stephen, Luke provides another summary of the church's remarkable growth.[22] Luke notes that "a large group of priests became obedient to the faith" (6:7), a remarkable statement considering that the strongest opposition to the church was coming from the high priest and the priestly leadership of Jerusalem. Luke's point is that the truth is breaking through even among those who most resist it.

The Ministry and Martyrdom of Stephen (6:8–8:1a)

Stephen's name means "crown" (*stephanos*),[23] which is appropriate since he was the first in the church to wear the martyr's crown. While Stephen was chosen to distribute food, he soon gained a reputation for his powerful preaching and miracles (6:8). Stephen's opponents, however, accuse him of blasphemy and speaking against the temple and the law (6:11–14).[24] Stephen's speech before the Sanhedrin is the longest in Acts, summarizing God's dealings with his people from Abraham to Solomon's building of the temple, with special emphasis on Moses and the exodus. The central theme is that Israel has consistently rejected God's messengers and now the Sanhedrin has done the same thing with Jesus. Stephen concludes: "You stiff-necked people with uncircumcised hearts and ears! You are always resisting the Holy Spirit. As your ancestors did, you do also. Which of the prophets did your ancestors not persecute? They even killed those who foretold the coming of the Righteous One, whose betrayers and murderers you have now become" (7:51–52).

Hearing Stephen's accusation, the assembly dissolves in rage. They drag Stephen out of the city and stone him to death. There are striking parallels between Stephen's death and the death of Jesus in Luke's Gospel: (1) Stephen has a vision of the Son of Man at the right hand of God (Acts 7:55–56), alluding to Ps 110:1; Jesus cites this same passage at his trial to confirm his coming vindication (Luke 23:69).[25] (2) As he is dying, Stephen commends his spirit to Jesus (Acts 7:59), just as Jesus did to the Father

[22] Cf. Acts 2:41, 47; 4:4; 5:14; 6:7; 9:31; 12:24; 16:5; 19:20; 28:31.

[23] The term refers to a wreath worn to indicate honor, status, or athletic victory, not a royal crown (*diadēma*).

[24] Luke calls them members of the Freedmen's Synagogue (6:9), probably meaning its founders were freed slaves. Like Stephen, they were Hellenistic Jews.

[25] While Ps 110:1 speaks of the Son of Man "sitting" at God's right hand, Stephen describes him as "standing," perhaps to welcome the martyr into his presence.

(Luke 23:46). (3) Stephen asks the Lord to forgive his murderers (Acts 7:60), just as Jesus did (Luke 23:34). As elsewhere throughout Acts, we see the church carrying forward "all that Jesus began to do and teach" (Acts 1:1).

Luke points out the seemingly incidental detail that the witnesses laid their clothes at the feet of a young man named Saul (7:58), adding in 8:1 that Saul gave approval to the execution. This sets the stage for Luke's transition to the missionary activities of the apostle Paul (chaps. 13–28).

The Witness of the Gospel to Judea, Samaria, and Beyond (Acts 8:1b–12:25)

The Persecution and Scattering of the Church (8:1b–3)

Stephen's execution sparks severe persecution against the church in Jerusalem, scattering "all except the apostles" throughout Judea and Samaria. The references to Jerusalem, Judea, and Samaria (8:1) recall Jesus's commission in 1:8 and hint for the reader that this persecution (like all opposition to the church in Acts) will serve to advance the gospel. The fact that the apostles are not included in the dispersion suggests that the primary targets were the Hellenistic Jewish-Christians, who were perhaps viewed as the radicals among the followers of Jesus.

Philip's Ministry to Samaria (8:4–25)

Luke notes the positive result of the persecution—"those who were scattered went on their way preaching the word" (8:4)—then illustrates this with the example of Philip, another one of the seven chosen to minister to widows.[26] Philip flees north to a city in Samaria, where his preaching and his miracles of exorcism and healing result in many Samaritans believing and receiving baptism. Luke notes in particular the case of a man named Simon, a powerful and popular local sorcerer and magician, who also believed and was baptized.

---

[26] This Philip is probably to be distinguished from Philip the apostle, one of the Twelve (Acts 1:13). See 21:8, where he is called "Philip the evangelist, who was one of the seven." I. H. Marshall, *The Acts of the Apostles: An Introduction and Commentary*, TNTC (Grand Rapids: Eerdmans, 1980), 135; J. B. Polhill, *Acts*, NAC (Nashville: Broadman, 1992), 181n13.

ANCIENT CONNECTIONS 2.3: THE SAMARITANS

The conflict between the Samaritans and the Jews has its roots in the division of Israel's united kingdom into Judah in the south and Israel in the north, following the death of King Solomon.[27] From the perspective of the Jews, the Samaritans were a half-breed and heretical race arising from intermarriage with pagan settlers brought in by the Assyrians following their conquest of Israel in 722 BCE (2 Kgs 17:24–41). The Samaritans, by contrast, viewed themselves as the true Israelites who had remained faithful to their ancestral land and religion.[28] They rejected the Jerusalem temple and built their own rival temple on Mount Gerizim (John 4:9, 20). They had their own version of the Scriptures (the Samaritan Pentateuch) and anticipated a Moses-like messianic figure known as the *Taheb* (cf. Deut 18:15). Animosity between the Jews and Samaritans grew exponentially during the Maccabean period, when the Hasmonean king John Hyrcanus (135–104 BCE) destroyed their temple and forcibly converted many Samaritans. During the Roman period, the Samaritans and Jews remained bitter enemies. For Luke, however, the Samaritans were an important transitional people between Jews and Gentiles. Luke shows special interest in them both in his Gospel (9:51–56; 10:29–37; 17:11–19) and here in Acts, where they become an important part of the eschatological people of God.

When the apostles in Jerusalem hear of the Samaritan response to the gospel, they send Peter and John to Samaria to investigate. Luke notes that though the Samaritans had been baptized, they had not yet received the Spirit (8:15–16). The Spirit only comes when Peter and John pray and lay hands on them (v. 17). Why this delay? Elsewhere in Acts people typically receive the Spirit when they believe and are baptized (Acts 9:17–18; 10:44–48; 19:2–7; cf. Eph 1:13; 1 Cor 12:13). The likely answer is the need for unity in the church. The Spirit was withheld until the apostles arrived (1) to confirm for the Jerusalem believers that the Samaritans were truly saved, and (2) to confirm for the Samaritans that they were dependent on the Jerusalem church.

---

[27] For more detailed background, see Robert T. Anderson, "Samaritans," in *ABD* 5:940–47; E. Nodet, *The Samaritans* (London: T&T Clark, 2023); R. Pummer, *The Samaritans: A Profile* (Grand Rapids: Eerdmans, 2016).

[28] Josephus, *Ant.* 11.8.6 §§340–41.

The history of the Jews and Samaritans was one of division and rivalry, each claiming to be the true people of God (see Ancient Connections 2.3: The Samaritans). There must be no similar division in the church of Jesus Christ. The same Spirit who baptized the Jerusalem believers on the Day of Pentecost united the Samaritans with the eschatological people of God.

When Simon the sorcerer sees the power of the Spirit coming through the laying on of hands, he offers the apostles money for this power, thinking of the commercial opportunities. Peter severely rebukes Simon for believing he can purchase this gift of God and calls for his repentance. Simon appears to repent and begs for prayer, but his motives seem to be self-preservation rather than authentic faith (see 8:24).[29]

Philip's Ministry to an Ethiopian Eunuch (8:26–40)

Following Philip's successful ministry in Samaria, an angel instructs him to go south on the desert road that runs from Jerusalem to Gaza, where another divine appointment awaits him. He encounters a eunuch, a high official of Candace, the Queen of Ethiopia.[30] The man has been to Jerusalem to worship, indicating he is a God-fearer, a Gentile who worshipped the true God of Israel. Prompted by the Spirit, Philip approaches the chariot and hears the man reading from Isaiah 53, a key prophetic passage related to the suffering of the Messiah. Confused by the passage, the man invites Philip up to explain it. Beginning with this text, "Philip proceeded to tell him the good news about Jesus" (8:35). When they come to a body of water, the man asks to be baptized.[31]

This episode, like the previous one, demonstrates the widening influence of the gospel and a preview of the coming Gentile mission. Considering that Christianity is sometimes associated with a Eurocentric worldview, it is significant that the first Gentile convert in Acts is an African. The account also illustrates the guiding role of the Holy Spirit, who directs Philip step-by-step. The many "coincidences"—a chance

---

[29] For later traditions about Simon as heretic in the early church, see R. F. Stoops, "Simon," in *ABD* 6:29–31.

[30] This is not modern Ethiopia (which is further south and east), but the ancient Nubian empire of Meroë, in what is modern southern Egypt and Sudan. This area is identified as "Cush" in the OT. The term "Candace" (*Kandakē*) was not a personal name, but the title for the queen or the queen mother.

[31] Our earliest and most reliable manuscripts of Acts do not include verse 37 (absent in 𝔓[45,74] ℵ A B C). It was undoubtedly added by a later copyist who felt the story was incomplete without an explicit confession of faith.

encounter on a deserted road; a curious and open God-fearing Gentile; a scroll of Isaiah, opened to the most important passage in Scripture on the suffering Messiah—are clearly the work of God.

**ANCIENT CONNECTIONS 2.4:
A "EUNUCH" OR AN "OFFICIAL"?**

The word "eunuch" originally referred to a castrated male, whose sexual status made him safe to oversee the king's harem. In time, however, the term came to be used more generally for a royal court official. Was this Ethiopian a true eunuch or simply a high governmental official? If the former, there may be additional theological significance here. Eunuchs were barred from full participation in Israel's religious life (Deut 23:1). Yet Isa 56:1–8 envisions the time of God's final salvation, when foreigners and eunuchs would be welcomed fully into the people of God. This fits the central theme of Luke-Acts, that Jesus is the Savior for all people everywhere, and especially those who are presently outsiders and outcasts.

After baptizing the Ethiopian, Philip is swept away by the Spirit and finds himself in the city of Azotus (ancient Ashdod). He then travels up the coast to Caesarea, preaching the gospel along the way. He evidently remained in Caesarea since in Acts 21:8–9 Paul and his associates (including the author—a "we" section) visit Philip and his family in Caesarea on Paul's return from his third missionary journey.

Saul Encounters the Risen Lord (9:1–31)

After describing Philip's successful ministry in Samaria and with the Ethiopian official, Luke returns to the story of Saul, who was introduced at the account of Stephen's stoning (7:58; 8:1–3). The dramatic transformation of Saul of Tarsus from persecutor to apostle becomes a cornerstone for Luke's apologetic purpose in Acts. Its narrative importance is evident in that Luke recounts it three times, once in narrative form (9:1–19) and twice in Paul's retelling (22:1–21; 26:1–29).[32] The second half of Acts deals almost exclusively with Paul's missionary journeys (chaps. 13–28). Luke seeks

[32] Paul also refers to it repeatedly in his letters (1 Cor 9:1; 15:8; Gal 1:12–17; Phil 3:4–7; 1 Tim 1:12).

to show Paul's loyalty to his Jewish identity, his faithfulness to the God of his ancestors, and his innocence in the court of Roman law. This apostle to the Gentiles was not a renegade Jew, but God's prime instrument for bringing this great salvation to the nations.

Luke begins where he left off in 8:3, with Saul's zeal in persecuting the church. He is "breathing threats and murder" (9:1; cf. Phil 3:6; 1 Tim 1:13). Viewing the Jesus movement as a heretical sect, Saul requests letters of reference from the high priest to arrest Jesus's followers in the synagogues of Damascus, about 180 miles north of Jerusalem. On the road Saul has a dramatic encounter (9:2–9). A bright light shines from heaven and a voice demands, "Saul, Saul, why are you persecuting me?" Saul asks, "Who are you, Lord?" and the response is, "I am Jesus, the one you are persecuting." Blinded by the light, Saul is led by his companions into Damascus, where the Lord sends a disciple named Ananias to complete his conversion (9:10–19). Saul regains his sight and is baptized as a believer. Soon thereafter, he begins to preach in the synagogues of Damascus, proclaiming his faith in Jesus as the Messiah and Son of God. Paul's testimony is so powerful that his former allies conspire to kill him. The Christian believers in Damascus, however, sneak him out of the city by night and send him to Jerusalem (9:20–25; cf. 2 Cor 11:32–33).[33]

The apostles in Jerusalem fear that Saul's newfound faith in Jesus is simply a ruse to capture them. Barnabas, however, vouches for Saul and brings him to the apostles (9:26–27). In Gal 1:19 Paul notes that he spent fifteen days with Cephas (= Peter) in Jerusalem on this visit and also met James, Jesus's brother.[34] As in Damascus, Saul's bold witness in Jerusalem results in a plot against his life. To calm the situation, the believers take him down to the port at Caesarea and put him on a ship to his home city of Tarsus (9:28–30). There he will remain for ten years. Luke concludes this section with another summary of the church's Spirit-empowered growth, this time emphasizing a period of relative calm after the turmoil of Stephen's martyrdom and Saul's conversion (9:31).

---

[33] In Paul's own account in Galatians, he says it was three years before he went to Jerusalem, with some of this time spent in Arabia (the Nabatean kingdom; Gal 1:17).

[34] *Petros* (Peter) is the Greek translation of the Aramaic *Qéphâ* (transliterated as *Kēphas* [Gk] or Cephas [English]). Both the Greek and Aramaic words mean "Rock," the nickname Jesus gave Peter (see John 1:42; Matt 16:18; Mark 3:15; Luke 6:14). In his letters, Paul refers to Peter as *Kēphas* eight times (1 Cor 1:12; 3:22; 9:5; 15:5; Gal 1:18; 2:9, 11, 14) and *Petros* only twice (Gal 2:7, 8).

Peter's Ministry in Lydda and Joppa (9:32–43)

Although Luke's focus has begun to shift to Saul/Paul, Peter continues to show up as a key representative of the Twelve and the Jerusalem church (9:32–43; 10:1–11:18; 12:1–23; 15:7–11). For Luke he remains a key link to Jesus and his original followers. As in the early chapters of Acts, Peter is seen performing miracles like Jesus, continuing Jesus's ministry (cf. 1:1). He first travels to Lydda, the OT city of Lod, where he heals a paralyzed man named Aeneas. The story recalls Jesus's healing of a paralyzed man in Luke 5:17–26. He then travels to Joppa on the Mediterranean coast, where he raises a woman named Tabitha (or Dorcas)[35] from the dead, recalling Jesus's raising of Jairus's daughter (Luke 8:41–56) and the son of the widow of Nain (Luke 7:11–17).

The Conversion of Gentiles: Cornelius and His Household (10:1–11:18)

Peter's ministry in Lydda and Joppa sets the stage for the longest single narrative in Acts, the conversion of Cornelius (10:1–11:18). It is characterized by much repetition, indicating its importance for Luke.[36] Cornelius is identified as a centurion living in Caesarea, a coastal city built by Herod the Great as the Roman military headquarters of Judea. Centurions commanded about 100 soldiers each and were considered the backbone of the Roman army. Cornelius is identified as devout and God-fearing (10:22). As we have seen, God-fearers in Acts are Gentiles who worship the one true God of Israel but have not converted fully to Judaism (cf. 10:35; 13:16, 26). In a vision, an angel tells Cornelius his prayers have been answered and that he must summon a man named Simon Peter from Joppa.

Meanwhile in Joppa, Peter too receives a message from God. While hungry and waiting for a meal to be prepared, he has a vision. A sheet descends from heaven full of "unclean" animals that were forbidden by the law of Moses to eat (Lev 11). When a voice calls on him to "Get up, Peter; kill and eat!" Peter refuses, thinking this is test of his piety. But the voice continues, "What God has made clean, do not call impure." The vision is repeated three times. As Peter is puzzling over its meaning, the messengers from Cornelius arrive, and the Spirit tells Peter to go with them. By the time Peter arrives at Cornelius's house the next day, he has figured out the vision. After Cornelius describes his own vision, Peter responds, "Now I truly understand that God

---

[35] Both Dorcas (in Greek) and Tabitha (in Aramaic) mean "gazelle."

[36] Notice that Cornelius's vision is recounted three times (10:3–8, 30–32; 11:13–14) and Peter summarizes the whole episode in 11:4–16. Peter alludes to it again in 15:8–10.

doesn't show favoritism, but in every nation the person who fears him and does what is right is acceptable to him" (10:34–35). He then begins to relate the story of Jesus to Cornelius and his family. To the amazement of the Jewish believers who are present, when Peter reaches the climax of his preaching that "everyone who believes in him receives forgiveness of sins," the Holy Spirit suddenly comes upon the Gentiles, and they begin speaking in tongues. Peter responds, "Can anyone withhold water and prevent these people from being baptized, who have received the Holy Spirit just as we have?" This emphasis on God's actions becomes Peter's repeated refrain and represents a key Lukan theme in Acts. It is God himself, not any human being, who chose the Gentiles and poured out his Spirit on them (11:1–3, 15–18; 15:7–11).

Gentile Outreach in the Church at Antioch (11:19–30)

Having introduced the beginning of the Gentile mission with the story of Cornelius, Luke now recounts another key event in the expansion of the gospel to Gentiles, the founding of the church at Antioch (11:19–21). He begins with a flashback to the time of Stephen's martyrdom. While most of those fleeing the persecution preached the gospel only to Jews, some Hellenistic Jewish-Christians from Cyprus and Cyrene go to Antioch in Syria and begin preaching to "Greeks," meaning Greek-speaking Gentiles. Many believe, and Antioch becomes the first church to incorporate Gentiles into its community.[37]

When the Jerusalem church hears of these developments, they send Barnabas to Antioch to investigate (11:22–24). Barnabas is an ideal choice. He is identified as a good man, "full of the Holy Spirit and of faith"—essential credentials for leadership in Acts[38]—and he has a track record of encouragement and reconciliation (4:36–37; 9:27). He is also a Hellenistic Jew himself, from Cyprus (4:36). Barnabas, in turn, goes to Tarsus to find Saul—no doubt aware of Saul's commission to preach to the Gentiles (9:15; 22:21). Barnabas brings Saul to Antioch, where they minister together for a year (11:25–26).

---

[37] If this episode occurred earlier, why did Luke recount it *after* the Cornelius episode? One likely reason was to highlight Peter's role in the Gentile mission. As Jesus's closest disciple and the chief spokesperson of the apostles, Peter's testimony carried great weight among Jewish Christians. By recounting Peter's role in the Cornelius episode first, Luke confirms that the Gentile mission in Antioch has God's stamp of approval.

[38] Acts 6:3, 5; 7:55; 11:24.

SIDEBAR 2.2: NAMING THE JESUS FOLLOWERS

Luke says that Jesus's disciples were first called "Christians" in Antioch (11:26). Before this time, the followers of Jesus were viewed as a sect within Judaism. But with the incorporation of Gentiles, the church begins to develop a distinct identity. In seeking a label, Luke reports that some chose "Christian" (*christianos*), meaning "Christ-follower" or "Christ-partisan."[39] The word was likely first used by outsiders, perhaps in a derogatory manner. It appears only three times in the NT (Acts 11:26; 26:28; 1 Pet 4:16). Luke's preferred terms are "brothers and sisters" (*adelphoi*),[40] "disciples/followers" (*mathētai*),[41] the "church/assembly" (*ecclesia*),[42] or people of "the Way" (*hē hodos*).[43]

The link between the churches in Jerusalem and Antioch is reinforced when a group of prophets comes down to Antioch from Jerusalem. One prophet, named Agabus (cf. 21:10–11), predicts a famine that will threaten the poverty-stricken and persecuted church in Jerusalem. In response, the Christians in Antioch collect relief funds and send them to Jerusalem with Paul and Barnabas (11:27–30). This is likely the Jerusalem visit Paul describes in Gal 2:1–10.[44] Later Paul will organize a similar relief effort with gifts from the churches of Greece and Asia Minor (Rom 15:25–28; 1 Cor 16:1–4; 2 Cor 8:1–9:15). From Paul's perspective, the Gentile churches are indebted spiritually to the mother church in Jerusalem and so ought to support her materially (Rom 15:26–27).

The Jerusalem Church Persecuted by Herod Agrippa I (12:1–25)

Before turning to the missionary journeys of Paul (chaps. 13–28), Luke records another wave of persecution against the Jerusalem church (12:1–25). "King Herod" here (12:1) is Herod Agrippa I, the grandson of Herod the Great. Agrippa was raised in Rome, where he developed strong ties with some of Rome's most influential future leaders.

---

[39] "Χριστιανός" in BDAG, 1090.

[40] Acts 1:15, 16; 6:3; 9:17, 30; 10:23; 11:1, 12, 29; 12:17; 14:2; 15:1, 3, 22, 32, 33, 36, 40; 16:2, 40; 17:6, 10, 14; 18:18, 27; 21:7, 17, 20; 22:13; 28:14, 15.

[41] Acts 6:1, 2, 7; 9:1, 10, 19, 25, 26, 38; 11:26, 29; 13:52; 14:20, 22, 28; 15:10; 16:1; 18:23, 27; 19:1, 9, 30; 20:1, 30; 21:4, 16.

[42] Acts 5:11; 8:1, 3; 9:31; 11:22, 26; 12:1, 5; 13:1; 14:23, 27; 15:3, 4, 22, 41; 16:5; 18:22; 20:17, 28. The term usually refers to a local assembly, but occasionally to all believers (9:31; 20:28).

[43] Acts 9:2; 19:9, 23; 22:4; 24:14, 22; cf. 16:17; 18:25–26.

[44] Some, however, claim that Galatians 2 describes the Jerusalem Council of Acts 15. See Galatians: Occasion.

Returning to Palestine, he drew on the patronage of the emperors Caligula (37–41 CE) and Claudius (41–54 CE) to gain greater authority. By 41 CE he reigned as "king of the Jews" over almost as much territory as his famous grandfather, including Judea, Samaria, Galilee, Transjordan, and the Decapolis. Agrippa also courted the favor of the Jewish religious leaders, gaining a reputation as a pious Jew. This was likely his motivation for arresting and executing the apostle James, brother of John (12:1–2). From Agrippa's perspective, the followers of Jesus were a heretical and dangerous sect. When the execution of James pleased the Jewish leadership, Agrippa went further, arresting Peter with the intention of holding a public trial after the Festival of Unleavened Bread (12:3–5).

But as so often in Acts, God had other plans, and an angel comes and releases Peter from prison. The story is full of color and detail, with ironic humor (12:6–19). Peter is presented as groggy and half-asleep, nearly oblivious to what is happening. This is *God's* deliverance, not Peter's escape! When Peter arrives at the house where believers are gathered in prayer for him, a servant girl named Rhoda is so excited to hear Peter's voice that she forgets to let him in. The gathered church, though praying earnestly for Peter's release, finds it impossible to believe that their prayers have been answered and ignore Rhoda's claim that Peter is at the gate.

The miraculous deliverance of Peter is another reminder of the central theme of Acts: The gospel is unstoppable because it is the work of God (5:39). This theme is reinforced in the narrative that follows. God judges King Agrippa with a gruesome death because of his arrogant and violent opposition to the church (12:20–23). Meanwhile, the work of God moves relentlessly forward (12:24–25).

ANCIENT CONNECTIONS 2.5: JOSEPHUS ON THE DEATH OF HEROD AGRIPPA I

The Jewish historian Josephus provides an account of Herod's gruesome death (ca. 44 CE) similar in many respects to Luke's account (*Antiquities* 19.8.2 §§343–52). Both place the event in Caesarea during a speech by Herod and both attribute the death to God's judgment for arrogantly accepting divine accolades from the crowd. Josephus adds the interesting detail that the people's amazement resulted when Herod's silver robe reflected the sun with a dazzling brilliance. Josephus also notes that just before collapsing, Herod looked up and saw an owl sitting on a rope, which he knew from previous experience was an omen of evil.[45]

[45] The earlier episode involving the sighting of an owl is in Josephus, *Ant.* 18.6.7 §§195–204.

The Gospel to the Ends of the Earth: The Journeys of Paul (13:1–28:31)

Paul's ministry in Acts has traditionally been divided into three missionary journeys, each of which sets out from his home base in Antioch. A "fourth" journey involves Paul's journey to Rome after his Jerusalem arrest.

First Journey: Cyprus and Galatia (13:1–14:28)

Second Journey: Macedonia and Achaia (15:36–18:22)

Third Journey: Ephesus and Asia Minor (18:23; 19:1–21:16)

Fourth Journey: Arrest in Jerusalem, transfer to Caesarea and Journey to Rome (21:17–28:31)

SIDEBAR 2.3: DID PAUL TAKE JUST THREE MISSIONARY JOURNEYS?

The traditional schema of "Paul's Three Missionary Journeys" (and a fourth journey to Rome) neatly summarizes Paul's travels as recounted by Luke in the book of Acts (see the maps on pp. 48 and 51; similar maps appear at the end of many Bibles). But Paul himself is unlikely to have described his ministry in this way. We know, for example, that after his conversion Paul travelled to "Arabia" (Gal 1:17), likely meaning the Nabatean kingdom southeast of Israel. Some have described this as a period of solitude and reflection, where Paul poured over Scripture and formed his theology. But Luke describes Paul as already preaching about Jesus immediately after his conversion (Acts 9:19–25), and Paul's own claim that agents of King Aretas of Nabatea tried to arrest him in Damascus (2 Cor 11:32–33) suggests Paul's time in Arabia was occupied with preaching rather than cloistered solitude. Paul also speaks of ministry in Illyricum (regions north of Greece; Rom 15:19), which are not mentioned in Acts. Judging from Paul's own "résumé" in 2 Cor 11:24–28 (see v. 26: "frequent journeys"), there were far more than three journeys! Nevertheless, for our survey of Acts and for establishing the chronology of Paul's letters, we will continue to use the traditional terminology of three journeys.

First Journey: The Gospel to Cyprus and Galatia (13:1–14:28)

Paul and Barnabas are called on their first missionary journey while working with the church in Antioch. They are worshiping and fasting when the Holy Spirit announces (probably through one of the prophets in the church [13:1]): "Set apart for me

Barnabas and Saul for the work to which I have called them" (13:2). As in the case of Peter's ministry to Cornelius, it is God himself, not any human being, who initiates the mission to the Gentiles. The leaders of the church "laid hands on" them (a sign of commissioning and support) and sent them off.

Barnabas and Saul travel from Antioch to the port of Seleucia, where they catch a ship to the island of Cyprus. Cyprus was Barnabas's homeland and so a natural starting point. Luke notes in passing that they brought along "John" as their helper. This is "John, also called Mark," who was introduced earlier as the son of Mary, the woman in whose home the Christians gathered to pray for Peter (12:12). After their famine relief visit to Jerusalem, Barnabas and Saul brought John Mark from Jerusalem to Antioch (12:25). In Col 4:10 we learn that John Mark was Barnabas's cousin, which helps to explain Barnabas's loyalty to him (see 15:37–39).

Starting in the city of Salamis in eastern Cyprus, the missionaries preach the gospel in synagogues throughout the island. In Paphos, Saul is opposed by a magician named Bar-Jesus (or, Elymas), an attendant to Sergius Paulus, the Roman governor (proconsul) of the island. Paul accuses Elymas of being in league with the devil, and the Lord strikes him blind (13:10–11). Seeing this act of power, Sergius Paulus believes the gospel (13:12).

It is in Cyprus that Luke notes that Saul was also known as "Paul" (13:9), and the name Paul is used from this point forward. Some have suggested that Saul adopted this name here, perhaps as a tribute to his convert, Sergius Paulus. More likely, this was one of Paul's Roman names from birth (see Ancient Connections 1.3: What's in a Name?), which he began using while working among the Gentiles. The order "Barnabas and Saul" (13:7) now changes to "Paul and Barnabas" (13:43) and remains so in most cases from here onward (13:46, 50; 15:2, 22, 35), as Paul takes the lead.

From Cyprus the group sails to Pamphylia, the region of modern-day south-central Turkey, landing in the city of Perga. At this point, Luke reports, John Mark returned to Jerusalem. The reason for his departure is not given, although Paul later refers to it as a desertion (15:38). Paul and Barnabas go on to the Roman province of Galatia, establishing churches in four cities: Pisidian Antioch, Iconium, Lystra, and Derbe.

At Pisidian Antioch,[46] Paul and Barnabas visit a local synagogue on the Sabbath, where they find both Jews and God-fearing Gentiles. Recognized by the synagogue

---

[46] Though located in Phrygia, the city was called "Pisidian Antioch" because it bordered on Pisidia.

leaders as qualified Jewish teachers, they are given the opportunity to speak (13:15).[47] Paul's message begins as a summary of Israel's history leading up to God's choice of David to be king. From there, he moves to God's promises to raise up the Messiah from David's line—a prophecy fulfilled in the coming of Jesus (13:16–41). The message at first elicits a positive response, and the missionaries are invited to return the next Sabbath (13:42–43). Yet this second visit does not go well. The size and enthusiasm of the crowd and the presence of many Gentiles provoke jealousy among the Jewish leaders, who reject Paul's message. Paul responds by saying that he is now turning to the Gentiles, quoting Isa 49:6 (cf. Luke 2:32 and Acts 1:8). A number of Gentiles believe, and the new community is established (13:44–49). The synagogue leaders, however, appeal to their Gentile supporters in the city and provoke persecution against the missionaries, who are forced to leave. The new believers, however, are "filled with joy and the Holy Spirit" (13:52)—key indicators in Acts of the arrival of God's eschatological salvation.

Luke's lengthy account here (13:13–52), his first description of Paul's synagogue preaching, establishes a common pattern for Paul's ministry in Acts: (1) Paul preaches in the local synagogue, where Jews and God-fearing Gentiles are gathered. (2) His message centers on the continuity between the old and the new. God's covenants to Israel have come fulfillment in the church through the life, death, and resurrection of Jesus the Messiah. Salvation and forgiveness of sins are now available to all who believe, both Jews and Gentiles. (3) A small number of Jews and a larger number of God-fearing Gentiles respond in faith. (4) Opposition arises against Paul and his companions, usually provoked by the Jewish leaders in concert with their Gentile supporters. Sometimes this results in departure from the synagogue for a new venue and other times in expulsion from the city. (5) Paul picks up and moves on to the next town, continuing to proclaim the gospel and launching small communities of Jesus followers. Setbacks consistently turn to success as the gospel moves relentlessly forward.

From Pisidian Antioch, Paul and Barnabas move on to Iconium. Many more believe there until, again, opposition from the Jewish community and their Gentile benefactors forces them to leave (14:1–7). They go to Lystra, where they encounter a different challenge. When Paul heals a man who is unable to walk, the pagan

[47] Most synagogues did not have a professional pastor or teacher. Rather, qualified elders and rabbis would be invited to give a homily following readings from the Law and the Prophets. Paul was a Pharisee (23:6) and Barnabas was a Levite (4:36), so both would likely have been viewed as qualified teachers.

crowd tries to worship them as gods, calling Barnabas "Zeus" and Paul "Hermes."[48] Horrified, Paul and Barnabas reject this false worship and point the way to the one true God. Yet when the Jews of Iconium and Pisidian Antioch hear about Paul's work in Lystra, they incite the crowd against him. A mob drags Paul out of the city and stones him, leaving him for dead (cf. 2 Cor 11:25). Remarkably, Paul gets up and the next day travels on to Derbe, where a large number of converts are won (14:8–20).

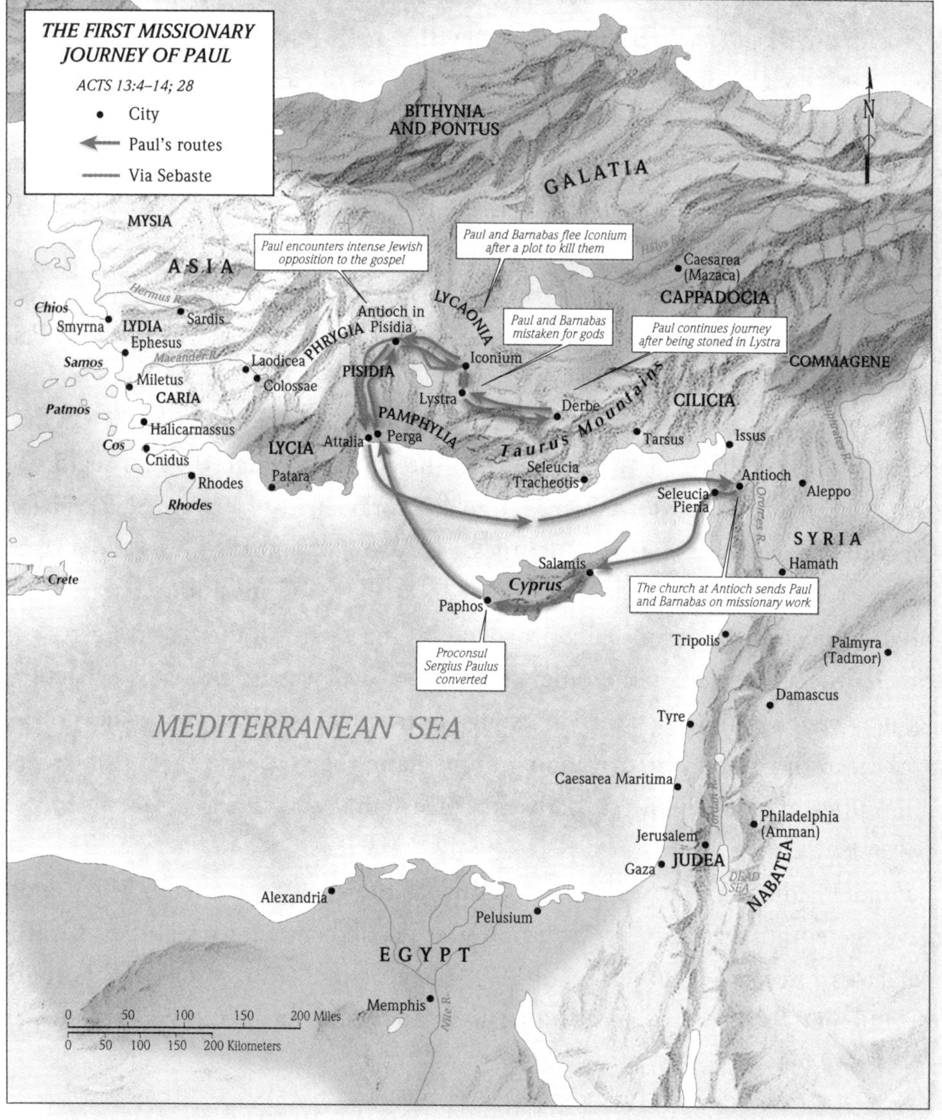

48 F. F. Bruce, *Acts*, NICNT, rev. ed. (Grand Rapids: Eerdmans, 1988), 275, suggests that Barnabas may have been called Zeus, the king of the gods, because of his dignified bearing, and Paul was called Hermes, the messenger of the gods, because he was the chief spokesperson.

ANCIENT CONNECTIONS 2.6: LEGENDS OF VISITING GODS

Tales of the gods secretly visiting human beings were common in the Greco-Roman world. One story with interesting parallels to Paul and Barnabas's visit to Lystra comes from the first-century Roman poet Ovid (ca. 43 BCE–17 CE), who relates how the gods Jupiter and Mercury (the Roman names for Zeus and Hermes) visit nearby Phrygia. They are refused hospitality by all the people until an old couple, Philemon and Baucis, welcome them into their humble home and share their meager provisions with them. In response, the gods punish the inhospitable neighbors by destroying them with a flood and reward the old couple by turning their cottage into a golden-roofed temple and making them its priests (Ovid, *Metamorphoses* 8.611–724). Perhaps when the people of Lystra saw Paul's healing, they did not want to make the same mistake and miss their opportunity for a gilded temple!

Paul and Barnabas then retrace their steps, appointing elders in the churches they have started. They return to (Syrian) Antioch and report to the church how God has opened the door of faith to the Gentiles (14:21–27). This influx of Gentiles into the church sets the stage for the Council of Jerusalem.

Galatians — Paul likely wrote Galatians around this time (ca. 49 CE), after Judaizers infiltrated the churches of Galatia.

The Jerusalem Council (15:1–35)

The question of the means of salvation for Gentiles (which is central in Paul's letter to the Galatians; see chapter 3) becomes a critical issue in the next episode, when some Jewish Christians (often called "Judaizers") come from Judea to the church at Antioch, Syria. They begin teaching that the Gentile Christians must be circumcised and keep the law of Moses to be saved (15:1, 5).[49] The leaders at Antioch decide that a delegation should go to Jerusalem to resolve this issue.

[49] In 15:5 they are identified as from "the party of the Pharisees." It is remarkable that even members of this conservative religious party were accepting Jesus as the Messiah (cf. the "large group of priests" in 6:7).

In Jerusalem, the Judaizers make their case for circumcision and Torah observance (15:5), and the apostles and elders meet to discuss the issue. Peter emphasizes the same point he repeatedly made in the Cornelius episode (10:44–48; 11:1–3, 15–18). It was God alone who instigated the Gentile mission. He poured out his Spirit on them, just as he had on the Jews. Furthermore, the Jews have never been able to fully keep the law. Why should the church place this impossible burden on the Gentiles (15:7–11)? Luke doesn't record the speeches of Paul and Barnabas. He just mentions that they bore witness to "all the signs and wonders God had done through them among the Gentiles" (15:12). As in the case of Jesus (2:22), the miracles confirm that this is the work of God.

James, the half-brother of Jesus and now leader of the Jerusalem church, renders the decision (or perhaps expresses the consensus). He affirms Peter's point that it was God who instigated the Gentile mission and that this was in line with the prophecy that God would one day return "and rebuild David's fallen tent . . . so the rest of humanity may seek the Lord" (15:16–17; citing Amos 9:11–12 LXX).[50] James concludes that the Gentiles should not be troubled with circumcision or keeping the OT law, but proposes that they be asked to abstain from four things: (1) eating food sacrificed to idols (cf. 1 Cor 8:7–13; 10:14–28; Rev 2:14, 20), (2) eating the meat of strangled animals (i.e., not drained of blood; cf. Gen 9:4; Lev 17:13–14), (3) consuming blood (cf. Lev 17:10–12), and (4) sexual immorality (15:13–21). These were actions especially repulsive to Jews and so sensitivity to them would encourage table fellowship between Jewish and Gentile believers.[51] Following James's lead, the council drafts a letter to the Gentile Christians in Antioch, Syria, and Cilicia with these guidelines. Two believers from Jerusalem, Judas Barsabbas and Silas, are chosen to accompany Paul and Barnabas in delivering the letter to Antioch (15:22–35).

---

[50] David's restored "tent" could refer to the church as a restored temple, but more likely refers to the restored "house" (= dynasty) of David, inaugurated through Christ's reign (see Luke 1:27, 69; 2:4; Acts 2:32–36). On the differences between the Greek LXX cited by James and the Hebrew Masoretic text, see Marshall, *Acts*, 267; Bruce, *Acts*, 293–94.

[51] Other possibilities are that these four things (1) reflect the prohibitions in Leviticus 17–18 for non-Israelites living in the land or (2) that they are all related to idolatry and so are meant to keep Gentiles from falling back into pagan practices. For detailed discussion of various options, see Craig S. Keener, *Acts: An Exegetical Commentary*, 4 vols. (Grand Rapids: Baker, 2014), 3:2258–79.

Second Journey: The Gospel to Macedonia and Achaia (15:36–18:22)

After a time of ministry in Antioch, Paul suggests to Barnabas that they return to visit the churches in Galatia established on their first journey. Barnabas agrees and in turn suggests they bring John Mark along. When Paul refuses because of Mark's prior desertion, Luke says, "They had such a sharp disagreement that they parted company, and Barnabas took Mark with him and sailed off to Cyprus" (15:39).[52] This embarrassing conflict suggests that Luke is not simply sugarcoating the history of the early church. He is willing to presents its struggles and conflicts as well as its successes.

In place of Barnabas, Paul chooses Silas, the Jerusalem leader who helped deliver the council's letter (15:22, 32, 40). They take the land route north through Syria and Cilicia to Galatia,[53] strengthening the churches and delivering the letter from the

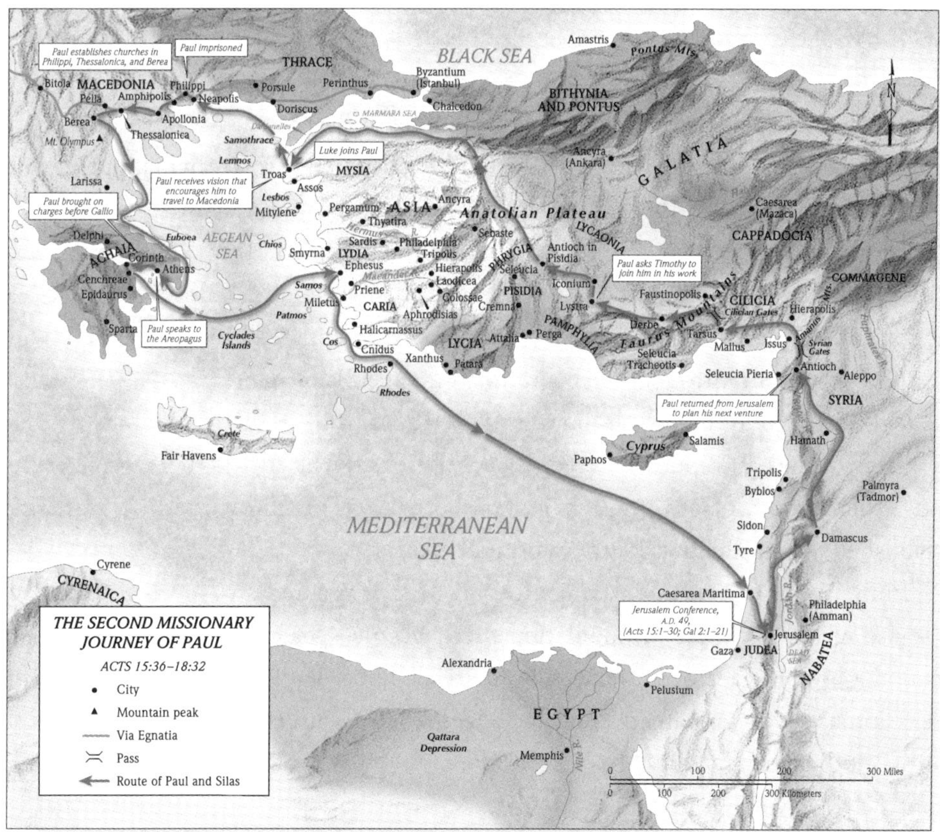

[52] Barnabas and Mark do not appear again in Acts. In his letters, Paul refers to Barnabas in Gal 2:11–13 and 1 Cor 9:6, and to Mark in Col 4:10; Phlm 24; and 2 Tim 4:11.

[53] Tarsus, Paul's hometown, was in Cilicia, so some of these churches may have been established during Paul's ten years there between Acts 9:30 and 11:25 (*ca.* 37–46 CE).

Jerusalem council. In Lystra they pick up a new associate, Timothy, a promising young believer who will become one of Paul's most trusted disciples.[54] The author reports that because Timothy had a Greek father and a Jewish mother, Paul had him circumcised. This at first seems shocking, since it would appear to contradict Paul's strong teaching in Galatians that circumcision is unnecessary for salvation (Gal 5:2, 3, 6, 11; 6:15). Luke, however, explains that Paul did this "because of the Jews who were in those places, since they all knew that his father was a Greek" (16:3). Timothy was considered Jewish because of his Jewish mother; but he was not circumcised because his Greek father would have forbidden it (Greeks viewed circumcision as mutilation). For Paul to bring Timothy along as an uncircumcised Jew would have opened Paul up to accusations that he was teaching Jews not to circumcise their children, which would have been catastrophic for Paul's claims to be a faithful Jew. The situation in Gal 2:3 with Titus, who was a Gentile, was entirely different. To support his circumcision would have been to accept that Gentiles needed to be circumcised (i.e., to become Jewish) to be saved—something Paul vehemently denied.

After continuing westward through Phrygia and Galatia, the missionaries try to turn south into the province of Asia and then north into Bithynia, but in both cases the Spirit prevents them.[55] In Troas, on the Aegean coast, Paul has a vision of a Macedonian man calling them to come over to Macedonia (16:9). They take a ship across the Aegean to the port of Neapolis and then travel to Philippi. The first "we" section in Acts begins in Troas (16:10), as the author apparently joins the group (see "Author" section in introduction, beginning on page 2).

On this "second" missionary journey (see sidebar 2.3), Luke recounts Paul's ministry in five cities: Philippi; Thessalonica and Berea, in Macedonia (northern Greece); and Athens and Corinth, in Achaia (southern Greece). The patterns and themes established during the first journey continue here.

Philippi was one of the leading cities of Macedonia and a proud Roman colony. Because of its small Jewish population there was no synagogue, but the missionaries find a Jewish place of prayer beside the river. There Paul gains his first convert in Macedonia: a woman named Lydia, a God-fearing Gentile and merchant who sold purple cloth from Thyatira. She believes the message, is baptized, and invites the missionaries to stay in her home (16:11–15).

---

[54] Cf. Phil 2:19–24; 1 Cor 16:10–11; 1 and 2 Timothy.

[55] It is not clear whether the Spirit's direction came from circumstances on the ground, a prophetic revelation, or some other means. But note the close connection between the "Holy Spirit" (16:6) and the "Spirit of Jesus" (16:7), indicating Jesus's deity.

As always, success brings opposition. One day while Paul and the others are going to the place of prayer, a slave girl begins to follow and harass them. Luke describes her as possessed by a demon, which enabled her to predict the future, making a large profit for her owners. Paul gets so annoyed at the girl's taunts that he turns and casts the demon out, infuriating the girl's owners, who have Paul and Silas arrested, beaten, and thrown in jail.[56] But as so often happens in Acts, God turns bad to good. That evening Paul and Silas are praying and singing hymns in their jail cell, when an earthquake occurs. Their chains fall off and the jail doors fly open. The jailer rushes in, preparing to commit suicide for allowing an escape, but Paul assures him that the prisoners are still there and leads him to faith in Christ.

ANCIENT CONNECTIONS 2.7: A "PYTHON SPIRIT"

Luke describes the slave girl of 16:16 as having a "python spirit" (*pneuma pythōna*). The term goes back to the Greek legend about Apollo, son of Zeus, who slayed the Python that guarded the underworld and so became Lord of the underworld. At the oracle sanctuary at Delphi, virgin priestesses of Apollo known as Pythia made prophecies about the future. In many sources, the priestess would prophesy from a subterranean tripod seat while in a state of ecstasy. In time the term "python-spirit" came to be used of others who channeled spirits to tell fortunes. Divination was big business in the Greco-Roman world, used to decide issues as common as marriage or business ventures and as momentous as war and peace.[57]

From Philippi, the team travels to Thessalonica, where Paul teaches in the synagogue for three consecutive Sabbaths. While some Jews believe, others are unpersuaded and provoke a mob action against the missionaries. The new believers send Paul and Silas away to Berea. At first, they receive a more favorable reception from the Jews in Berea, who "examined the Scriptures daily to see if these things were so" (17:11). Many believe, including a number of prominent Greek women and men.[58] Soon, however, the Thessalonian Jews come down to Berea and provoke opposition, so the believers take Paul to Athens. Timothy and Silas remain for the time being in Berea.

---

[56] See 2 Cor 11:25, where Paul says he was beaten with rods on three occasions.

[57] For details see the excursus in Keener, *Acts*, 3:2422–29.

[58] See Ancient Connections 4.1: Patronage in Thessalonica, p. 97.

In Athens, Paul splits his time preaching in the synagogue and the marketplace. When he begins to debate a group of Epicurean and Stoic philosophers,[59] they bring him to the Areopagus, the ruling council of Athens (17:16–21).[60] There Paul delivers his famous "Mars Hill" address. His message here is very different from that in the synagogue in Pisidian Antioch. Rather than introducing God's promises through the patriarchs of Israel, he begins by noting an altar he saw in Athens inscribed "To an Unknown God." He then says that what they worship in ignorance he now proclaims to them, the one true God, the self-sufficient creator and Lord of all things. Only the climax of the sermon is the same: God's vindication of Jesus through the resurrection. The response to this message is mixed. Some sneer at the absurdity of a bodily resurrection, while others are curious and wish to hear more. A few respond with faith and repentance (17:22–34).

Though Luke does not mention it, Timothy and Silas evidently join Paul in Athens, and he sends Timothy back to Thessalonica to check on the church there (1 Thess 3:1–2). Paul goes ahead on his own to Corinth, where he meets Priscilla and Aquila, a Jewish-Christian couple who had left Rome because of an edict from the emperor Claudius forcing Jews out of the capital (see Ancient Connections 2.8). Like Paul, Priscilla and Aquila are tentmakers by trade. The three work together, while Paul continues to preach on the Sabbath in the synagogue. Eventually, Timothy and Silas join him at Corinth, and Paul turns to full-time ministry (18:1–5). This intensified ministry results in greater opposition, and Paul is forced to leave the synagogue and meet next door in the house of a God-fearer named Titius Justus. In the face of this pressure, Paul receives a vision from God, telling him to keep on preaching since "I have many people in this city" (18:10). Paul remains in Corinth for eighteen months, a length second only to his time in Ephesus on his third journey (18:6–11).

---

[59] For details on these philosophical traditions, see Keener, *Acts*, 3:2584–95.

[60] Areopagus means "Hill of Ares," and refers to a prominent hill west of the Acropolis named after Ares, the Greek god of war. (It is sometimes called Mars Hill, since Mars was the Roman equivalent of Ares.) It is unclear whether Luke uses the term of the place or of the ruling Council of Athens that met there (or both). There is some evidence that in Paul's day the council met in the Royal Portico in the northwest corner of the Agora. In the Roman period the Areopagus remained a prestigious and venerable assembly, though its authority may have been primarily over religious and moral matters. See C. K. Barrett, *A Critical and Exegetical Commentary on the Acts of the Apostles*, 2 vols., ICC (Edinburgh: T&T Clark, 1998), 2:831; Bruce, *Acts*, 331. On the council's possible reasons for interrogating Paul, see Bruce W. Winter, "On Introducing Gods to Athens: An Alternative Reading of Acts 17:18–20," *TynBul* 47 (1996): 71–90.

	1 Thessalonians ca. 50–51 CE	Paul wrote 1 Thessalonians about this time, after Timothy visited the church and returned with a positive report that the church was thriving despite persecution.

	2 Thessalonians ca. 50–51 CE	Paul wrote 2 Thessalonians about this time to correct misconceptions in the church concerning the day of the Lord.

ANCIENT CONNECTIONS 2.8: THE EDICT OF CLAUDIUS

The Roman emperor Claudius (reigned 41–54 CE) was suspicious of the growing Jewish population in Rome and throughout his reign sought to limit their influence. Things came to a head in 49 CE with their expulsion from Rome. The Roman historian Suetonius (writing ca. 120) notes: "Because the Jews at Rome caused continuous disturbances at the instigation of Chrestus, he expelled them from the city" (*Life of Claudius* 25.4). Most scholars think that Suetonius was mistaken, thinking "Chrestus" (a common name, especially among slaves) was one of the ringleaders of the groups, when in fact it is a misspelling of *Christos* ("Christ") and refers to the sometimes-violent conflicts between Jews and Jewish Christians over whether Jesus was *the Christ*.[61]

Opposition from the Jewish community in Corinth comes to a head when some Jewish leaders bring Paul before Gallio, the Roman proconsul (governor) of Achaia, on charges of teaching contrary to the Jewish law. Before Paul can make his defense, Gallio dismisses the charge as religious rather than political ("questions about words, names, and your own law") and so outside his jurisdiction (18:12–17). This event is historically significant for two reasons. First, coming from a Roman court, the decision sets a legal precedent that Christianity was a sect within Judaism and so shared its status as a recognized religion. This likely lessened persecution (especially from the state), at least until the time of Nero (mid-60s CE). Second, while Luke seldom identifies events in his story with externally datable events, we know from an inscription

[61] Bruce, *Acts*, 347.

that Gallio was proconsul of Achaia from 51–52 CE.[62] So we can approximate the dates of Paul's ministry—both forward and backward—from this point.

After ministering in Corinth for eighteen months, Paul begins his journey home, taking Priscilla and Aquila with him (18:18). When they stop at Ephesus, in the province of Asia, Paul takes the opportunity to teach in the synagogue. The Jews there ask him to stay longer, but he declines, saying that he will try to return. This sets the stage for the "third" missionary journey, which will be focused on Ephesus and Asia Minor. Paul departs for home, leaving Priscilla and Aquila in Ephesus (18:21).

Before describing the details of Paul's third journey, Luke introduces a new character, Apollos, who shows up in Ephesus about this time. He is identified as a Jew from Alexandria, Egypt, an intelligent and gifted orator with a good knowledge of Scripture. Luke says he had been well instructed and taught accurately about Jesus, but only knew the baptism of John. This likely means that he knew about John's baptism of repentance (Luke 3:3), but not Christian baptism commanded by Jesus and practiced by the post-resurrection church (Matt 28:18–20; Acts 2:38).[63] Impressed by his abilities, Priscilla and Aquila take him aside and instruct him further. Eventually, Apollos is sent to Corinth, where his rhetorical skills are put to good use (18:24–19:1).

Third Journey: The Gospel to Asia Minor (18:23; 19:1–21:16)

After spending some time in Antioch (in Syria), Paul returns to Ephesus, where he has an extended three-year ministry (18:22–23; 19:1–41; 20:31). In Ephesus he encounters a group of a dozen "disciples" who, like Apollos, needed further instruction. These were followers of John the Baptist who believed John's message of repentance and the coming Messiah but knew nothing of Jesus or of the eschatological pouring out of the Holy Spirit. They are baptized in the name of Jesus, and when Paul lays hands on them they receive the Spirit and speak in tongues (19:1–7). As elsewhere in Acts, reception of the Holy Spirit marks confirmation of salvation and entrance into the new age of salvation.

Paul spends three months preaching in the synagogue in Ephesus, then under increasing opposition moves to the lecture hall of Tyrannus for two years. This was probably a school of rhetoric, which was rented out when available to traveling philosophers and teachers. Luke reports that from the city of Ephesus the gospel spreads throughout the province of Asia (19:10).

---

[62] For details see Bruce, *Acts*, 352; Barrett, *Critical and Exegetical Commentary*, 2:870–71.

[63] Bruce, *Acts*, 359.

1 Corinthians ca. 54 CE	Paul wrote 1 Corinthians from Ephesus about this time in response to problems in the church and questions sent to him.

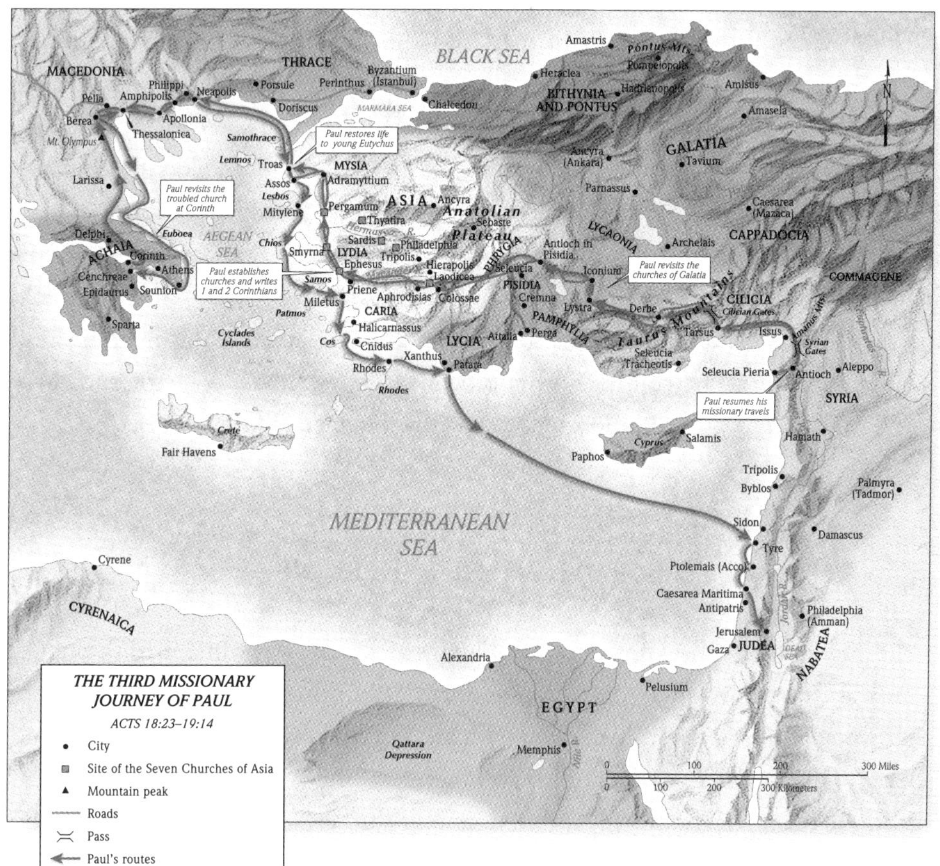

The dominant theme of Paul's Ephesian ministry in Acts is spiritual warfare (cf. Eph 6:10–20).[64] Paul's extraordinary ministry of healing (Acts 19:11–12) provokes some Jewish exorcists to attempt to mimic his success. In one almost farcical episode, seven sons of a Jewish priest named Sceva attempt to cast out a demon in the name of Jesus and Paul. The demon responds with ironic sarcasm: "I know Jesus,

[64] For the conflict with spiritual forces in Pauline theology, see Clinton E. Arnold, *Powers of Darkness: Principalities & Powers in Paul's Letters* (Downers Grove, IL: InterVarsity Press, 1992).

and I recognize Paul—but who are you?" The man with the demon then attacks the would-be exorcists, beating them up, and sending them fleeing naked and wounded (19:13–17).

This kind of spiritual power results in many converts to Christianity and a decline in the practice of magic. People gather to burn their books of magic spells (19:18–20), and the prosperous idol-making business begins to hurt financially. This provokes a backlash when the silversmiths of the city, led by a certain Demetrius, attempt to launch a riot against the Christians. Gathering in the amphitheater, they hold a kind of pep rally for the city's patron goddess, shouting for hours, "Great is Artemis of the Ephesians!" The situation finally calms when the clear-headed city clerk steps forward and quiets the crowd. He appeals to their civic pride by pointing out that the goddess Artemis and the magnificent city of Ephesus are far too great to be threatened by these men, who have done nothing to steal from their temple or to blaspheme Artemis's name. Provoking a riot will result in arrest and punishment from the Roman authorities. The courts and the proconsuls are available to settle such grievances. Persuaded by this common sense, the crowd disperses (19:23–41).

ANCIENT CONNECTIONS 2.9: "GREAT IS ARTEMIS OF THE EPHESIANS"

The goddess Artemis, known to the Romans as Diana, was worshiped throughout the Roman world as the virgin goddess of hunting. At Ephesus, however, her worship was apparently merged with an Anatolian fertility goddess, and she became the premier goddess of love and fertility. She is called the mother goddess, the queen of the world, and first among thrones. Ancient writers identify her temple as one of the Seven Wonders of the World.[65] It was four times the size of the magnificent Parthenon in Athens, approximately 450 feet long and 225 feet wide, with 127 columns. Inside was a massive statue of the goddess and an "image that fell from heaven" (19:35), probably a meteorite that was considered a representation of the goddess. The cult brought great wealth to the city, as tourists and pilgrims filled the city's lodgings and markets and bought images of the goddess and silver shrines depicting the goddess enthroned in her temple. People like Demetrius saw Paul and his anti-idol preaching of Christ's lordship as a serious threat to their prosperity.

---

[65] Clinton E. Arnold, "Acts," *ZIBBC* 2:414.

Shortly after the riot, Paul determines to visit the churches in Macedonia and Achaia before returning to Jerusalem. He heads north and crosses over into Macedonia to visit the churches in Philippi, Thessalonica, and Berea (20:1–2a).

	2 Corinthians ca. 56 CE	Paul wrote 2 Corinthians from Macedonia after being reconciled with the church at Corinth following a period of conflict and alienation.

From Macedonia, Paul heads south into Achaia, where he stays for three months, probably mostly in Corinth (20:2b–3).

	Romans ca. 56 CE	Paul wrote Romans during his time in Corinth to prepare the church in Rome for his visit and to solicit help in an evangelistic outreach to Spain.

From Corinth, Paul begins his journey to Jerusalem, accompanied by a group of leaders from various churches in Macedonia, Achaia, Asia, and Galatia (20:4–5). Although Luke does not tell us their mission, we know from Paul's letters that they are representatives of the Gentile churches of Asia and Greece who are accompanying Paul to Jerusalem carrying a collection of money for the poor and persecuted believers in Jerusalem (1 Cor 16:1–4; 2 Cor 9:1–5; Rom 15:25–28).

When Paul learns of a plot by his Jewish opponents to assassinate him while at sea (20:3), he chooses not to sail directly from Corinth, but instead travels by land north through Macedonia. The "we" section of Acts begins again at Acts 20:6 when Paul reaches Philippi. The previous one ended there several years earlier on Paul's second missionary journey (16:16). The author apparently stays with Paul from here to the end of the book (20:7, 8, 13–15; 21:1–17; 27:1–28:16).

From Philippi, Paul crosses over to Troas. In Troas, on the night before his departure, Paul delivers a long sermon that goes well into the night. A young man named Eutychus who is sitting on a windowsill drifts off to sleep and falls three stories to his death! Rushing down to him, Paul embraces him and Eutychus comes back to life (20:7–12). Again, we see Paul, like Peter earlier (cf. 9:36–42), replicating the miracles of Jesus and so confirming that the events in Acts carry forward what Jesus "began to do and teach" (1:1).

The next day, Paul sets sail again, arriving several days later in Miletus, a coastal town in Asia (20:13–16). From there Paul calls the elders of the church at Ephesus to him. Knowing that great danger awaits him in Jerusalem, he gives what he thinks will be his final message to them. This classic address on Christian leadership is the only speech in Acts that Paul gives to believers (20:17–38).

From Miletus, the group sails to Caesarea, with stops in Tyre and Ptolemais. In Caesarea, they stay at the home of Philip the evangelist, who was so instrumental in the salvation of the Samaritans and the Ethiopian eunuch (Acts 8:4–40). While in Caesarea, a prophet named Agabus (cf. 11:28) symbolically binds Paul's hands and feet with a belt and predicts that he will be arrested and bound in Jerusalem. Paul responds by affirming his willingness to give his life for the name of Jesus (21:1–14).

Fourth Journey: Paul's Arrest, Imprisonment, and Journey to Rome (21:17–28:31)

When Paul arrives in Jerusalem, he is greeted warmly by James and the church leadership and reports on the continuing success of the Gentile mission. To keep a good testimony among the Jewish Christians, he agrees to a plan to pay the expenses for some men who have taken a Jewish Nazirite vow (cf. Num 6:1–21). This action was evidently meant to squelch rumors that Paul opposed the Jewish law and was teaching that Jews should not circumcise their children or keep the law of Moses (21:16–25).[66]

While Paul is in the Jerusalem temple performing the prescribed purification rituals, some Jews from Asia recognize him. Having previously seen him in the city with Trophimus, an Ephesian and a Gentile, they accuse him of taking Gentiles into the temple building—a crime punishable by death (21:26–29). Enraged, the mob seizes Paul and tries to kill him, until soldiers from the Roman garrison intervene and take him into custody. Paul convinces the Roman commander he is not a notorious Egyptian terrorist (see Ancient Connections 2.2) and asks for an opportunity to address the crowd (21:30–40). The commander agrees and Paul speaks to the people, identifying himself as a faithful and zealous Jew, educated by the respected rabbi Gamaliel. They listen intently as he recounts his life leading up to his Damascus encounter with Jesus. Yet when he mentions his commission to preach the good news to the Gentiles, the crowd again becomes enraged. The soldiers grab Paul and take him away for questioning (Acts 22:1–29).

The next day, Paul is sent by the Romans to present his case before the Sanhedrin. Realizing that the council is made up of both Pharisees and Sadducees, Paul provokes an argument among these sects by announcing that he is on trial for preaching the

---

[66] Cf. Acts 18:18, where Luke presents Paul himself as fulfilling a similar vow.

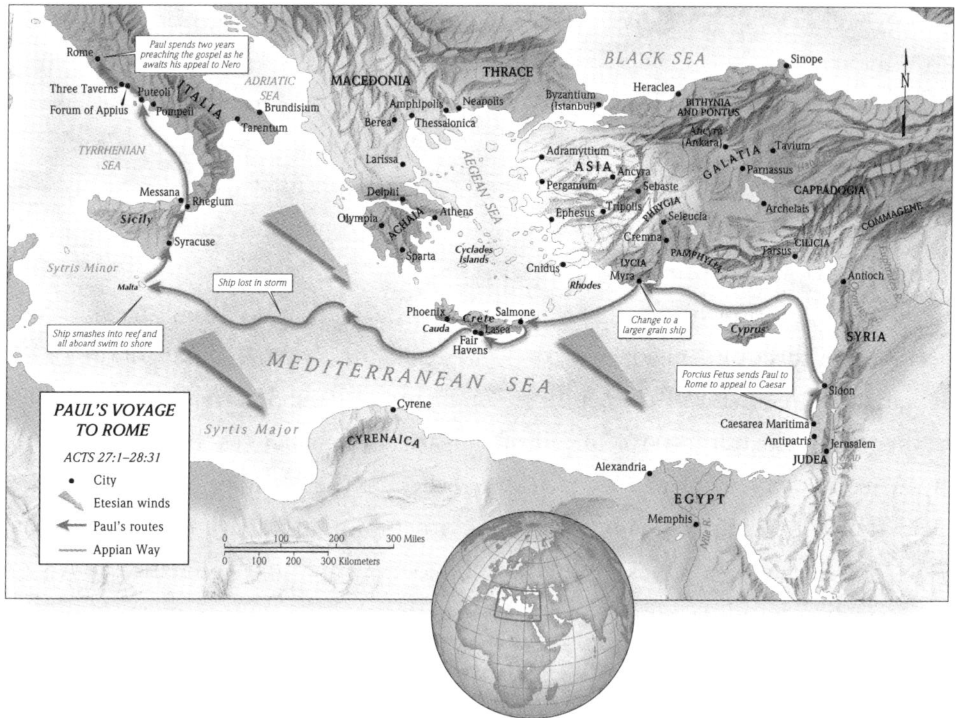

resurrection of the dead (Pharisees believed in a final resurrection; Sadducees did not). Such a violent debate erupts between the two that the Romans again intervene, taking Paul away under protective custody. On the following day, Paul is about to be taken for a second hearing before the Sanhedrin, when Paul is warned by his nephew of a Jewish plot to kill him on the way.[67] In response, the Roman commander sends Paul under heavy guard to the Roman headquarters in Caesarea on the Mediterranean coast (22:30–23:35).

Paul remains in custody in Caesarea for two years. During this time, he defends himself against his accusers before Felix, the Roman governor of Judea (24:1–26; ruled 52–59 CE); Festus, his successor as governor (25:1–12; ruled 59–62 CE); and finally, before King Herod Agrippa II and his sister Bernice,[68] who are visiting Festus (25:13–26:32). Paul's speeches in these three situations allow Luke to demonstrate the

---

[67] This brief but tantalizing reference to "the son of Paul's sister" (23:16) is the only reference in the NT to Paul's relatives.

[68] Herod Agrippa II was the great grandson of Herod the Great and the son of Herod Agrippa I, who had persecuted the church (12:1–25). Bernice was his sister, and the two were rumored to be in an incestuous relationship (Josephus, *Ant.* 20.7.3 §145; Juvenal, *Satires* 6.156–60). Later in Rome, Bernice became the mistress of Titus, the son of Vespasian and

innocence of Paul under Roman law and, more importantly, to show that the story of Jesus and his followers is the fulfillment of God's promises to Israel. These events also fulfill God's prediction to Ananias that Paul would become God's chosen instrument "to take my name to Gentiles, kings, and Israelites" (Acts 9:15; cf. Luke 21:12–15). When Festus considers sending Paul back to Jerusalem for trial, Paul exercises his right as a Roman citizen to appeal to Caesar. Festus responds, "You have appealed to Caesar; to Caesar you will go" (Acts 25:12).

The "we" section begins again at 27:1, as the journey to Rome begins. Luke describes the adventure-filled voyage in vivid detail, making special note of things like the name and regiment of the centurion in charge of Paul, descriptions of the ships, weather and sea patterns, ports of call, and a variety of challenges they face along the way. After a ferocious storm, they are shipwrecked on the island of Malta, where they spend three months, eventually catching another ship and arriving in Rome (Acts 27:1–28:16). The key themes throughout the journey are God's guidance, provision, and protection for his servants and Paul's consistent faithfulness, courage, and integrity in the face of adversity.

Luke concludes Acts with Paul under house arrest in Rome. He reports that after three days, Paul invites a group of Jewish leaders to hear him. He describes his situation, asserts his innocence, and, as throughout Acts, preaches the good news of Jesus to them. As elsewhere in the book, some Jews respond favorably while most reject the message. Paul responds with a warning of judgment from Isa 6:9–10 (Acts 28:26–27). In this way the book ends with three of Luke's key themes that have become familiar to the reader: (1) the rejection of the gospel by many in Israel (28:27); (2) the offer of salvation to the Gentiles, who will respond in great numbers (28:28); and, most importantly, (3) the unstoppable progress of the gospel. Luke concludes with the statement "Paul stayed two whole years in his own rented house. And he welcomed all who visited him, proclaiming the kingdom of God and teaching about the Lord Jesus Christ with all boldness and without hindrance" (28:30–31). Although the gospel messenger is in chains, the gospel message is unrestrained. It continues to go forth, "with all boldness and without hindrance."

---

conqueror of Jerusalem (Tacitus, *Histories* 2.2; Suetonius, *Titus* 7.1–2; Dio Cassius, *Roman History* 65.15.3–5; 66.18.2).

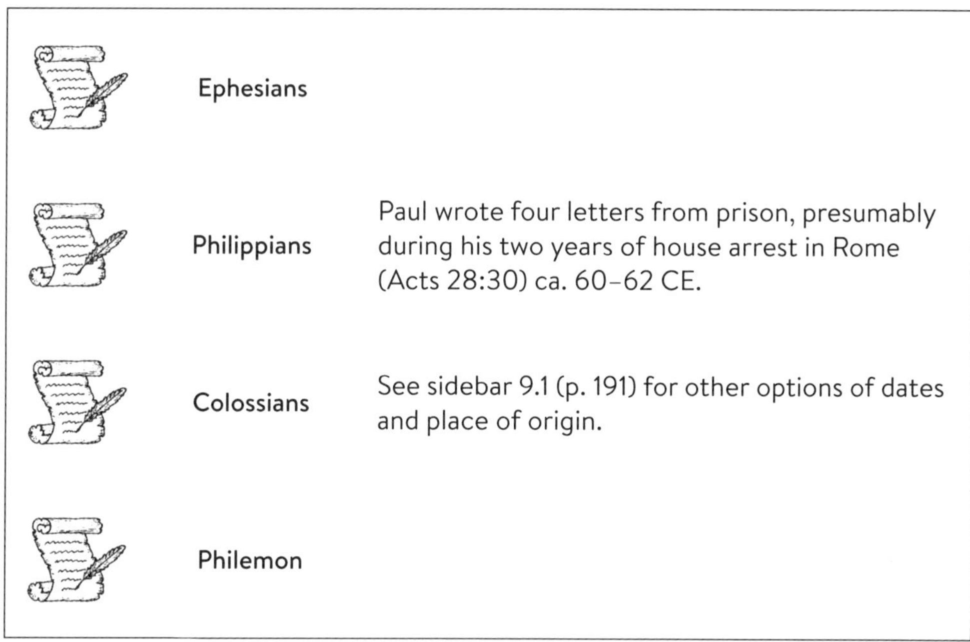

Ephesians	
Philippians	Paul wrote four letters from prison, presumably during his two years of house arrest in Rome (Acts 28:30) ca. 60–62 CE.
Colossians	See sidebar 9.1 (p. 191) for other options of dates and place of origin.
Philemon	

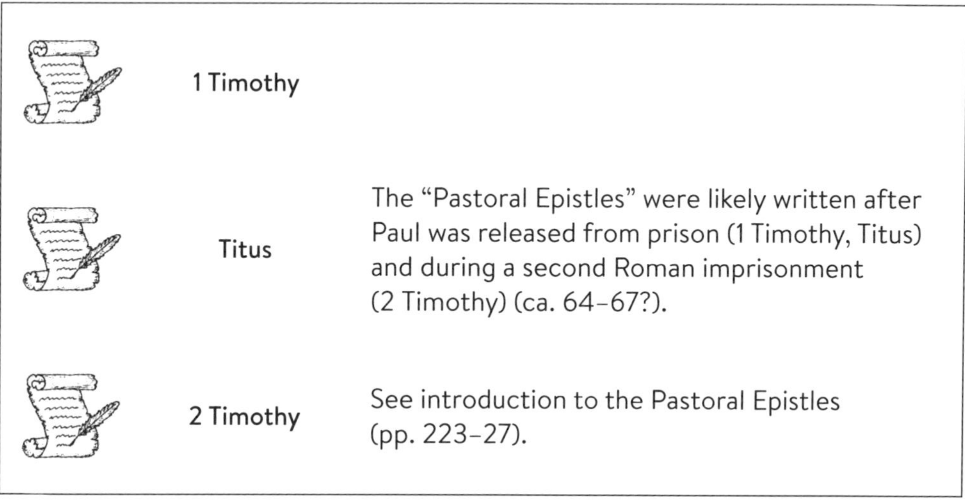

1 Timothy	
Titus	The "Pastoral Epistles" were likely written after Paul was released from prison (1 Timothy, Titus) and during a second Roman imprisonment (2 Timothy) (ca. 64–67?).
2 Timothy	See introduction to the Pastoral Epistles (pp. 223–27).

Old Testament Connections

Both Luke's Gospel and the book of Acts are permeated with citations, allusions, and themes from the Old Testament. This is in line with Luke's overall purpose in Luke-Acts, which is to demonstrate the continuity between the Old Testament people of God, the coming of Jesus the Messiah, and the church that is now proclaiming the good news of the salvation he has achieved. The Jesus movement is not a new religion. It is the continuation and fulfillment of God's plan of salvation for Israel and for the whole world. As the elderly Simeon says when Jesus's parents come to Jerusalem to dedicate Jesus to the Lord: "My eyes have seen your salvation. You have prepared it in the presence of all peoples—a light for revelation to the Gentiles and glory to your people Israel" (Luke 2:30–32; cf. Isa 49:6).

Luke's use of Scripture may be compared and contrasted with Matthew's. While both have a strong fulfillment motif focused on Jesus as the Messiah from the line of David, Matthew's scriptural citations come primarily in narrator comments about events in the story (e.g., "This was to fulfill what was spoken by the prophet . . ."[69]). Luke occasionally does the same thing (cf. Isa 40:3–5 in Luke 3:4–6), but more often citations are made by characters in the story. For example, Jesus reads Isa 61:1–2 in the Nazareth synagogue and then announces that this passage is now being fulfilled in his ministry (Luke 4:18–19). This pattern is especially true in Acts, where all of the explicit quotations with introductory formulas appear in the direct speech of narrative characters.[70] Peter, for example, cites Pss 69:25 and 109:8 with reference to the replacement of Judas (Acts 1:20). In his Pentecost sermon, Peter cites Joel 2:28–32 with reference to the coming of the Spirit (Acts 2:17–21) and Ps 16:8–11 as a prophecy of the resurrection of Jesus (Acts 2:25–28). This pattern continues in the speeches of Stephen (7:2–53), Paul (13:16–41), and James (15:13–21).

Luke's connections to Scripture go well beyond direct quotations. His story is permeated with OT themes and motifs. As we have seen, this is especially true of the Gospel birth narrative (Luke 1–2), which immerses the reader in OT themes. The story begins in the Jewish temple in Jerusalem, the center of Israel's religious life, where a priest named Zechariah offers incense before the Lord. He and his wife Elizabeth are "righteous in God's sight, living without blame according to all the commands and requirements of the Lord." Yet Elizabeth is barren and unable to have children until the Lord opens her womb—a common OT theme (1:5–7).[71] Other characters, like Joseph, Mary, Simeon, and Anna, are faithful and obedient Jews. These characters frequently break into hymns of praise, similar to the OT psalms.[72]

Luke's perspective on Scripture may be seen in two passages at the end of the Gospel. Jesus rebukes the two disciples he meets on the road to Emmaus for not

---

69 See Matt 1:22–23; 2:15, 17–18, 23; 4:14–16; 8:17; 12:17–21; 13:35; 21:4–5; 27:9–10.

70 Alan J. Thompson, "Acts, Book of," in *DNTUOT*, 7.

71 Gen 11:31 (Sarai); Gen 25:21 (Rebekah); Gen 29:31 (Rachel); Judg 13:2 (mother of Samson); 1 Sam 1:2 (Hannah).

72 Luke 1:46–55 (Mary); 1:67–79 (Zechariah); 2:14 (an army of angels); 2:29–32 (Simeon).

recognizing the prophets' predictions of the suffering role of the Messiah (Luke 24:25–26). "Then beginning with Moses and all the Prophets, he interpreted for them the things concerning himself in all the Scriptures" (24:27). This theme is expanded when Jesus appears to the eleven disciples later in the chapter:

> He said to them, "This is what I told you while I was still with you: Everything must be fulfilled that is written about me in the Law of Moses, the Prophets and the Psalms."
>
> Then he opened their minds so they could understand the Scriptures. He told them, "This is what is written: The Messiah will suffer and rise from the dead on the third day, and repentance for the forgiveness of sins will be preached in his name to all nations, beginning at Jerusalem" (24:44–47 NIV).

The whole story in Luke-Acts is thus presented as the fulfillment of Scripture, with a special emphasis on its apologetic and legitimizing role. The suffering role of the Messiah and the expansion of the gospel to the Gentiles—the two most controversial themes in Luke-Acts—both find their legitimization in the Hebrew Scriptures.

Gospel Connections

The traditional title of Acts is "the Acts of the Apostles." This is not quite right since the book does not provide a biography of the twelve apostles. Though the Twelve appear in the early chapters (especially Peter and John), they are absent in most of the book. Others have suggested a better title would be the "Acts of God," since Luke narrates the fulfillment of God's covenants and promises given to the Old Testament people of God.[73] Another suggested title is the "Acts of Jesus, Part 2," since Luke refers to Acts as a continuation of "all that Jesus began to do and to teach," as recorded in Luke's Gospel (Acts 1:1). Finally, the book has sometimes been labeled as the "Acts of the Holy Spirit." This is also appropriate since the Spirit is the church's guiding force in Acts. The pouring out of the Spirit on the day of Pentecost marks the beginning of the church and the dawn of the new age of salvation. Throughout Acts, the Spirit fills, empowers, and guides believers, assuring the success of the church in fulfilling Christ's commission to take the gospel message from Jerusalem to the ends of the earth.

---

[73] David E. Garland, *Acts*, TTCS (Grand Rapids: Baker, 2017), 8.

Life Connections

Many Christians read Acts looking for the model on how to run a church. Yet Luke's purpose was not to provide a handbook on church polity. For example, there is very little direction in Acts on the day-to-day functioning of the church, things like the structure and offices of church leadership (elders, pastors, deacons, overseers?), the format of a worship service and its liturgy, how and with what frequency to administer the Lord's Supper, who should be baptized (infants or only professing believers?) and with what mode (immersion, sprinkling, pouring?). Luke does not focus on these kinds of things because his purpose is *not* to provide an instruction manual for church polity. It is to demonstrate the truth of the gospel message by charting its unstoppable progress.

Yet while Acts is not a handbook on how to "do church," the book provides great insight into what a healthy church looks like. Throughout the book we see that the church is the Spirit-led and Spirit-directed community of God on earth. Acting in purity, love, and unity, the church is to bear testimony to Christ, to call all people to faith in him for the forgiveness of sins, and to proclaim the good news of salvation from Jerusalem to the ends of the earth.

Interactive Questions

1. What verse is identified as the theme of the book of Acts and also its outline?

2. What role does the Holy Spirit play in the book of Acts?

3. What is the significance of the day of Pentecost for the followers of Jesus?

4. What role does the ministry and martyrdom of Stephen play in the progress of the narrative in Acts?

5. What role does the ministry of Philip play in the progress of the narrative in Acts?

6. What is the significance of the Cornelius episode for the progress of the narrative in Acts?

7. What decision was made at the Council of Jerusalem, and why is this important for the expansion of the gospel in Acts?

8. In what ways is the conversion and missionary activity of Paul critical for Luke's narrative purpose in Acts? How does Luke want his readers to view Paul with reference to Judaism?

9. What patterns of ministry does Paul establish on his "first" missionary journey? Why does he go first to the synagogue?

10. How does the ending of the book of Acts illustrate its main themes?

11. How might reading the book of Acts benefit Christians today?

Study Resources

Barrett, C. K. *A Critical and Exegetical Commentary on the Acts of the Apostles*. 2 vols. ICC. Edinburgh: T&T Clark, 1994, 1998.

Bauer, David R. *The Book of Acts as Story: A Narrative-Critical Study*. Grand Rapids: Baker Academic, 2021.

Bock, Darrell. *Acts*. BEC. Grand Rapids: Baker, 2007.

Bruce, F. F. *Acts*. Rev. ed. NICNT. Grand Rapids: Eerdmans, 1988.

Fitzmyer, Joseph A. *Acts of the Apostles: A New Translation with Introduction and Commentary*. AB. Garden City, NY: Doubleday, 1998.

Garland, David E. *Acts*. TTCS. Grand Rapids: Baker, 2017.

Gaventa, Beverly. *Acts*. ANTC. Nashville: Abingdon, 2003.

Huffman, Douglas S. *The Story Continues: A Survey of the Acts of the Apostles*. Grand Rapids: Zondervan, 2024.

Jennings, Willie James. *Acts*. Belief: A Theological Commentary on the Bible. Louisville: Westminster John Knox, 2017.

Jervell, Jacob. *The Theology of the Acts of the Apostles*. New Testament Theology. Cambridge: Cambridge University Press, 1987.

Keener, Craig S. *Acts*. NCBC. Cambridge: Cambridge University Press, 2020.

———. *Acts: An Exegetical Commentary*. 4 vols. Grand Rapids: Baker, 2012–2015.

Longenecker, Richard N. *Acts*. EBC. Grand Rapids, Zondervan: 2007.

Marshall, I. Howard. *The Acts of the Apostles: An Introduction and Commentary*. TNTC. Grand Rapids: Eerdmans, 1980.

Maloney, Linda M., and Ivoni Richter Reimer. *Acts of the Apostles*. Wisdom Commentary Series. Collegeville, MN: Liturgical Press, 2022.

Padilla, Osvaldo. *The Acts of the Apostles: Interpretation, History and Theology*. Downers Grove, IL: IVP Academic, 2016.

Pervo, Richard. *Acts*. Hermeneia. Fortress, 2008.

Polhill, John B. *Acts*. NAC. Broadman, 1992.

Schnabel, Eckhard J. *Acts*. ZECNT. Grand Rapids: Zondervan, 2012.

Schreiner, Patrick. *Acts*. Christian Standard Commentary. Holman Reference, 2022.

———. *The Mission of the Triune God: A Theology of Acts*. Wheaton, IL: Crossway, 2022.

Walton, Steve. *Acts 1–9:42*. WBC 37A. Grand Rapids: Zondervan, 2024.

———. *Reading Acts Theologically*. London: Bloomsbury, 2022.

Witherington, Ben. *The Acts of the Apostles: A Socio-Rhetorical Commentary*. Grand Rapids: Eerdmans, 1997.

THE LETTERS OF PAUL

MISSIONARY LETTERS

Galatians

1 and 2 Thessalonians

1 Corinthians

2 Corinthians

Romans

3

Galatians

Probably written from Antioch, Syria, ca. 49 CE

For freedom, Christ set us free. Stand firm, then,
and don't submit again to a yoke of slavery.

—Galatians 5:1

Outline

I. Introduction (1:1–10)
   A. Prescript: Paul's Authority (1:1–5)
   B. The Problem: Desertion from the True Faith (1:6–10)
II. The Personal Argument (1:11–2:21)
   A. Paul Received His Gospel by Revelation from God (1:11–24)
   B. Paul's Gospel Was Recognized by the Apostles (2:1–10)
   C. Paul's Rebuke of Peter (2:11–14)
   D. Transition: The Nature of the Gospel (2:15–21)
III. The Theological Argument: The Failure of Law Observance (3:1–4:31)
   A. You Gentiles Received the Holy Spirit by Faith (3:1–6)

B. Jews Have Always Been Saved by Faith: The Example of Abraham (3:7–9)
C. The Law Cannot Save; It Only Condemns (3:10–25)
D. Children of God through Faith (3:26–4:7)
E. Paul's Personal Appeal (4:8–20)
F. Allegory of Two Covenants (4:21–31)

IV. The Practical Argument (5:1–6:10)
A. A Call to Freedom (5:1–15)
B. Living by the Spirit (5:16–6:10)

V. Conclusion and Benediction (6:11–18)

Author, Occasion, Message

Author

The author identifies himself as "Paul, an apostle" (1:1), and this attribution is almost universally accepted today.

Occasion: North or South Galatian Theories?

Paul addresses the letter to "the churches in Galatia," but there is a debate over where these churches are. The term "Galatia" could be used in two different ways. One was of the ethnic region of north central Asia Minor named after the Gauls (or Celts) who had settled there. In 25 BCE, however, the Romans established the province of Galatia, which extended much further southward. The north Galatian theory claims that Paul is writing to ethnic Galatians in the north. The south Galatian theory says that Paul is writing to churches in the south, including Pisidian-Antioch, Iconium, Lystra, and Derbe, the four he and Barnabas established on their first missionary journey (Acts 13–14).

This debate affects the possible dates of Galatians. If Paul is writing to the south, the letter could have been written as early as 49 CE, shortly after the first journey (or any time after that).[1] If Paul is writing to the north, he must have written later, during or after the second or third journeys. We should note that while this debate is

[1] Some scholars hold to a south Galatian audience, but date the letter later, during or after the second missionary journey. See, for example, M. Silva, *Explorations in Exegetical Method: Galatians as a Test Case* (Grand Rapids: Baker, 1996), 131–32.

important historically with regard to the recipients and the date of the letter, it does not change the letter's essential message and theme.

Through most of church history, scholars have tended to favor the north Galatian theory. The strongest argument for this view is that Luke does not refer to the churches established during the first journey as located in "Galatia." His first reference to Galatia occurs during the second missionary journey, when Paul and Silas are said to travel through "Phrygia and Galatia" (Acts 16:6; cf. 18:23). Another argument for north Galatia is the similarity between events recorded in Gal 2:1–10 and the Jerusalem Council in Acts 15, especially the focus on the demand for Gentile circumcision (Gal 2:3; Acts 15:5). This would push the date of the letter forward, after the council and so during or after the second or third missionary journeys.

While the north Galatian theory has been popular throughout church history, the majority of contemporary scholars favor south Galatia. The following evidence favors this view:

(a) In geographical descriptions, Paul normally uses the names of Roman provinces. For example, in 1 Corinthians 16, he refers to Galatia (v. 1), Macedonia (v. 5), Achaia (v. 15), and Asia (v. 19), all of which are Roman provinces. So "the churches of Galatia" in Gal 1:2 probably also means the Roman province, which included the four churches started in Acts 13–14.

(b) There is no explicit mention in any of Paul's letters of churches or individuals from the north Galatian region. It is uncertain whether Paul founded churches there or even traveled there.

(c) In the letter to the Galatians, Paul refers to only two visits to Jerusalem, the visit when he met Peter and James (1:18) and his second visit in response to "a revelation" (2:2). Correlated with Acts, these would seem to be his first visit in Acts 9:26 and the famine visit with Barnabas in 11:28–30. Paul's point in Galatians seems to be that these were his *only* two visits to Jerusalem, evidence that he did not receive his gospel from the Jerusalem apostles. The claim that Gal 2:1–10 must be the Jerusalem Council is partly answered by the fact that Paul identifies this as a private meeting (2:2), while the Jerusalem Council was a more public event.

(d) There is no mention in Galatians of the decrees established at the Jerusalem Council. If these decrees had already been issued (a necessity for the north Galatian theory), it seems likely Paul would have introduced the council's decision as evidence that Gentiles did not need to be circumcised.

(e) Paul refers to Barnabas in the letter as though the Galatians know him (Gal 2:1, 9, 13). But Barnabas accompanied Paul only on his first journey, when the south Galatian churches were established. This argument is partially neutralized by the fact that Barnabas (like Peter and James) was a well-known figure in the early church, even to those he had not personally met (see 1 Cor 9:6; Col 4:10).

In short, the south Galatian theory seems to align more closely with Paul's own statements in Galatians and elsewhere, making it the preferred view.

Message

The general situation Paul is responding to in Galatians seems clear enough. Certain individuals are "troubling" his Galatian churches (1:7), teaching that Gentiles need to be circumcised and to keep the Jewish law to be saved. Paul is furious and responds with great passion, denouncing the false teachers and calling the Galatians to remain faithful to the true gospel: Salvation comes through faith in Jesus Christ, not by the "works of the law."

But what are the "works of the law"? Were Paul's opponents teaching legalism—that good works are necessary for salvation? Or were they teaching Jewish exclusivity—claiming that Gentiles needed to first become Jews to be saved? These questions have become part of a much larger scholarly debate concerning the nature of first-century Judaism and Paul's response to it. For the issues and possible solutions, see sidebar 3.1.

SIDEBAR 3.1: THE NEW PERSPECTIVE ON PAUL

The so-called New Perspective on Paul represents a scholarly revolution of sorts in how many scholars view first-century Judaism and the theology of the apostle Paul. While drawing ideas from earlier scholars,[2] the movement's launch can be traced to the groundbreaking work of E. P. Sanders in his 1977 volume, *Paul and Palestinian Judaism.*[3] Sanders claimed that the common view of first-century Judaism as a legalistic religion of salvation by works was incorrect. This distortion can be traced especially to the Protestant Reformers, who viewed first-century Judaism through the lens of their opposition to the Roman Catholic Church. Sanders asserted that, contrary to the claims of the Reformers, the Jews of Jesus's day were *not* legalists who believed they could earn salvation by obedience to the law. Rather, Jews considered their membership in the people of

---

[2] Frequently cited as a precursor is Krister Stendahl, "The Apostle Paul and the Introspective Conscience of the West," *HTR* 56, no. 3 (1963): 199–215.

[3] E. P. Sanders, *Paul and Palestinian Judaism: A Comparison of Patterns of Religion* (Philadelphia: Fortress Press, 1977).

God to be the result of a covenant of grace that God had established with them. Obedience to the law was not the means of salvation, which came by God's gracious choice, but was the way that Israel *maintained* its covenant relationship with God. Sanders coined the term "covenantal nomism" to describe this perspective. According to Sanders, when Paul came to believe that Jesus was the Messiah, he faced a dilemma. If Jesus was the way of salvation, then the Jewish law could not be. Paul resolved this problem through a backwards argument "from solution to plight." The solution is that Jesus is the Messiah. If this is true, there must be a problem with Israel's present condition (the plight). Paul claimed this problem was legalism—Israel was trying to be saved by their own effort, rather than by God's grace.

Sanders's perspective received a wide range of responses, from outright rejection, to affirmation, to qualification. Two of the most important responses were those of James D. G. Dunn and N. T. Wright.[4] Dunn, who was responsible for coining the term "New Perspective on Paul," argued that Sanders was essentially right about Judaism being a religion of grace but was wrong about Paul's response. According to Dunn, the "works of the law" that Paul rejected were not legalistic attempts to earn salvation. They were rather the boundary markers or badges of identity that determined what it meant to be Jewish, including especially circumcision, Sabbath observance, and obedience to dietary laws. Paul is essentially arguing that you don't need to become Jewish to be part of the eschatological people of God. In the new age and under the new covenant inaugurated by Jesus's life, death, and resurrection, salvation is available to all people through faith in Jesus the Messiah, regardless of their ethnic identity. Like the phrase "works of the law," the key Pauline term "justification" also takes on new meaning in the New Perspective. The traditional meaning is that God "declares righteous" those who depend wholly on God's grace. N. T. Wright, by contrast, defines justification as being "reckoned by God to be a true member of his family."[5] It is the verdict of God at the final judgment concerning who really is a member of the people of God through faith.

---

[4] Originally published in James D. G. Dunn, "The New Perspective on Paul," *BJRL* 65 (1983): 95–122; republished in Dunn, *Jesus, Paul and the Law: Studies in Mark and Galatians* (London: SPCK, 1990), 183–214; Dunn, *The New Perspective on Paul*, rev. ed. (Grand Rapids: Eerdmans, 2008).

[5] N. T. Wright, *Justification: God's Plan and Paul's Vision* (Downers Grove, IL: IVP, 2009), 119, 121.

As with most groundbreaking ideas, there are insights to be gleaned as well as cautions to be observed from the New Perspective. Most scholars today acknowledge that Sanders and company have provided an important corrective to the sweeping claim that first-century Judaism was a legalistic religion of works (and to the anti-Semitism that has often accompanied such claims). There is much grace to be found in the Jewish literature of this period. At the same time, Sanders was selective in pointing to texts that emphasized God's gracious choice and downplayed those that suggest obedience to the law can earn merit before God.[6] Of course this kind of legalism is not unique to Judaism. In many Christian contexts, teaching about free grace appears side-by-side with legalistic practice.

Balance is also needed in identifying Paul's response. In support of the New Perspective, there is no doubt that Paul is arguing against Jewish exclusivity and that the inclusion of the Gentiles *as Gentiles* is central to his theology. The Judaizers were teaching that since God's covenant was with the people of Israel, believers in Jesus the Messiah must first become *Jews* to receive the blessings of that covenant. And this required circumcision (for males) and the other requirements of the Mosaic law (cf. Acts 15:1). Against this view, Paul emphatically asserts that in the new age of salvation, faith in Jesus alone brings salvation. The stipulations of the old covenant—including circumcision, Sabbath observance, dietary laws, and so on—have been fulfilled in Christ and are no longer binding on the people of God. In Christ "there is no Jew or Greek" (Gal 3:28), so that "both circumcision and uncircumcision mean nothing; what matters instead is a new creation" (6:15).

At the same time, Paul's response includes opposition to *both* Jewish exclusivity *and* legalism. There are Pauline texts that go beyond the question of ethnicity and speak more generally of the danger of seeking merit before God through righteous actions (cf. Rom 4:4–5; Eph 2:8–9). It seems to me that Paul is mounting a two-pronged response to the claims of the Judaizers. First, in the new creation, the law has been fulfilled in Christ so that Jewish exclusivity is at an end. All people—Jews and Gentiles alike—are justified by faith alone

---

[6] See especially D. A. Carson, Mark Seifrid, Peter T. O'Brien, eds., *Paul and Variegated Nomism*, vol. 1, *The Complexities of Second Temple Judaism* (Grand Rapids: Baker 2001); Thomas Schreiner, *The Law and Its Fulfillment. A Pauline Theology of Law* (Grand Rapids: Baker, 1993), 114–21; Stephen Westerholm, *Perspectives Old and New on Paul: The "Lutheran" Paul and His Critics* (Grand Rapids: Eerdmans, 2004), 208–28.

through God's grace, so becoming Jewish is not necessary for salvation. Second, Paul argues, claiming that such "works of the law" are necessary for salvation in fact *amounts to legalism*, attempting to be saved by *works*. This disqualifies one for salvation, since it is trusting in oneself rather than Christ's finished work on the cross. All stand guilty before a righteous and perfect God and are wholly dependent on God's grace for salvation.

Interpretive Overview of Galatians

Introduction (1:1–10)

Prescript: Paul's Authority (1:1–5)

Galatians begins in typical first-century letter-writing style, with the author's name and credentials followed by the recipients and a greeting. Paul's defense of his gospel starts in his very first line. He identifies himself as an "apostle," meaning a "messenger" or one sent with a message or task. Yet Paul clarifies he was *not* sent by any human authority, but "by Jesus Christ and God the Father who raised him from the dead" (1:1). He will develop this point in detail in verses 11–24, emphasizing that the truth of his gospel is confirmed because it came from God himself.

The recipients are "the churches of Galatia." As noted in the introduction, this likely refers to the churches started during Paul's first missionary journey, in Pisidian Antioch, Iconium, Lystra, and Derbe (Acts 13–14).

The Problem: Desertion from the True Faith (1:6–10)

At this point in his letters, Paul typically provides a prayer of thanksgiving to God for the church and its ministry.[7] Yet in Galatians, this thanksgiving is missing. Paul is clearly disturbed and skips such niceties, launching immediately into his urgent reason for writing. He expresses shock that the Galatian Christians are so quickly deserting the good news that he had preached to them and are turning to a "different gospel." Paul quickly qualifies that there is no such thing as another gospel. There is only one true gospel! The Judaizers are preaching a lie, a *false gospel*. Paul drives this point home with hyperbole, proposing the absurd scenario that even if he were to

[7] Cf. Rom 1:8; 1 Cor 1:4; etc.

return and preach a different gospel to them or, even more absurdly, if an angel from heaven were to descend and preach a different gospel, they must not accept it. He goes so far as to pronounce a curse on anyone who would preach a different gospel (1:8–9). The false gospel of the Judaizers imperils the salvation of anyone who hears it, because it denies the one true way of salvation—God's grace received through faith.

The Personal Argument (1:11–2:21)

Paul Received His Gospel by Revelation from God (1:11–24)

Paul's first major defense of his gospel is autobiographical. He makes two main points. First, Paul asserts that the gospel he is preaching was not given to him by any person, but by a direct revelation from God (vv. 11–12). He offers two proofs of this: (1) First is the radical transformation of his life (vv. 13–16). Paul reminds the Galatians that in his former life, he was a zealous persecutor of the church. What could account for Paul's radical transformation? Only God's divine intervention in an encounter with the resurrected Christ. (2) The second proof that Paul's gospel came from God was the fact that he did not receive it from the apostles in Jerusalem or the churches of Judea (1:17–24). After his Damascus Road experience, Paul did not go to Jerusalem, but to Arabia. Only after three years did he come to Jerusalem, where he stayed with Peter (Cephas) for just fifteen days.[8] He also met James, but none of the other apostles. Paul's point is that he was preaching his gospel long before he had any contact with the Jerusalem apostles.[9] He did not receive it from them.

Paul's Gospel was Recognized by the Apostles (2:1–10)

The truth of Paul's gospel is not only confirmed by its source in God (1:11–24), but also by its acknowledgement by the Jerusalem apostles (2:1–10). Although Paul's message did not come from these apostles (1:1, 11–12, 17–24), it is important to his argument that they *affirmed* his ministry. After all, they were the original followers of Jesus and had been commissioned by him. Paul writes that fourteen years after his conversion, he returned to Jerusalem for a second time (2:1). As noted in the introduction, this was likely the famine visit of Acts 11:27–30; 12:25. Paul says he went to Jerusalem at God's direction ("according to a revelation," 2:2) in part to confirm that

---

[8] On Peter/Cephas, see chap. 2, note 34.

[9] See sidebar 2.3 for evidence of Paul's preaching before his first visit to Jerusalem.

he "was not running . . . in vain" (v. 2).[10] In other words, he wanted to confirm that he and the Jerusalem apostles were on the same page and working toward the same goal. This was confirmed in two ways.

First, Paul's associate Titus was not compelled to be circumcised, even though he was a Greek (2:3). Evidently, some of the Judaizers, whom Paul calls "false brothers" (v. 4), were conspiring behind the scenes to require Titus's circumcision. Paul would have none of it and writes that "we did not give up and submit to these people for even a moment, so that the truth of the gospel would be preserved for you" (v. 5). This was a huge win for Paul (and Titus!), since it amounted to acknowledging that Titus was a true believer even though he was a Gentile and uncircumcised—the very issue now in dispute in Galatia.[11]

A second confirmation that Paul's gospel was recognized by the apostles was their confirmation of his apostolic commission (2:6–10). Although they "added nothing to my message" (2:6 NIV)—which, as Paul has just established, came directly from God—they recognized and affirmed that God had given Paul a mission to take the good news to the Gentiles, just as Peter and the others had a commission to take it to the Jews (2:7–9). By extending to Paul and Barnabas the "right hand of fellowship" (v. 9), they accepted them as equals and friends. Their only request was that Paul would "remember the poor" (v. 10), that is, provide support for the persecuted and poverty-stricken church in Jerusalem.[12]

Paul's Rebuke of Peter (2:11–14)

In verse 11 the tone changes, as Paul introduces one more incident related to the Jerusalem apostles. After the positive affirmation that Gentiles did not need to be circumcised to be part of the people of God, Paul and Barnabas returned to Antioch (cf. Acts 12:25). Peter (= Cephas) subsequently visited Antioch and participated regularly in fellowship meals with Gentiles. Yet when some Judaizers came from Jerusalem and criticized him for participating in meals that were not kosher, Peter backed down

---

[10] This "revelation" (Gal 2:2) was likely the prophecy of Agabus in Acts 11:28, further evidence that Gal 2:1–10 is describing the famine visit of Acts 11 rather than the Jerusalem Council of Acts 15.

[11] See discussion of Acts 16:3 (p. 52) for why Paul was willing to circumcise Timothy but not Titus.

[12] This was Paul's mission on the present famine visit and would be a key emphasis on Paul's third missionary journey, where he gathered a collection for the Jerusalem church from the Gentile churches of Greece and Asia Minor (1 Cor 16:1–4; 2 Cor 8–9; Rom 15:25–27).

and withdrew from the Gentiles.[13] Paul reports that "the rest of the Jews" and "even Barnabas" were led astray by this hypocrisy (2:13). Paul publicly confronted Peter for first acknowledging that salvation came by faith apart from the law but then withdrawing from fellowship with Gentiles who did not follow the law.

Transition: The Nature of the Gospel (2:15–21)

It is difficult to tell how much, if any, of verses 15–21 is a continuation of Paul's dialogue with Peter (v. 14) and how much is his commentary for the Galatians. In either case, Paul asserts that you cannot have it both ways, affirming that salvation comes by faith in Christ and then requiring adherence to the works of the law. Paul says in verses 19–20 that he has been "crucified with Christ" so that now Christ lives in him, accomplishing what Paul could not. This is the essence of Paul's gospel. In our sinful state, we are spiritually helpless and unable to save ourselves. Through faith in Christ, we die with him and are raised with him to new life. His resurrection life becomes ours (cf. Rom 6:1–14). This section serves as a transition from Paul's personal or autobiographical arguments (chaps. 1–2) to his theological ones (chaps. 3–4).

SIDEBAR 3.2: "FAITH IN CHRIST" OR "THE FAITHFULNESS OF CHRIST"

The Greek genitive phrase *pistis christou* has traditionally been translated as "faith in Christ," an objective genitive (Christ is the object of our faith). But in recent years a number of scholars have argued that since *pistis* can also mean "faithfulness," the phrase should be translated "faithfulness of Christ," a subjective genitive (Christ is the subject who acts faithfully).[14] The subjective genitive provides greater emphasis on Paul's teaching that salvation comes through

---

[13] Paul calls this delegation from Jerusalem "certain men . . . from James" (Gal 2:12). James, Jesus's half brother, had become an influential leader in the Jerusalem church (Gal 1:19; 2:9; cf. Acts 12:17; 15:13–21; 21:18–26) and for many represented conservative Jewish Christianity. See the discussion of Acts 15:13–21; 21:18–26 in chapter 2.

[14] See G. Howard, "The 'Faith of Christ,'" *ExpTim* 85 (1974): 212–15; Richard B. Hays, *The Faith of Jesus Christ: An Investigation of the Narrative Substructure of Galatians 3:1–4:11*, SBLDS 56 (Chico, CA: Scholars, 1983); Morna D. Hooker, "Πίστις Χριστοῦ," *NTS* 35 (1989): 321–42; Kevin W. McFadden, *Faith in the Son of God: The Place of Christ-Oriented Faith Within Pauline Theology* (Wheaton, IL: Crossway, 2021). A summary of the arguments for both views can be seen in Thomas R. Schreiner, *Galatians*, ZECNT (Grand Rapids: Zondervan, 2010), 163–66.

Christ's actions alone. Compare the NIV and the NET Bible on seven passages below, where *pistis christou* or related phrases appear.

While this perspective has increased in popularity in recent years, the majority of Pauline scholars still favor the objective genitive ("faith in Christ").[15] Among popular English translations, only the NET, the CEB, and the NRSVue consistently adopt the subjective genitive. Some versions place this reading in footnotes (cf. NIV, CSB, NRSV).

This question is an important one with reference to the meaning (and translation) of these texts, but it does not fundamentally change Paul's theology. Those who argue for "faith in Christ" still recognize that for Paul salvation is achieved by Christ's work alone. And those who argue for "the faithfulness of Christ" acknowledge that these and many other passages still teach that salvation is received by faith. Indeed, in several passages where the genitive phrase appears, Paul also uses the verb *pisteuō* ("believe," "have faith") to refer explicitly to those who believe/have faith in Christ (see Rom 3:22; Gal 2:16; 3:22).

	NIV (Objective Genitive)	NET (Subjective Genitive)
Rom 3:22	This righteousness is given through **faith in Jesus Christ** to all who believe.	the righteousness of God through the **faithfulness of Jesus Christ** for all who believe.
Rom 3:26	so as to be just and the one who justifies those who have **faith in Jesus.**	so that he would be just and the justifier of the one who lives because of **Jesus' faithfulness.**
Gal 2:16	know that a person is not justified by the works of the law, but by **faith in Jesus Christ**. So we, too, have put our faith in Christ Jesus that we may be justified by **faith in Christ** and not by the works of the law . . .	yet we know that no one is justified by the works of the law but by the **faithfulness of Jesus Christ.** And we have come to believe in Christ Jesus, so that we may be justified by the **faithfulness of Christ** and not by the works of the law . . .

[15] See for example, J. D. G. Dunn, *Romans*, WBC (Dallas: Word, 1988), 1:166–67; Schreiner, *Galatians*, 163–66; Douglas J. Moo, *Galatians*, BECNT (Grand Rapids: Baker, 2013), 160–61.

Gal 2:20	The life I now live in the body, I live by **faith in the Son of God** . . .	So the life I now live in the body, I live because of the **faithfulness of the Son of God** . . .
Gal 3:22	. . . so that what was promised, being given through **faith in Jesus Christ**, might be given to those who believe.	. . . so that the promise could be given—because of the **faithful-ness of Jesus** Christ—to those who believe
Eph 3:12	In him and through **faith in him** we may approach God with freedom and confidence.	in whom we have boldness and confident access to God by way of **Christ's faithfulness.**
Phil 3:9	. . . not having a righteousness of my own that comes from the law, but that which is through **faith in Christ** . . .	not because I have my own righ-teousness derived from the law, but because I have the righteous-ness that comes by way of **Christ's faithfulness** . . .

The Theological Argument: The Failure of Law Observance (3:1–4:31)

Having demonstrated that his gospel came directly from God and that it was affirmed by the Jerusalem apostles, Paul now turns to a full-scale defense of the doctrine of justification by God's grace through faith.

You Gentiles Received the Holy Spirit by Faith (3:1–6)

Using strong language ("You foolish Galatians!"), Paul reminds the Galatians that they received the Holy Spirit, the ultimate mark of authentic salvation, by faith in Jesus, not by the works of the law. Why would they now start over and try to earn it for themselves?

Jews Have Always Been Saved by Faith: The Example of Abraham (3:7–9)

Since Paul's opponents were claiming circumcision was necessary to be part of the people of God, Paul points to the example of Abraham, the founding father of the Jewish nation. According to Gen 15:6, Abraham was declared righteous not because of his works, but because he believed God. This shows that it is those who have faith, not those who are circumcised, who are the true children of Abraham. The inclusion of the Gentiles by faith was promised already to Abraham in God's covenant with him: "All nations will be blessed through you" (3:8; Gen 12:3).

The Law Cannot Save; It Only Condemns (3:10–25)

If salvation comes by faith, it cannot also come by obeying the law. Paul follows with a three-fold indictment of the law. First, depending on the works of the law to be saved only brings condemnation, since Deut 27:26 pronounces a curse on "Everyone who does not do everything written in the book of the law" (3:10). For those who believe, however, Christ redeems them from this curse by taking that curse upon himself (3:10–14, citing Deut 21:23). Second, God's covenant with Abraham represents a divine promise, which cannot be cancelled or invalidated by the law that was given 430 years later (3:15–18). Third, the law's true purpose was never to bring salvation. Rather, the law was given as a "guardian" (see Ancient Connections 3.1) to provide guidance and protection until the promise could be fulfilled through Abraham's seed (= Christ). The law could only point out sin; it had no power to deliver people from sin's power (3:19–25).

ANCIENT CONNECTIONS 3.1: THE LAW WAS GUARDIAN (*PAIDAGŌGOS*) UNTIL OUR FULL ADOPTION (*HUIOTHESIA*)

Two concepts from the Greco-Roman world are important to understand Paul's discussion in Galatians 3–4. The first is a "guardian" (*paidagōgos*), which refers to the slave who served as attendant or childminder for the children of a wealthy Greco-Roman household. This guardian was responsible for their care, discipline, and education until they moved into their full role as heirs of the household. Under this guardianship, the heirs had no greater authority than a slave. The second concept is "adoption as sons" (*huiothesia*). At times an influential leader who had no qualified heir would adopt a promising youth as his son and heir. Octavian, who became Caesar Augustus, the first emperor of Rome, was the adopted son of Julius Caesar. Paul says we were under the law as our guardian until we received full adoption as heirs of God (3:24–4:7).

Children of God through Faith (3:26–4:7)

With the law as mere guardian, people remained slaves under sin's power. The coming of Christ marked the fulfillment of God's promise to Abraham and the dawn of the new age. Through his death and resurrection, Jesus did what the law could not do, defeating the power of sin and death. Now justified through faith in him, believers are "clothed with Christ" (3:27). They are no longer under a guardian or trustee but become children of God and full heirs of the promise (3:26; 4:4–7; cf. Rom 8:15). As heirs rather than slaves, human distinctions that formerly divided people and excluded some from full participation in the covenant have now been removed in Christ, so that "There is no Jew or Greek, slave or free, male and female; since you are all one in Christ Jesus" (3:28).

Paul's Personal Appeal (4:8–20)

Paul next returns to a personal appeal to the Galatians. They were once enslaved by false gods but have now been set free in Christ. Why would they possibly become slaves again to the legalistic stipulations of the law? Paul reminds them of the depth of their love for one another, how he ministered sacrificially to them, and how they welcomed him like an angel, and even like Christ himself. Now that he is being defamed by the false teachers, who are trying to put a wedge of separation between Paul and the Galatians, he is in pain like a woman in labor, as though he is giving spiritual birth to them for a second time (4:19).

Allegory of Two Covenants (4:21–31)

From this allusion to birth, Paul launches into an allegory drawn from the story of Abraham, who had two sons, Ishmael through Hagar a slave, and Isaac through Sarah his wife. Here Hagar symbolizes adherence to the law given at Mount Sinai and the legalism reflected in the earthly Jerusalem and the Judaizers who came from there. Sarah was a free woman and so represents the promise given to Abraham and the destination of those saved by faith, the heavenly Jerusalem. Just as Ishmael persecuted Isaac, so these Judaizers were persecuting the children of promise. Paul calls on the Galatians to reject the false teachers and, just like God commanded Abraham, to "drive out the slave and her son" (4:30, quoting Gen 21:10).

The Practical Argument: (5:1–6:10)

A Call to Freedom over Slavery (5:1–15)

Paul here turns from a theological argument to a practical one. He writes, "For freedom, Christ set us free. Stand firm, then, and don't submit again to a yoke of slavery" (5:1). There are two ways to live life: in freedom or in slavery. Freedom comes through a relationship with Christ and the transforming presence of the Spirit. It can be defined as "faith [in Christ] working through love [for God and others]" (5:6). Slavery, by contrast, can come in two forms. The first is slavery to the law and its stipulations. Some of the Galatians were getting circumcised and keeping the law to make sure they were saved. This is "just in case" theology. Just in case faith in Christ is not enough. Paul responds that if you get circumcised, "Christ will not benefit you at all" (5:2). This is because trying to save yourself is the opposite of trusting in Christ for salvation. Anyone who starts down that road, "is obligated to do the entire law" (5:3). And that is impossible. Paul expresses grief that, while the Galatians had started so well in their faith, they were now turning to legalism. Sarcastically, he wishes those who were encouraging them to get circumcised would do it to themselves, going "the whole way and emasculate themselves!" (5:12 NIV).

While one kind of slavery is seeking salvation by returning to the law, another form of slavery is indulging in the flesh. Paul says, "For you were called to be free, brothers and sisters; only don't use this freedom as an opportunity for the flesh, but serve one another through love" (5:13). Some Galatians were evidently claiming that their freedom in Christ allowed them to live any way they wanted, even in selfish indulgence and exploitation of others. Paul says that this is just another form of slavery and is self-destructive (5:15). True freedom comes by living in the power of the Spirit, which results in loving God and loving others. This is the true fulfillment of the law.

Living by the Spirit (5:16–6:10)

What does it look like to live by the power of the Spirit? Paul provides two lists contrasting the "works of the flesh" with the "fruit of the Spirit." These are the actions and attitudes that result from dependence on self versus dependence on Christ. The works of the flesh are "sexual immorality, moral impurity, promiscuity, idolatry, sorcery, hatreds, strife, jealousy, outbursts of anger, selfish ambitions, dissensions, factions, envy, drunkenness, carousing, and anything similar" (5:19–21). The fruit of the Spirit is "love, joy, peace, patience, kindness, goodness, faithfulness, gentleness, and self-control" (5:22–23). Love heads the list and sums them all up (cf. 1 Cor 13:1–13; Rom 13:9–10).

Finally, Paul unpacks some ways this "fruit" can be lived out in practical actions: restoring those who have sinned (6:1), carrying one another's burdens (6:2), evaluating oneself honestly (6:3–5), encouraging those who teach (6:6), and doing good to others, especially fellow believers (6:9–10).

Conclusion and Benediction (6:11–18)

Paul has evidently been dictating this letter to a secretary and now takes the pen in hand to write his conclusion (6:11). He warns the Galatians again against those who would try to compel them to be circumcised. Although these false teachers boast about imposing the law on others, they themselves fail to keep it. In contrast, Paul says "I will never boast about anything except the cross of our Lord Jesus Christ" (6:14). It is Christ's work alone that has brought salvation. In the end what counts is not whether one is circumcised, but whether one has become part of the new creation through faith in Christ (6:15). It is for this gospel and no other that Paul has suffered so much (6:17). Paul's closing words are more than just a trite formula. They sum up the gospel: "Brothers and sisters, the grace of our Lord Jesus Christ be with your spirit. Amen" (6:18).

Old Testament Connections

While Paul uses various arguments to show that his gospel is the authentic one, his most important evidence is the testimony of Scripture.[16] Citing Gen 15:6, he points out that "Abraham . . . believed God, and it was credited to him for righteousness" (Gal 3:6). It was Abraham's faith, not his works, that saved him. God's promise to bless all nations through Abraham (Gen 12:3; 18:18; 22:18) is fulfilled when Gentiles become children of Abraham by being justified by faith in the same way Abraham was (Gal 3:7–9).

---

[16] For Paul's use of the OT in general, see Richard B. Hays, *Echoes of Scripture in the Letters of Paul* (New Haven, CT: Yale University Press, 1989). For Galatians in particular, see Roy E. Ciampa, *The Presence and Function of Scripture in Galatians 1 and 2*, WUNT 2/102 (Tübingen: Mohr Siebeck, 1998); Moisés Silva, "Galatians," in *CNTUOT*, 785–812; Matthew S. Harmon, "Galatians, Letter to the," in *DNTUOT*, 258–61.

Scripture affirms not only salvation by faith but also the impossibility of salvation by works. Paul cites Deut 27:26 in Gal 3:10 to argue that anyone who does not perfectly keep the law is cursed. For this reason, only those who are made righteous *by faith* will live (citing Hab 2:4 in Gal 3:11).[17] The basis for our salvation is also presented in the OT Scriptures. Christ redeemed us from the curse of the law by becoming a curse for us (Gal 2:13). That Christ took on the curse for us is confirmed by Deut 21:23, "Cursed is everyone who is hung on a pole" (Gal 3:13).

Gospel Connections

Throughout the history of the church, Paul's strong assertions that people are justified by faith in Christ alone and not by works (Gal 2:16; Rom 3:28) have often been set against the equally strong assertions by James that, "faith, if it does not have works, is dead" (Jas 2:17). Do these two represent opposing factions within the early church, or can we harmonize their perspectives?

A closer look reveals that Paul and James are not nearly as far apart as some claim. First, they are addressing different problems in the church. James is responding to complacent Christians, who are using the doctrine of God's free grace as an excuse to sin. Paul, by contrast, is responding to Judaizers, Jewish Christians who are claiming that salvation comes through obedience to the Mosaic law or through identification with the covenant people of Israel.

The two are also using key terms differently, such as "faith," "works," and "justify/justification." James says, "What good is it . . . if someone *claims* to have faith but does not have works? Can *such faith* save him?" (Jas 2:14, emphasis mine). The faith James is referring to here is mere profession, unaccompanied by life change. For Paul, by contrast, faith is authentic trust in Christ for salvation. Similarly, works for James are the post-conversion works that are evidence of a life transformed by the gospel. For Paul, the "works of the law" are either attempts to earn merit before God (traditional view) or trust in one's identity as part of God's covenant people (New Perspective on Paul). Finally, for Paul to be justified means to be declared righteous by God on the basis of Christ's sacrificial death on the cross. For James, by contrast, to be justified means that one's salvation is confirmed by the evidence of a transformed life. Abraham's salvation was confirmed when he obeyed God and was willing to offer Isaac as a sacrifice (Jas 2:21).

---

[17] On the nature of Paul's gospel-centered exegesis here, see Francis Watson, "Gospel and Scripture: Rethinking Canonical Unity," *TynBul* 52 (2001): 161–82.

Paul in no way downplays the importance of good works. Like James, he asserts that life change accompanies true conversion. Even when he emphasizes salvation by faith alone, the accompanying works are not far behind. In Eph 2:8–9 he insists that we are saved by grace apart from works, but then adds, "For we are his workmanship, created in Christ Jesus for good works" (Eph 2:10). Similarly, in Phil 2:12–13, he says, "work out your own salvation with fear and trembling," but quickly clarifies, "For it is God who is working in you."

Life Connections

The close relationship between faith and works is the reason that hypocrisy is such a destructive thing to our Christian witness. Hypocrisy is claiming to be one thing but acting in a way that denies this. Jesus never criticized the religious leaders of his day for being too righteous. He condemned them for claiming to be righteous while neglecting God's greatest commands, like practicing justice and mercy (Matt 23:23). Too often today Christians are known more for their anger, hatred, pride, and argumentative nature (all works of the flesh: Gal 5:19–21) than for their love, joy, peace, patience, kindness, goodness, faithfulness, gentleness, and self-control—the fruit of the Spirit (5:22–25). That is a denial of the transforming power of the gospel.

Interactive Questions

1. What are the circumstances that compelled Paul to write the letter to the Galatians?

2. What is the debate concerning the recipients of the letter? What implications does this have with reference to the letter's date?

3. What is the debate concerning the nature of the false teaching? How does the New Perspective on Paul relate to this debate?

4. What two proofs does Paul offer to show that his gospel came directly from God?

5. In what two ways does Paul demonstrate that the Jerusalem apostles accepted the authenticity of his gospel?

6. What is the debate related to the translation of the genitive phrase "faith in Christ" or "faithfulness of Christ"?

7. How does Paul use the example of Abraham to show that salvation comes by faith and not by works?

8. Paul says the law was never intended to bring salvation. What was its purpose?

9. Paul warns the Galatians not only of returning to slavery to the law but also of returning to slavery to what?

10. What are the works of the flesh? What are the works of the Spirit? Why does Paul use these words ("flesh"/"Spirit") to describe them, and how does this relate to the message of Galatians?

11. How might reading this letter benefit Christians today?

Study Resources

Bruce, F. F. *The Epistle to the Galatians*. NIGTC. Grand Rapids: Eerdmans, 1982.
deSilva, David A. *Galatians*. NICNT. Grand Rapids: Eerdmans, 2018.
Dunn, James D. G. *The Epistle to the Galatians*. BNTC. Peabody, MA: Hendrickson, 1993.
Fung, Ronald Y. K. *The Epistle to the Galatians*. NICNT. Grand Rapids: Eerdmans, 1988.
George, Timothy. *Galatians*. NAC. Nashville: Broadman & Holman, 1994.
Greene-McCreight, Kathryn. *Galatians*. BTCB. Ada, MI: Brazos Press, 2023.
Gupta, Nijay K. *Galatians*. SGBC. Grand Rapids: Zondervan, 2023.
Jervis, L. Ann. *Galatians*. UBNT. Peabody, MA: Hendrickson, 1999.
Keener, Craig. *Galatians*. NCBC. Cambridge: Cambridge University Press, 2018.
———. *Galatians: A Commentary*. Grand Rapids: Baker Academic, 2019.
Longenecker, Richard N. *Galatians*. WBC. Dallas: Word Books, 1990.
Martyn, J. Louis. *Galatians: A New Translation with Introduction and Commentary*. AB 33A. New York: Doubleday, 1997.
Moo, Douglas J. *Galatians*. Baker Exegetical Commentary on the New Testament. Grand Rapids: Baker Academic, 2013.
Oakes, Peter. *Galatians*. Paideia. Grand Rapids: Baker Academic, 2015.
———, and Andrew Boakye. *Rethinking Galatians: Paul's Vision of Oneness in the Living Christ*. London: T&T Clark, 2021.
Schreiner, Thomas R. *Galatians*. ZECNT. Grand Rapids: Zondervan, 2010.
Witherington, Ben, III. *Grace in Galatia: A Commentary on Paul's Letter to the Galatians*. SRC. Grand Rapids: Eerdmans, 1988.

4

1 and 2 Thessalonians

Written from Corinth ca. 51–52 CE

For who is our hope or joy or crown of boasting in the presence of our Lord Jesus at his coming? Is it not you?

—1 Thessalonians 2:19

Outlines

1 Thessalonians

I. Introduction (1:1–10)
   A. Greeting (1:1)
   B. Thanksgiving (1:2–10)
II. Paul's Relationship with the Thessalonian Church (2:1–3:13)
   A. In Establishing the Church (2:1–16)
   B. In the Circumstances of the Letter (2:17–3:13)
III. Instructions for the Church (4:1–5:22)
   A. On Pleasing the Lord (4:1–12)
   B. On Questions Related to Christ's Return (4:13–5:11)

   C. Additional Instructions (5:12–22)
IV. Conclusion (5:23–28)

2 Thessalonians

I. Introduction (1:1–12)
   A. Greeting (1:1–2)
   B. Thanksgiving and Prayer (1:3–12)
II. Instruction Related to Christ's Return (2:1–12)
III. Encouragement to Faithfulness and Prayer (2:13–3:5)
IV. Warning against Lazy and Disruptive Members (3:6–15)
V. Conclusion (3:16–18)

Author, Occasion, Message

Author

Both 1 and 2 Thessalonians claim to come from "Paul, Silas, and Timothy" (1 Thess 1:1; 2 Thess 1:1 NIV). This fits well what we know from Acts, since Silas and Timothy were Paul's companions on his second missionary journey (Acts 15:36–18:22), when 1 and 2 Thessalonians were presumably written. While 1 Thessalonians is almost universally viewed as an authentic Pauline letter, more doubts have been raised about 2 Thessalonians. Some reasons for this are that 1 Thessalonians has a very warm and personal style, while 2 Thessalonians is more formal and distant. Second Thessalonians repeats almost verbatim many phrases from 1 Thessalonians, suggesting to some a later imitator. Other small differences in style and theology have been noted.[1] While good arguments can be made on both sides, there is no compelling reason for a pseudonymous author to have composed 2 Thessalonians. The second letter works well as Paul's attempt to clear up certain issues left unresolved by the first.

Occasion and Message

Thessalonica was a prominent seaport and the capital of the Roman province of Macedonia. It was located on the Via Egnatia, the main road from Rome to the East.

---

[1] For fuller discussion, see D. A. Carson and Douglas J. Moo, *An Introduction to the New Testament*, 2nd ed. (Grand Rapids: Zondervan, 2005), 534–42.

The city had a large Jewish population, and this Judaism had attracted many Gentile God-fearers. Paul, Silas, and Timothy came to the city after their eventful ministry in Philippi (Acts 16:11–40; 17:1). According to Luke's account in Acts, Paul engaged in discussions in the synagogue for three successive Sabbaths. Some Jews and a large number of God-fearing Greeks responded to the gospel (Acts 17:2–4). This resulted in opposition from the Jewish leadership, who provoked a riot. When the crowd could not find Paul, they dragged his host Jason and other believers before the city council, where they accused them of insurrection—claiming Jesus was a rival king to Caesar. Fearing for the lives of the missionaries, the Thessalonian believers took them by night to Berea (Acts 17:5–10).

While at first Paul and Silas received a more positive response from the Bereans, opponents from Thessalonica soon pursued them there, again forcing Paul to flee (Acts 17:10–14). The believers took Paul to Athens, where Silas and Timothy eventually joined him. Paul then sent Timothy back to check on the church in Thessalonica (1 Thess 3:1–2). Paul was extremely anxious that these new spiritual children would buckle under the pressure of suffering and persecution. After his address to the philosophers at the Areopagus in Athens (Acts 17:16–34), Paul continued on to Corinth, where Timothy finally joined him (Acts 18:1, 5; 1 Thess 3:6). Paul was thrilled with Timothy's report. Far from abandoning the faith, the Thessalonians were standing firm and growing stronger. Paul was delighted and sat down to write a letter of praise and thanksgiving to the Thessalonian church. Paul wrote the letter from Corinth around 51 CE.

The main theme of 1 Thessalonians is encouragement for a thriving church. Despite their spiritual youth, the church was thriving and growing. Paul writes to express his love for the church, his spiritual children, and to praise them for their strength, maturity, and endurance. He then encourages them to bigger and better things—even greater faith, hope, and love!

The date and circumstances of 2 Thessalonians is murkier. Sometime after writing 1 Thessalonians, Paul received reports concerning both new and continuing problems in the church. Most significantly, there had been a misunderstanding (or intentional misrepresentation; see 2:2) of Paul's teaching about the day of the Lord (1 Thess 5:1–11). Perhaps because of the severity of persecution, some thought that God's final judgment on the world had already begun. Paul corrects their misconceptions (2:1–17) while continuing to encourage them for their faith and endurance. He also returns to an issue discussed in his first letter, intensifying criticism of some who are refusing to work and are living off the charity of others.

Interpretive Overview

1 Thessalonians

Introduction (1:1–10)

Paul's greeting identifies his associates as Silvanus (a Latin form of Silas) and Timothy and the recipients as "the church of the Thessalonians."[2] Cross referencing to Acts allows us to locate the letter on Paul's second missionary journey, when these two were his traveling companions (Acts 15:40; 16:1) and the church at Thessalonica was established (Acts 17:1–10).

Paul launches into a long thanksgiving, setting the tone for the letter by praising the Thessalonians for their faith and endurance. The manifestation of three great Christian virtues in their lives—work produced by *faith*, labor motivated by *love*, and endurance inspired by *hope*—confirms God's choice of them. By following the model of Christian character demonstrated by Paul and his associates, they endured persecution and have now become an example for all the believers in Macedonia and Achaia. Everyone is talking about their transformation from idol worshippers to servants of the living and true God, as they await God's Son, who rose victorious from the grave and will return to rescue believers from the coming wrath (1:2–10).

Paul's Relationship with the Thessalonian Church (2:1–3:13)

Paul's thanksgiving for the Thessalonians' faith and endurance transitions smoothly into a discussion of the founding of the church. He reminds his brothers and sisters that, despite having experienced severe persecution in Philippi, he and his companions boldly preached the gospel to the Thessalonians. In doing so, they acted with great integrity, never out of greed or impure motives. They worked overtime to support themselves financially so as not to be a burden to the Thessalonians. The Thessalonians, for their part, received the gospel message not as merely human words, but for what it was—the word of God! They became imitators of the churches in Judea, suffering at the hands of their fellow Gentiles in the same way that the Judean Christians had suffered at the hands of their fellow Jews. This persecution by those

[2] In the NT Luke always uses the Greek *Silas* (Acts 15:22, 27, 32, 40; 16:19, 25, 29; 17:4, 10, 14, 15; 18:5), while Paul (and Peter) uses the transliterated Latin *Silouanos* (2 Cor 1:9; 1 Thess 1:1; 2 Thess 1:1; cf. 1 Pet 5:12).

Jews, first against Jesus and now against his church, was resulting in God's judgment against them (2:1–16).

Having reminded the church of the missionaries' love and integrity in founding the church, Paul turns to discuss the circumstances that followed. When violent opposition forced them to leave, they tried repeatedly to return. But Satan blocked their way. Paul doesn't say how, whether by illness, human opponents, direct demonic opposition, or other circumstances. In any case, when Paul could stand it no longer, he stayed in Athens and sent Timothy to strengthen and encourage the church. Now, as Paul writes, Timothy has just returned with a glowing report on the faith of the Thessalonians. The church is thriving! Their faith and love are undiminished and they long to see Paul in the same way he longs to see them. While Paul was dying inside, now he truly lives, since they are standing firm in the faith. Paul concludes with a prayer for the church, asking God to open the way for him to return to them, to increase their mutual love for one another, and to keep them holy and blameless before God the Father at the return of Jesus Christ (2:17–3:13).

Instructions for the Church (4:1–5:22)

After expressing his joy from Timothy's good report, Paul turns to some matters of instruction. He is their founding pastor and has a stake in their continued spiritual growth. Repeatedly, he first encourages them in how well they are doing and then spurs them on to bigger and better things.

On Pleasing the Lord (4:1–12)

While they are living moral lives that please God, he encourages them to be even more holy and blameless. They must control their bodies and not pursue lustful passions like unbelieving Gentiles. They must never take advantage of their brother or sister in this area of sexual purity (4:1–8). The same instruction relates to their love for one another. They are doing exceptionally well in loving not only their own but also believers throughout Macedonia. But Paul encourages them on to bigger and better things (4:9–12).

On Questions Related to Christ's Return (4:13–5:11)

Paul's brief stay in Thessalonica meant that his teaching had been limited in some areas. One of these concerned the return of Christ. While Paul had taught that their salvation would be complete when Christ returned, some of the Thessalonians were concerned that friends and family who died before Christ's coming would miss out on this salvation. Paul responds by correcting the church on the nature of Christ's return and the resurrection. When Christ descends from heaven at his return, those who have died "in Christ" (that is, as believers) will be raised from their tombs in glorified bodies. Only after that will those of us who are still alive be caught up together with them in the clouds to meet the Lord in the air. From that time on, we will always be with the Lord (4:13–18).

Paul turns from this teaching that was not well understood by the church to other teaching that they knew well. This concerns the day of the Lord, God's great and final judgment. While it would come "like a thief in the night," taking most people by surprise, they were children of light, who were alert and well prepared for the day of judgment. As elsewhere, Paul commends them for doing well in this area, then calls them to do even better. They are to stay spiritually awake, equipped with the spiritual armor of God—faith, love, and hope—and encouraging one another.

ADDITIONAL INSTRUCTIONS (5:12–22)

Paul concludes his instruction with a list of exhortations: honor your leaders; live at peace among yourselves; warn those who are idle and lazy; comfort and encourage those who are weak; be patient with everyone; never repay evil with evil; rejoice always; pray constantly; be thankful for everything; don't stifle the Spirit; don't despise prophecies; test everything; hold to the good; avoid all evil.

Conclusion (5:23–28)

The letter ends with a prayer that the church would be holy, sound, and blameless when Christ returns. This is possible because God is faithful and will do this through them. Paul then asks for prayer and encourages the church members to greet one another with a holy kiss and to read this letter to the whole church. He concludes with a benediction: "The grace of our Lord Jesus Christ be with you."

ANCIENT CONNECTIONS 4.1: PATRONAGE IN THESSALONICA

On several occasions in Acts, Luke notes that those who responded to the gospel included "a large number of God-fearing Greeks and quite a few prominent women" (Acts 17:4; cf. 13:50; 16:14; 17:12, 34). Readers might wonder why this special mention of women. The answer likely goes back to the idea of patronage, a kind of social relationship common in both ancient and modern societies. Social status in the Greco-Roman world was quite static, and everyone knew their place, from the lowest slave to the highest emperor. To violate one's social status was viewed as going against the divine order of things. So how could someone obtain something that was beyond their means? Part of the answer was patronage, whereby a person of higher status (a patron or benefactor) would provide needed resources for a client, a person of lower status. In return the client owed the patron love, loyalty, honor, and obedience. Patron-client dynamics were common in virtually all relationships of life, whether familial, social, economic, religious, or political. In Luke's Gospel, for example, we learn of a certain Roman centurion who had been a patron to the Jews of Capernaum, providing resources to build their synagogue. The Jewish elders honor him by asking Jesus to heal his servant (Luke 7:1–10).[3] We have literary and inscriptional evidence of this kind of patronage throughout the Mediterranean region, where God-fearing Gentiles provided patronage and support to Jewish communities.[4] Such influential Gentile relationships were especially important in this case, since the Jews were at times a persecuted minority and so needed influential friends in high places.

In this context, one can imagine how disturbing it would be for the Jewish leaders of Thessalonica to see their Gentile benefactors—especially prominent women, who often had greater interest in religion and more time for

---

[3] For a description of Greco-Roman patronage, see Bruce J. Malina and Richard L. Rohrbaugh, *Social-Science Commentary on the Synoptic Gospels* (Minneapolis: Fortress, 1992), 326–29.

[4] See W. Schrage, *TDNT* 7:813 for examples. The erection of a Jewish "place of prayer" (*proseuchē*) by a Gentile is attested in W. Dittenberger, *Orientis graeci inscriptiones selectae* (Leipzig: Hirzel, 1903–1905), §96; cited by Joseph A. Fitzmyer, *The Gospel according to Luke*, 2 vols., AB 28 (New York: Doubleday, 1985), 1:652; J. M. Creed, *The Gospel according to St. Luke* (London: Macmillan, 1965), 101.

philanthropy—being wooed away by an itinerant rabbi Paul, who was preaching the disturbing message that a certain crucified teacher named Jesus was the Messiah! From the letter of 1 Thessalonians, we can see some of the accusations they were making against Paul, charging him with deceit, flattery, financial exploitation, and even abandonment (1 Thess 2:3–12). Paul responds forcefully that the Thessalonians knew better—that he and the other missionaries had acted with absolute honesty, integrity, and out of intense parental love for their new spiritual children. Although for a time they had been torn away from the church because of persecution, they longed to return and be with them and to encourage them in their faith (2:17–3:13).

2 Thessalonians

Introduction (1:1–12)

The greetings and thanksgiving of 2 Thessalonians are very similar to the first letter. Paul thanks God for the Thessalonians' growing faith and love and their continued perseverance in the face of persecution. An added dimension is a strong emphasis on God's justice and the reality that he will "pay back trouble to those who trouble you" (1:6 NIV). This judgment will take place at the return of the Lord Jesus and will result in glory for God's people but everlasting destruction and expulsion from God's presence of those who are disobedient and do not know God. Paul concludes with a prayer that God would make the Thessalonians worthy of his calling and that "the name of our Lord Jesus will be glorified by you" (1:12).

Instruction Related to Christ's Return (2:1–12)

This section appears to be the primary reason Paul is writing. Some of the Thessalonians had become unsettled by reports—supposedly from Paul—that the day of the Lord (God's final judgment) had already begun. Paul is uncertain whether this false report came in the form of a prophecy, an oral message, or a forged letter (2:2).

Paul's answer is basically to calm down; do not be deceived; this day of judgment has not yet arrived. He offers two reasons why they know this: (1) The great "apostasy" (or rebellion) has not yet come and (2) the "man of lawlessness" has not been revealed (2:3). Paul does not clarify what he means by the apostasy, but other passages speak of a great turning away from God in the last days (Matt 24:10–12; 1 Tim 4:1–2;

2 Tim 3:1–5). Paul describes the "man of lawlessness" as one "doomed to destruction," who will set himself up in God's temple and proclaim himself to be God (2 Thess 2:3–4). As an ally of Satan, he will perform deceiving signs and wonders but will be destroyed by Christ at his Second Coming (2:8–10). (See Ancient Connections 4.2, Old Testament Connections, and New Testament Connections in this chapter.) This lawless one will deceive many. In addition, God will send a "strong delusion so that they will believe the lie" (2:11). It is a common theme in Scripture that in his sovereignty God uses even the evil actions of sinners to accomplish his good purposes. Consider Pharaoh, for example, whose heart God hardened after Pharaoh had repeatedly hardened his own heart and rejected God's command (Exod 9:34–35; 10:20).

SIDEBAR 4.1: WHAT IS THE RESTRAINER? (2 THESS 2:6)

Paul argues in 2 Thessalonians 2 that the day of the Lord clearly has not yet arrived, since the man of lawlessness has not yet been revealed. He adds, "And you know what currently restrains him" (2:6). While Paul had apparently taught the Thessalonians what this restraining force was, he does not tell us! (This is one of our challenges when reading the NT letters, namely that we are only hearing one side of the conversation.) Speculation as to the identity of this restraining force includes (1) the Roman government, or more specifically the emperor; (2) government in general, which provides law and order (Romans 13); (3) God himself, or God through the Holy Spirit; (4) Paul and the present proclamation of the gospel, which must first go to all nations (cf. Mark 13:10). Others find none of these satisfying and propose a different translation of the Greek "what restrains him" (*to katechon*) as "what empowers (or possesses)" him, and the answer is "the mystery of lawlessness" that is already at work in the world (2:7).[5]

Encouragement to Faithfulness and Prayer (2:13–3:5)

In contrast to the coming apostasy and deception, Paul thanks God for the faith of the Thessalonians, who were loved by God and chosen by him for salvation. He encourages them to stand firm and remain faithful to the truths they have been taught. He

[5] See Gene L. Green, *The Letters to the Thessalonians*, PNTC (Grand Rapids: Eerdmans, 2002), 314–17.

prays that their hearts may be encouraged and strengthened by the Lord Jesus Christ and God our Father. He also requests prayer for himself and his associates that the word of God may spread rapidly and that they may be protected from evil people.

Warning against Lazy and Disruptive Members (3:6–15)

As a final exhortation, Paul picks up a theme that he touched on in the first letter. There he had told the Thessalonians "to lead a quiet life, to mind your own business, and to work with your own hands" (1 Thess 4:11) and to "warn those who were idle" (5:14). He had also pointed to his own example of "working night and day so that we would not burden any of you" (2:9). The situation must have deteriorated because Paul is even more forceful here. He warns the church to keep away from certain believers who are idle and disruptive. These people are "busybodies" (3:11), who are not living by the standard of hard work that Paul and the other missionaries set. They must learn to work quietly and provide for themselves. Paul goes so far as to say, "If anyone isn't willing to work, he should not eat" (3:10).

The nature and context of this laziness and disruptive behavior is uncertain. A number of scholars have proposed that the heightened eschatological expectations at Thessalonica resulted in some people quitting their jobs and living off others while they waited for the Lord's return.[6] Others suggest that the church's identify as a spiritual family was resulting in new relational dynamics, with some poorer members expecting support and patronage from wealthier members.[7] Whatever the reason, Paul insists that all who are able to work should do so. As in his discussion of spiritual gifts elsewhere, he insists that all members should do their part for the common good (cf. Rom 12:4–8; 1 Corinthians 12–14).

Conclusion (3:16–18)

Paul concludes with a prayer that the Thessalonians would experience the Lord's peace and his presence (3:16). He then takes pen in hand and provides a concluding greeting and benediction in his own hand, confirming the authenticity of the letter. He ends with a benediction, "The grace of our Lord Jesus Christ be with you all."

---

[6] See F. F. Bruce, *First and Second Thessalonians*, WBC (Dallas: Word Books, 1982), 91.

[7] Green, *Letters to the Thessalonians*, 342.

Old Testament Connections

The letters of 1–2 Thessalonians have no explicit citations from the OT.[8] This may be due in part to the predominantly Gentile background of the church (1 Thess 1:9; 2:14). Yet, as with all of Paul's letters, their "vocabulary, metaphors, and theological framework . . . betray the influence of the OT in both small and significant ways."[9] While this OT influence can be illustrated with any number of themes,[10] consider Paul's language with reference to eschatology (teaching about the end times), which plays such a prominent role in the Thessalonian correspondence.

(1) Paul's prayer that the Thessalonians will be found blameless and holy "when our Lord Jesus comes with all his holy ones" (3:13 NIV) alludes to Zech 14:5, which speaks of the time when "the Lord my God will come and all the holy ones with him." Note how seamlessly Paul equates the coming of *Jesus the Messiah* with the expected return of the *Lord God*. These kinds of equations were no doubt part of the reason for the early church's strong and early affirmation of the deity of Christ. (2) The descent of the Lord from heaven "with the trumpet of God" (1 Thess 4:16) recalls OT passages associated with the day of the Lord, God's final judgement, where the trumpet blast calls the people of God to eschatological battle (cf. Isa 27:13; Joel 2:1; Zeph 1:14–16; Zech 9:14). (3) Similarly, Paul's affirmation that believers will be caught up to meet Christ "in the clouds" (1 Thess 4:17) recalls OT imagery where clouds indicate a theophany.[11] Most important in this regard is Dan 7:13, where "one like a son of man" comes "with the clouds of heaven." (4) The description of the "man of lawlessness" in 2 Thess 2:3–4 similarly echoes the language of Daniel concerning Antiochus IV Epiphanes, the prototype of the Antichrist (See Ancient Connections 4.2). Many more examples could be cited, but these are enough to show that even without explicit OT citations, the Thessalonians letters are thoroughly immersed in the world of the Hebrew Scriptures.

---

[8] Robert J. Cara, "Thessalonians, First and Second Letters to the," in *DNTUOT*, 845.

[9] Jeffrey A. D. Weima, "1–2 Thessalonians," in *CNTUOT*, 871–89; quote from 871. Cf. E. S. Steele, "The Use of Jewish Scriptures in 1 Thessalonians," *BTB* 14, no. 1 (1984): 12–17.

[10] Cara, "Thessalonians," *DNTUOT*, 845, points to Paul's perspective on eschatology, calling and election, holiness/sanctification, working versus idleness, kinship/family, and imitation, all of which are influenced to a greater or lesser extent by the Hebrew Scriptures.

[11] See Exod 13:21–22; 14:19–20, 24; 16:10; 19:9, 16–17; Lev 16:2; Num 9:15–22; 10:11–12; 1 Kgs 8:10–12; 2 Chron 5:13–14; 6:1; Neh 9:12, 19; Ps 97:2; Isa 19:1; Ezek 1:4–28 (Weima, "1–2 Thessalonians," *CNTUOT*, 880).

Gospel Connections

Paul's eschatology of 1–2 Thessalonians not only has its background in the Hebrew Scriptures, but has parallels throughout the NT. Here is a small sampling:

The Antichrist/Man of Lawlessness (2 Thess 2:3–12). See Ancient Connections 4.2: Antiochus IV "Epiphanes."

The Great Apostasy (2 Thess 2:3). In Jesus's end-time discourse on the Mount of Olives he speaks of a time when "many will fall away, betray one another, and hate one another" (Matt 24:10–12). Paul elsewhere speaks of a great departure from the faith that will occur "in later times" (1 Tim 4:1–2) and "in the last days" (2 Tim 3:1–5).

The Coming (Parousia) of Christ (1 Thess 1:10; 2:19; 3:13; 4:13–18; 5:23; 2 Thess 1:7–10; 2:8). In addition to many other references in Paul (1 Cor 1:7–8; 4:5; 11:26; Phil 3:20–21; Col 3:4; 1 Tim 6:14; 2 Tim 4:1, 8; Titus 2:13), the return of Christ is predicted by angels at Jesus's ascension in Acts (1:11) and affirmed elsewhere in Acts (3:19–21). Jesus speaks of the return of the Son of Man in his Olivet Discourse (Matt 24:27–44; Mark 13; Luke 21) and elsewhere (Matt 16:27–28; Luke 12:40) and promises to return for his disciples in his farewell discourse in John's Gospel (John 14:1–3). The general epistles have many references to Christ's return (Heb 9:28; Jas 5:7–9; 1 Pet 1:7, 13; 5:4; 2 Pet 1:16; 3:3, 4, 8–14; 1 John 2:28; 3:2; Jude 14, 15). In the book of Revelation, Christ's return is repeatedly announced (Rev 1:7; 3:11) and narrated as he comes riding on a white horse with the armies of heaven (19:11–21).

The Resurrection of the Dead (1 Thess 4:13–18). The hope for end-time resurrection of the dead (see Dan 12:2) is referred to by Paul often in his letters (Rom 8:11; 1 Cor 6:14; 2 Cor 4:14; 5:1–5; Phil 3:10–11, 20–21) and discussed in detail in 1 Cor 15:12–52. Jesus is also identified by Paul as the "firstborn" from the dead (Rom 8:11, 29; Col 1:18) and the "firstfruits" (the present evidence of the future harvest) of the resurrection for all believers (1 Cor 15:20). Elsewhere in the NT, Jesus speaks of the resurrection frequently in the Synoptics (Mark 12:18–27 pars.; Luke 14:14; 20:35–38) and in John (5:21–29; 6:39–54; 11:23–25). In Acts the proclamation of the resurrection is often met with skepticism and unbelief (4:2; 17:18, 32; 23:6, 8; 24:15; 26:8). The "first" resurrection of martyred saints is described in Rev 20:4–6.

The Final Judgment/Day of the Lord (1 Thess 5:1–11; 2 Thess 1:7–10; 2:1–12). The day of the Lord is specifically referred to in a number of NT passages (1 Cor 5:5; 2 Cor 1:14; 2 Pet 3:10). Many others speak of God's final judgment (Luke 17:22–37; Rom 2:5–16; 14:10–12; 1 Cor 3:13; 6:2; 2 Cor 5:10; 2 Tim 4:1, 8; etc.).

ANCIENT CONNECTIONS 4.2: ANTIOCHUS IV "EPIPHANES": PROTOTYPE OF THE ANTICHRIST

The OT book of Daniel and the apocryphal books of 1–2 Maccabees describe the rise of the Syrian king Antiochus IV, whose attempts to paganize Judaism in the second century BCE provoked the Maccabean revolt. Antiochus called himself "Epiphanes"—meaning "the Divine One," but his enemies mocked him as "Epimanes," meaning "madman."[12] Daniel describes Antiochus's desecration of the temple: "His forces will rise up to desecrate the temple fortress. They will abolish the regular sacrifice and set up the abomination of desolation" (Dan 11:31; cf. 1 Macc 1:54–57; 2 Macc 5–7). "He will exalt and magnify himself above every god, and he will say outrageous things against the God of gods" (Dan 11:36–37; cf. Dan 7:25–27; 8:8–9; 9:27; 11:36–45).

Through these evil actions, Antiochus became the model and prototype for the "Antichrist." In his discourse on the Mount of Olives, Jesus referred to "false Christs" who would arise before the coming of the Son of Man (Matt 24:24–27) and recontextualized Daniel's "abomination of desolation" for the end of the age (Mark 13:14; Matt 24:15). Paul similarly draws on this Danielic imagery when he describes the "man of lawlessness" who "opposes and exalts himself above every so-called god or object of worship, so that he sits in God's temple, proclaiming that he himself is God" (2 Thess 2:3–4). The lawless one will deceive with "every kind of miracle, both signs and wonders serving the lie" (2 Thess 2:9), but "the Lord Jesus will destroy him with the breath of his mouth and will bring him to nothing at the appearance of his coming" (2 Thess 2:8–9). There are many parallels between this man of lawlessness, the coming "Antichrist" in the Johannine letters (1 John 2:18; cf. 2:22; 4:3; 2 John 7), and the "beast" from the sea in the book of Revelation (Rev 11:7; 13:1–18; 19:19–20). The beast, too, will be accompanied by false miracles and signs, but will be destroyed by Christ when he returns on a white horse with the armies of heaven (Rev 19:11–21). Scholars debate whether this "Antichrist" represents an individual, a nation, or the evil world system. They also debate whether his coming is related to events surrounding the destruction of Jerusalem in 70 CE or to the still future second coming of Christ.

[12] Polybius, *Histories* 26.1–14.

Life Connections

While the Thessalonian letters have a lot to say about eschatology (see above), their central theme is not eschatology; it is encouragement. Paul is thrilled that, despite persecution and trials of various kinds, the church is thriving. The letters are filled with joyful praise, words of support, and encouragement. The church is certainly not perfect, and Paul instructs them in various areas of needed growth, but before he does that, he expresses his joy and relief at their spiritual vitality and heaps praise and encouragement on them for how well they are doing. This is an important leadership principle for today. Whether in the context of parenting, business, or Christian ministry: encouragement before criticism!

Interactive Questions

1. Describe the circumstances surrounding the establishment of the church at Thessalonica.

2. What events led to the writing of the letter? (Why did Paul leave Thessalonica? What were his concerns after he left? How did he seek to make up for his absence?)

3. What report did Timothy bring back to Paul from the church at Thessalonica?

4. What was Paul's purpose in writing 1 Thessalonians?

5. In what ways does he defend his ministry with the Thessalonians?

6. What concerns did the Thessalonians have about Christ's return and how does Paul respond?

7. What question about the day of the Lord provoked Paul to write a second letter to the Thessalonians? What does he tell them?

8. What does Paul say to the Thessalonians about those who are idle and refuse to work?

9. What are some suggestions concerning the situation that prompted this instruction?

10. How might reading these letters benefit Christians today?

Study Resources

Bruce, F. F. *First and Second Thessalonians*. WBC. Dallas: Word Books, 1982.

Fee, Gordon D. *First and Second Letters to the Thessalonians*. NICNT. Grand Rapids: Eerdmans, 2009.

Gaventa, Beverly Roberts. *First and Second Thessalonians*. Louisville: Westminster John Knox, 1998.

Green, Gene L. *The Letters to the Thessalonians*. PNTC. Grand Rapids: Eerdmans, 2002.

Gupta, Nijay K. *1–2 Thessalonians*. NCCS. Eugene, OR: Wipf & Stock, 2016.

Holmes, Michael W. *1 and 2 Thessalonians*. NIVAC. Grand Rapids: Zondervan, 1998.

Johnson, C. Andrew. *1 and 2 Thessalonians*. THNTC. Grand Rapids: Eerdmans, 2016.

Kim, Seyoon, and F. F. Bruce. *1 & 2 Thessalonians*. 2nd ed. WBC. Grand Rapids: Zondervan, 2023.

Malherbe, Abraham J. *The Letters to the Thessalonians: A New Translation with Introduction and Commentary*. AB. New York: Doubleday, 2000.

Marshall, Molly T. *1 and 2 Thessalonians*. Belief: Theological Commentary on the Bible. Louisville: Westminster John Knox, 2022.

Shogren, Gary. *1 and 2 Thessalonians*. ZECNT. Grand Rapids: Zondervan, 2012.

Wanamaker, Charles. A. *The Epistles to the Thessalonians: A Commentary on the Greek Text*. NIGTC. Grand Rapids: Eerdmans, 1990.

Weima, Jeffrey A. D. *1 and 2 Thessalonians*. BECNT. Grand Rapids: Baker, 2014.

Witherington, Ben, III. *1 and 2 Thessalonians. A Socio-Rhetorical Commentary*. Grand Rapids: Eerdmans, 2006.

5

1 Corinthians

Written from Ephesus ca. 55–56 CE

So, whether you eat or drink, or whatever you do, do everything for the glory of God.
—1 Corinthians 10:31

Outline

I. Introduction (1:1–9)
  A. Greeting (1:1–3)
  B. Thanksgiving (1:4–9)
II. Paul's Response to Reports from Corinth (1:10–6:20)
  A. The Problem of Divisions in the Church (1:10–4:21)
  B. The Problem of Not Confronting an Immoral Situation (5:1–13)
  C. The Problem of Lawsuits between Believers (6:1–11)
  D. The Problem of Immorality in General (6:12–20)
III. Paul's Response to the Letter from Corinth (7:1–16:4)
  A. Concerning Marriage (7:1–40)
  B. Concerning Food Sacrificed to Idols (8:1–11:1)

C. Concerning Head Coverings in Worship (11:2–16)
D. Concerning Abuse of the Lord's Supper (11:17–34)
E. Concerning Spiritual Gifts (12:1–14:40)
F. Concerning the Resurrection (15:1–58)
G. Concerning the Collection for Jerusalem (16:1–4)

IV. Conclusion
A. Travel Plans of Paul and his Companions (16:5–12)
B. Recognition of Leaders (16:15–18)
C. Final Greetings and Benediction (16:19–24)

Author, Occasion, Message

Author

The author identifies himself as Paul the apostle, together with "Sosthenes our brother" (1:1). Paul's authorship of 1 Corinthians is affirmed by virtually all scholars.

Occasion

Paul founded the church at Corinth on his second missionary journey (Acts 18:1–18). On his third journey, Paul spent about three years in Ephesus, establishing churches in Asia Minor (Acts 18:23–21:14). While ministering in Ephesus, Paul began to hear of problems in the church at Corinth. One of these problems concerned sexual immorality, and Paul seems to have written a short letter, now lost, to correct it (see 1 Cor 5:9). The church was also suffering from serious rivalries and divisions, something reported to Paul by "Chloe's people" (1:10–12), perhaps servants or business associates of a church member named Chloe. Around this time, a delegation also arrived from Corinth with a financial gift from the church (Stephanas, Fortunatus, and Achaicus; 16:17). These men may have also brought a list of questions from the church, since Paul seems to be answering these in the letter (7:1, 25; 8:1; 11:2; 12:1; 15:1; 16:1). These reports and requests prompted Paul to write this letter we call "1 Corinthians." It was intended to deal with various problems in the church and to answer the questions from the church.

One major question concerning the occasion of 1 Corinthians is whether Paul's primary purpose in writing is (1) to provide pastoral oversight by answering questions from the church and responding to problems the church is having, or (2) whether by engaging these topics he is *already responding to a growing challenge to his authority* in the church—a challenge that will blow up into full-scale revolt and eventual reconciliation in the events leading up to his writing of 2 Corinthians (see "Occasion," in chap. 6, pp. 136–37).[1]

Message

At the surface level, the church at Corinth was an impressive and influential congregation, boasting spiritual wisdom and knowledge, strong rhetorical and teaching skills, and an impressive array of spiritual gifts (1:5–7). Yet the church was plagued by spiritual immaturity, immorality, and division. Paul addresses a number of problems in the church, including factions resulting from exalting human leaders (1:10–4:21); sexual immorality (5:1–13; 6:12–20); personal conflicts that denied the reconciling power of the gospel (6:1–11); misconceptions about marriage, singleness, and divorce (7:1–40); idolatry and the danger of spiritual pride (8:1–11:1); issues of wealth, status, arrogance, and cultural superiority that were impairing the church's worship (11:2–14:40); and misconceptions related to the resurrection (15:1–58).

For Paul the antidote to all these problems is the transforming and reconciling power of the gospel. Though a stumbling block for Jews and foolishness to Gentiles, the cross of Christ is the power of God and the wisdom of God (1:22–24). Paul calls believers to a life of humility and love that exalts the name of Christ and brings glory of God.

ANCIENT CONNECTIONS 5.1: CORINTH: CROSSROADS OF COMMERCE AND CULTURE

Much of our knowledge of ancient Corinth comes from two Greek travelers and geographers, Strabo (ca. 64 BCE–ca. 24 CE), who wrote a seventeen-volume work called *Geography*, and Pausanias (ca. 110–ca. 180), who wrote the ten-volume *Description of Greece*.[2] The city of Corinth was strategically located in

[1] The latter is the primary thesis of Gordon Fee in *The First Epistle to the Corinthians*, NICNT, rev. ed. (Grand Rapids: Eerdmans, 2014), 6–17, and throughout. Fee writes, "The basic stance of the present commentary is that the *historical situation* in Corinth was primarily *one of conflict between the church and its founder*" (p. 6).

[2] For access to references to Corinth in these writers and other historians, see Jerome Murphy-O'Connor, *St. Paul's Corinth: Texts and Archaeology* (Collegeville, MN: Liturgical Press, 2002).

Achaia on the narrow isthmus between the Saronic Gulf and the Ionian Sea. The port of Lechaeum lay to the northwest on the Saronic Gulf and Cenchreae to the southeast on the Ionian Sea. Corinth became prosperous and powerful as a key crossroads for commerce and culture. Merchants who did not want to take the dangerous voyage around Achaia would drag their ships and cargo on rollers the four miles across the isthmus on a rock-cut track known as the *diolkos*.[3] The city had a natural defense in the Acrocorinth, a mountain that towered 575 meters (1500 ft.) above the city.

Disaster for the city came in 146 BCE, when Corinth led the Achaian League of city states in revolt against their Roman overlords. The Roman legions under the command of Lucius Mummius marched against the city and destroyed it, killing the men and selling the women and children into slavery. Corinth lay in ruins for over a century, until 44 BCE, when it was refounded by Julius Caesar as a Roman colony. The city was repopulated primarily with colonists from Rome, especially freedmen, who developed into a thriving middle class. Its strategic location made it one of the wealthiest and most culturally diverse cities of Greece. The city had athletic contests—the Isthmian games—that were second only to the Olympics and an outdoor theater that held 14,000 people. Temples were scattered throughout the city.

The city's reputation for immorality was legendary. Strabo claimed the temple of the goddess Aphrodite housed 1,000 sacred prostitutes (*Geog.* 8.6.20c). The Greek term *korinthiazesthai* ("to act like a Corinthian") was coined by the writer Aristophanes to refer to sexual promiscuity, and Plato used *korinthia koré*, "a Corinthian girl," to mean a prostitute.[4] Some caution must be exercised before applying these statements directly to New Testament Corinth, since they were made concerning the old Greek city, which was destroyed almost 200 years before Paul visited Corinth.[5] But it seems clear that much of the old was reproduced in the new, and Corinth remained a place of moral and spiritual decadence. It is not surprising that a church trying to thrive in such a setting would face many challenges.

---

[3] The emperor Nero attempted to dig a canal through the isthmus but failed. A canal was eventually completed in modern times (1893), but it cannot accommodate large ships.

[4] Murphy-O'Connor, *St. Paul's Corinth*, 56–57.

[5] Murphy-O'Connor, 57.

Interpretive Overview

Introduction (1:1–9)

Paul begins his letter in typical Greco-Roman style, identifying himself as author ("Paul, called as an apostle . . ."), naming the recipients ("To the church of God at Corinth . . ."), and his typical greeting ("Grace to you and peace . . ."). Paul notes he is writing together with "Sosthenes our brother," who may be the synagogue leader from Corinth mentioned in Acts 18:17. Sosthenes may be functioning as Paul's secretary.

In the thanksgiving that follows (1:4–9), Paul expresses gratitude to God that the Corinthians are "enriched . . . in all speech and all knowledge" and that they "do not lack any spiritual gift." Ironically, Paul will criticize the Corinthians for their weakness in these very areas, pride in human wisdom (chaps. 1–4) and their misuse of spiritual gifts (chaps. 12–14). One's strengths can become weaknesses when used for selfish means.

Paul's Response to Reports from Corinth (1:10–6:20)

The Problem of Divisions in the Church (1:10–4:21)

After his greeting, Paul begins by addressing the greatest problem in the church, divisions and disunity manifested especially in claims of allegiance to different Christian leaders. Some were saying, "I belong to Paul," others, "I belong to Apollos," "I belong to Cephas," or even "I belong to Christ" (1:10–12). We don't know for certain the nature of these allegiances. Paul's supporters may have been those who remained loyal to the apostle because of his role as founder of the church. Apollos's supporters may have been Greeks who valued his Alexandrian education and eloquence (cf. Acts 18:24–26). Cephas's (Peter's) followers may have been Jewish Christians who felt loyal to the Jerusalem apostles and the mother church there. Most puzzling are those who claimed loyalty to Christ. Isn't this where our loyalty as Christians should be? Perhaps these were claiming their superior spiritual wisdom that came directly from Christ.

Paul will have none of it. The divisions caused by such party loyalty are incompatible with the gospel message. Christians have only one allegiance, to Christ himself, who was crucified for us and in whose name we were all baptized. Paul downplays his own role in baptizing the Corinthians, even forgetting how many of them he baptized (1:14–16)! What matters in Christian leadership is not powerful rhetoric or the number of loyal fans, but the transforming power of the cross of Christ (1:17).

This message of the cross, Paul says, seems like foolishness to the people of the world who are dying in their sins, but is recognized as the power of God by those who have experienced its ability to save (1:18–19). All the world's great "wisdom," epitomized in Paul's day by the Jewish scribe's expertise in the Mosaic law and the Greek philosopher's rhetorical skills, is foolishness when compared to God's wisdom. The Jews longed for a powerful, miracle-working Messiah to free them from the bondage of Rome. Greeks sought for wisdom to comprehend the mysteries of life. A humiliated and crucified Messiah was of little use to either. Yet to those who had experienced God's saving power, the cross of Christ was both power to overcome evil and the wisdom to provide true knowledge of God (1:18–25).

The paradox of God's power and wisdom could be seen in the Corinthians themselves. They came mostly from the lower classes. They were not brilliant philosophers, powerful military leaders, or royal heirs to the throne. God chose things that were foolish in the eyes of the world to shame the wise, and things that were weak to shame the strong. As a result, no one could boast about their own abilities or standing before God. They could only boast in the Lord, whose wisdom, righteousness, holiness, and redemption becomes ours in Christ (1:26–31).

Just as this paradox of wisdom and power was illustrated in the calling of the Corinthian church, so it was illustrated in Paul himself. When he came to Corinth to establish the church, he did not come with great charisma or rhetorical skills. He came "in weakness, in fear, and in much trembling" (2:3). Paul may here be referring to his arrival in Corinth after visiting Athens, where "he was deeply distressed" by the city's idolatry (Acts 17:16). Or he may be referring to his early ministry in Corinth (18:1), a city of paganism and decadence. Paul did not wow his audience with the "persuasive words of wisdom" of the Greek philosophers. But he had something much greater, the power of God's Spirit (1 Cor 2:1–5).

While the world's wisdom leads to nothing, there is a true wisdom that comes from God. It is not "a wisdom of this age" (2:6) but is rather God's wisdom and a "mystery." The Greek word *mystērion* is used by Paul of something previously unknown but now revealed by God's Spirit to his people. In this case the mystery is the cross. For the world's rulers, the cross meant Jesus's defeat and death. But for believers it means victory and salvation (2:6–9).

But how can we know this mystery? As mere human beings, it is impossible. Yet God has revealed it to us through his Spirit, who is living within us (2:10–16). This is an amazing truth and is central to so much of Paul's theology. Paul quotes Isa 40:13, an OT passage that speaks of God's sovereignty and transcendence: "Who has known the Lord's mind, that he may instruct him?" (2:16) The answer to this rhetorical question in Isaiah is, "No one!" But that is not Paul's conclusion. Astonishingly, he answers, "*We can!*" This is because "we have the mind of Christ" (v. 16). With God's Spirit living within us, we have direct access to God's truth.

Having identified the reality of the Spirit in a believer's life, Paul next turns to how the presence of the Spirit should be manifested in the life of the church (3:1–3). Unfortunately, the Corinthians remained spiritually immature. They were like babies who could only drink milk rather than eat solid food. Rather than living "in the power of the Spirit" (*pneumatikos*), they were still "worldly," or "fleshly" (*sarkinos*), living in the power of the "flesh" (*sarx*). The Greek term *sarx* (traditionally translated "flesh") is a technical term for Paul that refers to our sinful selves apart from Christ's transformation through the Spirit.

The Corinthians' tendency to exalt human leaders arose from the immaturity of living in the power of the flesh instead of the Spirit. A mature, Spirit-informed perspective recognizes that Christian leaders are merely servants of God and coworkers with one another, fulfilling whatever roles God has given them. Paul introduces two metaphors to illustrate this. The first is agricultural, with leaders portrayed as field hands. Paul planted the field (= the Corinthian church), and Apollos watered it, but God made it grow. The second metaphor is construction workers. Paul laid the foundation—which is Christ himself—and others have built upon it. Those who build well and whose work stands the test of fire will be rewarded. Those who build poorly and with shoddy materials will receive no reward but will barely escape with their lives (3:4–15). Paul then extends the metaphor by identifying the building as a temple. The church is God's holy temple, where he dwells through his Spirit. Those who destroy God's temple through pride and ambition will suffer God's judgment (3:16–17). In light of the reality that we are merely God's servants and that God's wisdom infinitely exceeds ours, there should be no boasting about human leaders. All believers belong to Christ alone and have everything they need in him (3:18–23).

Paul concludes his call for unity by describing the role of the apostles and how the Corinthians should relate to them. The Corinthians had become prideful about their spiritual abilities and their wisdom. But Paul says that true apostles are servants of Christ, entrusted with God's "mysteries" (thing revealed by God). Their ultimate responsibility is to be faithful to him. Human judgments matter little, since we will all be judged by God at Christ's return (4:1–5). This was Paul's point with his metaphors related to himself and Apollos: All leaders are merely servants of God, a principle clearly taught in Scripture (which Paul has been quoting throughout this section—1:19, 31; 3:19, 20). There is no reason, therefore, to go "beyond what is written,"[6] that is, beyond what Scripture says (4:6). Pride is ruled out since everything we have is from God (4:7).

Paul drives this point home by ironically contrasting the pride of the Corinthians with the humility of true apostles. The Corinthians are acting like they have arrived spiritually, like triumphant kings already assuming their thrones (4:8). By contrast the apostles are like prisoners of war at the end of a Roman victory parade, condemned to be executed (4:9). The Corinthians claim all the marks of Greco-Roman status: wisdom, power, honor. The apostles are viewed as the opposite: foolish, weak, and dishonored. They are "the scum of the earth, like everyone's garbage" (4:10–13).

After such strong language, Paul clarifies his purpose: "I'm not writing this to shame you, but to warn you as my dear children." He reminds the Corinthians that though they have many teachers, he is their one spiritual father (4:14–15). And as their father, he calls on them to imitate him. Though he hopes to come soon, he is sending Timothy for now to remind them of his life and teaching (4:16–17). While a good father always acts out of love for his children, love involves discipline. So Paul asks: "Should I come to you with a rod, or in love and a spirit of gentleness?" (4:18–21). This section suggests that there is already a growing conflict between Paul and some of the church's leaders, who are challenging his authority (see "Occasion" on pp. 108–9 of this chapter).

The Problem of Not Confronting an Immoral Situation (5:1–13)

After his call for unity (chaps. 1–4), Paul turns to address a second problem in the church. This is a case of sexual immorality so egregious that it is even condemned in the pagan world. A man in the church is in a sexual relationship with his stepmother![7] Yet instead of responding with deep sorrow and acting to discipline the man, the church is acting proud (5:2). This could mean they were proud *despite* the man's actions (they were tolerating it), or it could mean they were proud *because* of it (they were condoning it). Elsewhere in the letter we see evidence that the Corinthians were justifying bad behavior by claiming they had complete freedom in Christ (6:12).

Paul responds by calling the Corinthians to come together to discipline the man and expel him from the fellowship (5:2, 5, 7, 13). At that time, Paul will be present with

---

[6] This is likely a rabbinic slogan that Paul is quoting, meaning "Scripture teaching on this is all you need."

[7] Such behavior was forbidden in the OT law (see Lev 18:8; 20:11; Deut 27:20) and is denounced by Jewish writers (e.g., Josephus, *Ant.* 3.12.1, §274; Philo, *Special Laws* 3.12–21) and Greco-Roman writers alike (e.g., Gaius, *Institutes* 1.63; Cicero, *Pro Cluentio* 5.27).

them in spirit. In the name and power of Jesus, they are to "hand that one over to Satan for the destruction of the flesh, so that his spirit may be saved in the day of the Lord" (5:5). There are various interpretations of this statement.[8] (1) Some say "destruction of the flesh" means physical death as God's discipline. (2) Others see it as some kind of physical affliction to his body, leading to the man's repentance. (3) A third possibility is that, as often in Paul, flesh means "sinful self," and its destruction means that God's discipline will result in the man's repentance. In any case, the goal of this discipline is not retribution but restoration ("so that his spirit may be saved").

To reinforce his command, Paul draws several analogies to the Jewish Passover. He first cites what was probably a popular proverb, "a little leaven leavens the whole batch of dough" (5:6). Just as leaven permeates through a lump of dough, so leaving sin unchecked will encourage it to spread. Building on this, Paul calls the church to "clean out the old leaven . . ." (v. 7a), recalling the Passover practice of removing leaven (symbolizing sin) from the home (Exod 12:19). This Passover imagery in turn recalls for Paul the most important Passover symbol, "For Christ our Passover lamb has been sacrificed" (v. 7b). The salvation provided by Christ's sacrifice allows us to celebrate a new Passover with the "unleavened bread of sincerity and truth" rather than "the leaven of malice and evil" (v. 8).

Paul concludes this section by correcting a misunderstanding that arose from an earlier letter he wrote (5:9, 11), which called the church not to associate with sexually immoral people. In that letter he was *not* referring to the people of the world, but to believers who refused to repent. While God will judge outsiders, the church must take responsibility for its own (5:9–13).

The Problem of Lawsuits between Believers (6:1–11)

Paul next turns to another issue that was causing divisions in the church at Corinth. Believers were suing each other in the city courts (6:1). These lawsuits compromised the testimony of the church and contradicted the reconciling power of the gospel. In response, Paul encourages the church to resolve its own conflicts. He makes two main arguments. First, believers should be better than this (6:2–6). Using a greater-to-lesser argument, he points out that as heirs of God's great salvation, believers will

[8] For various interpretations, see Fee, *First Epistle to the Corinthians*, 228–35; A. C. Thiselton, "The Meaning of σάρξ in 1 Cor. 5:5: A Fresh Approach in the Light of Logical and Semantic Factors," *SJT* 26 (1973): 204–28.

judge the world, both people and angels.[9] Surely they are competent to judge such trivial cases (vv. 2–4)! With subtle sarcasm, he reminds the Corinthians how they have been boasting of their great wisdom. "Can it be that there is not one wise person among you who is able to arbitrate between fellow believers?" (vv. 5–6). Second, lawsuits are a lose/lose prospect. Whether or not they win their court battle, they have already lost the spiritual war. This is because such disputes deny the reconciling power of the gospel. "Why not rather be wronged?" says Paul, "Why not rather be cheated?" (6:7). Instead of adopting Jesus's attitude of self-sacrificial love and righteousness, they are acting like the people of the world—the unrighteous who will not inherit God's kingdom. He launches into a list of sins characteristic of unbelievers. They were once like this, but they have now been washed, sanctified, and justified in the name of Jesus Christ and by the power of the Spirit. Their lives should reflect this transformation (6:8–11).

The Problem of Immorality in General (6:12–20)

After responding to the question of lawsuits, Paul returns to the issue of sexual immorality raised by the case of incest in chapter 5. Sexual promiscuity was common in the Greco-Roman world (see Ancient Connections 5.2), and some of the men in the Corinthian church were evidently continuing to visit prostitutes. Paul argues that this behavior is destructive to their spiritual life and contrary to the gospel. Their bodies are the temple of the Holy Spirit and so should be used to bring glory to God.

ANCIENT CONNECTIONS 5.2: GREEK SEXUAL VALUES

"Mistresses we keep for the sake of pleasure, concubines for the daily care of our persons, but wives to bear us legitimate children and to be faithful guardians of our households."

Demosthenes, *Orations* 59.122 (fourth c. BCE)

Paul cites and then responds to several slogans that Corinthian church members were using to justify their behavior. The first was, "Everything is permissible for me." This slogan likely arose in response to Judaizers claiming that Christians were bound by the OT law. The response was, "Everything is permissible for me," meaning "I

[9] See Matt 19:28; 2 Tim 2:12; Rev 20:4.

am not bound by these laws." Paul agrees in part, but sharply qualifies the slogan. True, believers are not under the law, but this does not mean they can do anything they want. To the slogan "Everything is permissible," Paul provides two important qualifications: "But not everything is beneficial" and "but I will not be mastered by anything." Food and alcohol, like sex, are not prohibited by God, but they can be destructive and addictive when abused.

In 6:13 Paul cites another Corinthian slogan, "Food for the stomach and the stomach for food, and God will destroy them both" (NIV).[10] This slogan is similar to the first ("everything is permissible for me"), since it is saying that foods themselves no longer defile. But the second part of the slogan goes further. Some of the Corinthians were not just saying "we are not under the law." They were also claiming that what they did with their bodies in the physical world was irrelevant to their spiritual state.[11] Only the spiritual world matters because God will do away with both food and stomach. While Paul here cites a slogan related to food, the next line ("the body is not for sexual immorality") shows that the Corinthians were applying it further. "Food" became a euphemism for the pleasures of sex: "Sex for the body and the body for sex, but God will do away with both." They were saying "I can sleep with a prostitute with my body, and it doesn't affect my spiritual state at all."

Paul disagrees. First, your body is not your own. It belongs to the Lord (vv. 13, 19). The church is the bride of Christ, and as believers we are united to Christ in a spiritual union. And as in marriage, "The two will become one flesh" (6:16; Gen 2:24). To have sex with a prostitute is to unite spiritually with her and so distort this one-flesh relationship with Christ. Second, contrary to the slogan, the body is not destined for destruction. It is destined for resurrection (v. 14). Unlike in later Gnosticism (see Ancient Connections 10.1, p. 206), the physical world is not a bad thing; it is a good thing (Gen 1:31). It is destined for restoration, not for destruction (Rev 21–22). In light of this, Paul calls on the church to "Flee sexual immorality!" (1 Cor 6:18). Our individual body (like the church as a whole; 3:16) is a temple of the Holy Spirit, the place where God's presence dwells (6:19). Its value is inestimable, since it was purchased with the blood of Christ. It is essential, therefore, to glorify God with our bodies (6:20).

---

[10] The CSB stops the quote after the second "food" (cf. NLT), while the NIV (cf. NET) continues it up to "both." The latter is more likely. The Corinthians were claiming that the physical world was destined for destruction, so what they did in it was irrelevant to their spiritual state or destiny.

[11] This perspective may be called "proto-Gnostic," since it would become a central part of the second-century heresy known as Gnosticism. See Ancient Connections 10.1.

Paul's Response to the Letter from Corinth (7:1–16:4)

After dealing with problems at Corinth that had been reported to him, Paul turns to questions brought to him from the church. This transition is signaled in the phrase, "Now in response to the matters you wrote about" (7:1). These questions relate to marriage (chap. 7), food sacrificed to idols (chaps. 8–10), propriety in worship (chap. 11), spiritual gifts (chaps. 12–14), the resurrection (chap. 15), and the collection he is making for the poor in Jerusalem (16:1–4).

CONCERNING MARRIAGE (7:1–40)

In chapter 7 Paul responds to a number of questions related to marriage, divorce, and singleness. These questions were evidently sparked by the claim of some that celibacy was a higher spiritual state than marriage and that sexual relations were spiritually defiling. As in 6:12, Paul begins with a Corinthian slogan, which he partly agrees with but sharply qualifies. The slogan is "It is good for a man not to have sexual relations with a woman" (7:1 NIV).[12] Paul agrees that celibacy and singleness are good things. Indeed, throughout this chapter Paul celebrates singleness, since it allows undistracted devotion to the Lord (7:1, 7, 8, 26–28, 32–34). But that doesn't mean marriage is wrong. Especially in light of the many sexual temptations in society, "each man should have sexual relations with his own wife, and each woman should have sexual relations with her own husband." Marriage is the norm for most Christians (7:2, 8–9). Paul then goes on to describe each spouse's sexual responsibilities. "A wife," he says, "does not have the right over her own body, but her husband does." This was the norm in both Greco-Roman and Jewish society. Wives were considered the sexual property of their husbands and were expected to remain faithful to them and meet their needs.[13] Shockingly, however, Paul then says that the reciprocal is also true: "In the same way, a husband does not have the right over his own body, but his wife does." This is a relationship of mutuality, where each partner should seek to please and meet the needs of the other person (7:3–4). Abstinence should be practiced only by mutual consent and for a limited period (7:7).

---

[12] The Greek idiom is, "It is good for a man not to touch a woman," with touch being a euphemism for sexual relations.

[13] See Num 30:3–16, where a woman could not make a vow, such as a vow of abstinence, unless the male authority in her life (either her father or her husband) approved it. Men, by contrast, had the freedom to make their own vows (Num 30:1–2).

Paul next moves on to questions of separation and divorce (7:10–16). It should be noted that when Paul says "not I, but the Lord" in 7:10, he is referring to what Jesus himself taught about marriage and divorce. And when he says in v. 12, "I (not the Lord)," he is teaching something Jesus did not specifically address (marriage to an unbeliever). Paul is *not* saying in either case that his own words do not carry authority or that they are less authoritative than Jesus's (see 7:40b).

Paul first affirms what Jesus taught (cf. Matt 5:31–32; 19:3–12; Mark 10:2–12; Luke 16:18), which is that marriage ought to be a lifelong commitment: "A wife is not to leave her husband . . . and a husband is not to divorce his wife" (1 Cor 7:10–11). He adds that if separation does occur, a wife should remain unmarried or be reconciled to her husband. Paul makes an exception in the case of an unbelieving spouse. If the unbeliever leaves, the believing spouse should let them leave. But if the unbeliever is willing to stay, the believer should remain in the marriage, since the believer "sanctifies" or "makes holy" the unbeliever. Paul is not saying that the believer's presence automatically saves the unbeliever. Rather, while some Corinthians claimed that an unbeliever *defiled* a marriage, Paul says the opposite is true: A believer brings holiness to that marriage. This is a powerful image. While in the Old Testament, Israel was meant to be separate from the nations to avoid defilement, in the New Testament the church is salt and light, a transforming presence in the world.[14]

Third, Paul turns to a variety of issues related to marriage and singleness (7:17–40). He first calls believers to be content in whatever state they are in, whether married or single, Jew or Gentile, slave or free (7:17–24). He next turns to the question of "virgins," or whether single people should pursue marriage (7:25–38). While it is good to marry, Paul favors singleness for two main reasons: The first is expressed variously as "because of the present distress" (v. 26), "the time is short" (v. 29 NIV), and "this world in its current form is passing away" (v. 31). Christians are living at the "culmination of the ages" (10:11 NIV) inaugurated by Christ's death and resurrection, giving us a new perspective on life and an urgency to everything we do. The second reason is to allow wholehearted devotion to the Lord, especially in light of the many responsibilities of marriage (7:32–35). Paul concludes by pointing out that a widow is free to marry, but only to another believer ("in the Lord"). Again, however, Paul encourages singleness: "But she is happier if she remains as she is, in my opinion," adding that his words carry authority: "And I think that I also have the Spirit of God" (7:39–40).

---

[14] Notice that when Jesus touches a man with leprosy, Jesus does not become defiled, but rather brings holiness and healing (Matt 8:1–4 pars.).

CONCERNING FOOD SACRIFICED TO IDOLS (8:1–11:1)

Following his response to questions related to marriage and divorce, Paul turns to another question from Corinth. This was whether Christians should eat food that had been offered to an idol. Much of the food sold in the marketplaces in Corinth and throughout the Greco-Roman world had been offered as a sacrifice to a god. The Corinthians were struggling with whether it was acceptable to eat such food. Paul first responds with an overall principle: "Knowledge puffs up, but love builds up" (8:1). This "knowledge" is the awareness that there is one true God and that idols are nothing. For the one who knows this, eating food sacrificed to idols is no big deal, since no god is being worshiped. Yet some believers, because of their background in idol worship, experience eating such food as worshipping a pagan deity. So, Paul says, if your actions cause your brother or sister to sin, love dictates that you should abstain (8:1–13).

Paul next illustrates this principle by showing how he is willing to give up his own rights to reach more people for Christ. As an apostle of Jesus Christ, he has certain rights, such as being financially compensated for his ministry and bringing a believing wife along on his missionary journeys—as Peter and other apostles did.[15] Just as workers in any occupation, whether soldiers, farmers, or shepherds, deserve compensation, so also ministry workers should be compensated. This is a biblical principle, as God commanded Israel not to muzzle an ox while it treaded out grain (v. 9; cf. Deut 25:4), and priests in the temple were allowed to eat a portion of the sacrifice (cf. Lev 6:16, 26; Deut 18:1) (9:1–14).

While Paul has all these rights, he has given them up for the sake of the gospel. It is his joy and reward to preach the free gospel of grace free of charge! Though he is free, Paul becomes a slave to everyone to win more people to Christ. To the Jews, he became like a Jew, to win the Jews; to Gentiles, he became like a Gentile, to win the Gentiles. To the "weak" (those who would sin in eating idol food), he becomes "weak," abstaining in the same way. He does all these things for the sake of the gospel, to share in its blessings (9:15–23).

This theme of sacrifice for the gospel leads into an athletic metaphor, where Paul describes the motivation and discipline necessary to successfully live out the Christian life. Like an athlete, believers must run with their eyes on the prize. While our salvation means resting in God's grace, we also strive to live with purpose, passion, and self-discipline (9:24–27).

---

[15] That Peter was married is also attested in Mark 1:30 pars.

Paul has been speaking about his freedom in Christ and his willingness to give up that freedom to protect those who are vulnerable. Now he addresses what it means to take this freedom too far and fall into idolatry. He points to the negative example of Israel in the wilderness. Though God delivered them from Egypt and gave them enormous spiritual blessings, they became idolaters, adulterers, and complainers. As a result, they experienced God's judgment. The Corinthians should expect the same if they practice idolatry and immorality at pagan feasts (10:1–22).

Paul concludes his discussion on food sacrificed to idols by giving more general principles and discussing specific contexts in which idol meat may be permissible. He first repeats from 6:12 his response to the Corinthian slogan "Everything is permissible," by reminding believers, "but not everything is beneficial." While previously adding, "but I will not be mastered by anything" (6:12), now he adds a new principle, "but not everything builds up" (10:23). Our goal should be to seek the best for others (10:24). Although previously Paul told the Corinthians that they must *not* eat idol food at pagan temples since that is to worship with demons (10:14–22), he now provides a more nuanced response for other contexts. They *can* eat idol meat bought in the marketplace without any problem, since there is no worship involved and since "the earth is the Lord's, and all that is in it" (10:25–26; citing Ps 24:1). They *can also* eat such food when it is served at a private dinner party. The only exception is when someone announces that this is food offered to an idol. In that case, you should abstain, since to eat would be to participate in the worship of that deity—at least in the mind of that person (10:27–30).

Paul concludes these three chapters with several guiding principles (10:31–11:1): (1) Do everything for God's glory (10:31). (2) Do not cause others to stumble, whether Jews or Greeks or fellow church members (10:32). (3) Seek to benefit others, not just yourself (10:33). (4) Imitate the example that Paul has set for them, as he follows the example of Christ (11:1).

Concerning Head Coverings in Worship (11:2–16)

In the next four chapters (11–14), Paul addresses questions from the church related to public worship, including head coverings in worship (11:2–16), bad behavior at the Lord's supper (11:17–34), and the misuse of spiritual gifts (chaps. 12–14). In the first, Paul instructs men to pray or prophesy with their heads uncovered, while women are to pray or prophesy with their heads covered (11:5). Paul's general point here seems clear enough: Christianity greatly raised the status of women, treating them as equal to men in bearing the image of God and in joining in worship (cf. comments on 7:4

above). In the church at Corinth, however, some women were expressing their freedom in Christ in culturally disruptive ways. Paul encourages them to avoid distractions by observing social norms with reference to head coverings.

While this much is reasonably clear, our limited knowledge of the cultural context and the specifics of the situation at Corinth makes this one of the most difficult passages in the NT to interpret. Some key interpretive questions include, (1) What is the cultural background that requires head coverings (or long hair) during worship? Is this about avoiding pagan worship styles? Promoting modesty over promiscuity? Stressing God-ordained gender-distinctions? (2) Are Paul's concerns primarily about head coverings (11:4–10) or about long versus short hair (11:13–15)? (3) Are Paul's guidelines for husbands and wives or for men and women generally? (The Greek uses the same word for man/husband [*anēr*] and for woman/wife [*gynē*]). (4) Does the figurative use of "head" refer primarily to the man's *authority over* the woman, or the man (Adam) as the *source of* the woman (see 11:8–12)? (5) Is the head covering a symbol of the woman's own authority to pray and prophesy (v. 10) or a symbol of the man's authority over the woman? (6) What does it mean that the man is the "image and glory of God," while woman is the "glory" of man (11:7)? (7) What does "because of the angels" in v. 10 mean? (8) How does "nature itself" (v. 14) point to long hair as disgraceful for men? Is this an appeal to nature or to culture?[16]

With so many difficult questions concerning the meaning of the text in its original context, the application of the text for today becomes even more difficult! Is the text a call for (1) female head covering in worship? (2) Submission of women to men in worship? (3) Proper reverence for all in worship (whatever form that takes in a particular culture)? In passages like this, humility and charity towards others may be the most important qualities an interpreter brings to the text. It seems to us in this case Paul's previous admonitions to seek the best for others and to honor one another above self should take precedent over dogmatic assertions about head coverings and their implications.

Concerning Abuse of the Lord's Supper (11:17–34)

Some of the divisions in the church at Corinth were related to the gap between rich and poor. This was manifesting itself especially in a communal meal that the church

[16] For these and other questions, see the detailed discussions in Fee, *First Epistle to the Corinthians*, 542–86; Anthony C. Thiselton, *The First Epistle to the Corinthians: A Commentary on the Greek Text*, NIGTC (Grand Rapids: Eerdmans, 2000), 799–848.

traditionally shared in conjunction with the Lord's Supper. In the Greco-Roman world, formal meals or dinner parties were rituals of social status (see Ancient Connections 5.3). Who you ate with and the quality of your food was determined by your social status. In line with these Greco-Roman values, the elite rich in the Corinthian congregation were bringing their own meals and eating them before the poor arrived. By the time the church had gathered, half the congregation was hungry while the other half was drunk! Paul is horrified that the Lord's Supper, which should have been an occasion of unity, had become an arena for selfishness, prejudice, and division.

In the midst of this discussion, Paul recounts Jesus's own institution of the Lord's Supper (11:23–26), an episode that also appears in all three Synoptic Gospels (Matt 26:26–29; Mark 14:22–25; Luke 22:17–20). Paul's account here is the earliest written record of the event, since 1 Corinthians was almost certainly written before the Synoptics. The words here are closest to Luke's account, with references to the "new covenant in my blood" and to "do this . . . in remembrance of me" (Luke 22:19–20).

Paul warns the church that those who partake of the Lord's Supper "in an unworthy manner" will be guilty of sinning against the body and blood of the Lord. Self-examination is therefore necessary, since God will judge those who do not show honor to the body of Christ, his church. God's judgment could already be seen in that many of the Corinthians were sick, and some had even died (11:27–32). In conclusion, Paul encourages the church to wait for each other before they eat. If someone is hungry, they should eat before they come (11:33–34).

ANCIENT CONNECTIONS 5.3: MEALS AS RITUALS OF SOCIAL STATUS

We have examples from the Greco-Roman world where different meals were served to people of different social status at the same banquet. The former (from Martial, ca. 40–103 CE) is a perspective from someone of lower status; the latter (from Pliny, ca. 61–113 CE) of one from higher status. [17]

> Since I am asked to dinner . . . why is not the same dinner served to me as to you? You take oysters fattened in the Lucrine lake, I suck a mussel through a hole in the shell; you get mushrooms, I take hog funguses; you tackle turbot, but I brill. Golden with fat, a turtledove gorges you with

[17] Both cited by Fee, *First Epistle to the Corinthians*, 600n61.

its bloated rump; there is set before me a magpie that has died in its cage. Why do I dine without you although, Ponticus, I am dining with you? The dole has gone; let us have the benefit of that; let us eat the same fare. (Martial, *Epigram* 3.60; cf. 1.20; 4.85; 6.11; 10.49)

It would take too long to go into the details . . . of how I happened to be dining with a man though no particular friend of his whose elegant economy, as he called it, seemed to me a sort of stingy extravagance. The best dishes were set in front of himself and a select few, and cheap scraps of food before the rest of the company. He had even put the wine into tiny little flasks, divided into three categories, not with the idea of giving his guests opportunity of choosing, but to make it impossible for them to refuse what they were given. One lot was intended for himself and for us, another for his lesser friends (all his friends are graded) and his and our freedmen. (Pliny, *Epistula* 2.6)

Concerning Spiritual Gifts (12:1–14:40)

The third issue related to public worship is the use of spiritual gifts. While the church at Corinth had a rich array of spiritual gifts (1:7), some members were exalting certain gifts above others and expressing pride in the superiority of their own gifts. Their worship services were becoming increasingly chaotic, discouraging authentic worship and providing a poor witness for unbelievers.

Paul begins by reminding the Corinthians that when they were pagans, they were led astray by lifeless idols that could not speak. Now, however, the living God spoke to them through his Spirit. The confirmation that we are hearing the true Spirit of God is the centrality of Christ, expressed in the confession that "Jesus is Lord" (12:1–3). While the church is united around one Spirit and one Lord, the Spirit gives a variety of gifts to enrich and edify the people of God. Among these gifts are wisdom, knowledge, faith, healing, miracles, prophecy, tongues, and the interpretation of tongues (12:4–11; see sidebar 5.1 for lists of gifts). Paul illustrates this "unity through diversity" with the metaphor of the body. Just as the human body has many parts that all function together for the common good, so the body of Christ—the church—has many individuals with different gifts, all functioning together to accomplish God's purposes. No gifts are independent of the others and *all* the gifts are essential for the proper functioning of the body (12:12–24). This mutuality should create unity in the church. When one member suffers, all suffer, and when one member is honored, all should rejoice with them (12:25–26). Although the Corinthians were seeking certain gifts above others, Paul emphasizes that it is God who assigns gifts, and all the gifts are essential. Not everyone has every gift (12:27–30). In what at first sounds like a contradiction, Paul tells the Corinthians to "desire the greater gifts" (12:31a). Are some gifts greater than others?

SIDEBAR 5.1: LISTS OF SPIRITUAL GIFTS IN THE NEW TESTAMENT

Eph 4:11	1 Cor 12:28–30	1 Cor 12:8–10	Rom 12:6–8	1 Pet 4:11
1. apostles	1. apostles			
2. prophets	2. prophets	2. prophecy	2. prophesying	
3. teachers	3. teachers		3. teaching	
4. evangelists				
5. pastors				
	6. miracles	6. miracles		
	7. tongues	7. tongues		
	8. interpretation of tongues	8. interpretation of tongues		
	9. healing	9. healing		
	10. helps			
	11. administration			
		12. wisdom		
		13. knowledge		
		14. faith		
		15. discerning of spirits		
			16. serving	16. serving
			17. encouraging/ exhorting	
			18. giving	
			19. leadership	
			20. showing mercy	
				21. speaking

Numbering of gifts is meant only to show alignment between the lists.

Before describing these "greater gifts," Paul pauses his discussion of spiritual gifts to show them "an even better way" (12:31b), which is the way of love (13:1–13). Love is expressed through building others up rather than exalting oneself. If the fundamental purpose of spiritual gifts is to *build up the church*, then even the most powerful use of those gifts is useless unless they are practiced with love (13:1–3). This kind of love is not a feeling but an action, and Paul uses fifteen verbs to describe it: Love is patient; it is kind; it does not envy; it is not boastful, arrogant, rude, self-seeking, or irritable. It does not keep a record of wrongs and finds no joy in unrighteousness but rejoices in the truth. It bears all things, believes all things, hopes all things, endures all things. It never ends. While all other spiritual gifts are temporary and will disappear at Christ's return, faith, hope, and love will remain. And the greatest of these is love.

After this great interlude on the "better way" of love, Paul returns to his discussion of spiritual gifts, addressing the specific problems at Corinth. Church members were apparently exalting the gift of tongues, which was an impressive gift in the context of public worship. Yet, Paul argues, when everyone speaks in tongues and no one interprets, the service becomes chaotic, and only the tongue-speaker is edified. By contrast, when someone prophesies, everyone understands and so the church as a whole is edified. In the same way, if an unbeliever comes in and hears only tongues, they will say, "You are out of your minds." However, if they hear prophecy, they will say, "God is really among you!" (14:1–25).

Paul therefore provides certain guidelines for tongue-speaking and prophesying, calling the church to order and peace in a way that edifies the body and advances the gospel (14:26–40). Everything should be done in a way that builds up the church. Only two or three people should speak in tongues, one after another, and someone should interpret for each. If no interpreter is present, they should remain silent and speak only to God. Two or three prophets may speak, one by one, and others evaluate. Since "God is not a God of disorder but of peace . . . everything is to be done decently and in order" (14:33, 40).

Concerning the Resurrection (15:1–58)

The last major theological issue Paul deals with concerns the resurrection from the dead. While some Greeks believed in the immortality of the soul, few believed that the dead would rise bodily from the grave. Some in the Corinthian church were evidently challenging Paul's teaching about the resurrection of the dead.

Paul begins by reiterating his essential gospel message: "that Christ died for our sins according to the Scriptures, that he was buried, that he was raised on the third day according to the Scriptures" (15:3–5). Central to the apostolic gospel was the atoning death of Christ and his bodily resurrection. And there is overwhelming evidence for Christ's resurrection. Jesus was seen alive by Peter (Cephas), by the Twelve, and by more than 500 people, many of whom were still alive when Paul writes. The resurrected Christ was also seen by Jesus's half-brother James, by all the apostles, and finally, by Paul himself at his Damascus Road experience (15:1–11).

If Christ has indeed been raised from the dead, Paul asserts, then it is absurd to claim that there is no bodily resurrection. On the other hand, if Christ has *not* been raised from the dead, then Christianity is a sham and so is our faith. We are false witnesses and still dead in our sins (15:12–19). But, as the resurrection appearances confirm, Christ has indeed been raised! He is the "firstfruits," the present evidence of the future harvest, and so the guarantee that we too will be raised. Just as all humanity died in Adam, so all humanity will be made alive in Christ, who is the second Adam (15:20–23). In this way Christ's defeat of death marks the beginning of the end times, which will come to completion when he defeats every earthly power, including death, and turns the kingdom over to his heavenly Father (15:24–28). Paul concludes this section by providing additional arguments for the resurrection (15:29–34): If the dead are not raised, why are some people baptized for the dead (v. 29)?[18] If the dead are not raised, why should Christians be willing to suffer persecution and martyrdom for their faith (vv. 30–32a)? If the dead are not raised, why not just live life for pleasure? (v. 32b, citing Isa 22:13).

A second question related to the resurrection raised at Corinth concerned the nature of the resurrection body (15:35–49). Some were mocking the idea that our physical bodies will be raised from the dead (like zombies?!). Paul responds by describing the nature of the resurrection body. It will be a new body but in some sense related to the old, just as a plant is related to the seed from which it grew (15:36–38). It will be a different kind of body, just as heavenly bodies differ from earthly bodies (15:39–41). While our present body is corruptible, dishonored, weak, and natural, our resurrection body will be incorruptible, glorious, powerful, and spiritual. Just as our present body bears the image of fallen Adam, so our heavenly body will bear the image of the glorified Christ (15:42–49). As the "firstfruits of those who have fallen

---

[18] This is one of the most puzzling statements in Paul's letters. He may be referring to (1) proxy baptism for believers who had died before being baptized or perhaps (2) new converts who were viewed as replacing those who had died. See Fee, *First Epistle to the Corinthians*, 845–50.

asleep" (15:20, 23) and the "firstborn from the dead" (Col 1:18), his resurrection body is the prototype for ours.

Paul finally takes up a question that naturally arises from his discussion: How will this transformation occur? or perhaps, What happens to those who are still alive when Christ returns? (15:50–58). He responds that although we will not all die, we will all be "changed." When Christ returns, the last trumpet will sound and the dead in Christ will be raised in immortal, incorruptible bodies, while those who are still alive will be instantly transformed into these same resurrection bodies. At that moment, Christ's victory will be complete as sin and death will be destroyed forever (vv. 54–57; citing Isa 25:8; Hos 13:14). In light of this reality, Paul calls the church to faithfulness and to action: "be steadfast, immovable, always excelling in the Lord's work, because you know that your labor in the Lord is not in vain" (v. 58).

Concerning the Collection for Jerusalem (16:1–4)

The last issue Paul deals with concerns the collection for the poor Christians in Jerusalem. Throughout Paul's third missionary journey, he has been gathering this collection (cf. 2 Cor 8–9; Rom 15:25–29). Paul first repeats guidelines he has given to other churches. They should start early, setting aside money weekly as their income allows. This will avoid the embarrassment of having to rush to take the collection when Paul arrives (16:1–2). When he arrives, Paul will provide letters of introduction for those who will accompany the money to Jerusalem, and Paul himself might go with them (16:3–4).

Conclusion

Paul closes his letter with news, exhortation, commendations, and greetings (16:5–24). He first notes his travel plans and the plans of other associates. He intends to stay in Ephesus until Pentecost because the Lord has opened up opportunities (and challenges) for ministry there. He then plans to come to Corinth after visiting the churches in Macedonia, perhaps staying with them through winter (16:5–9). Meanwhile, he is sending Timothy to them. Paul warns them to treat Timothy well, not with contempt, and to send him on his way in peace (16:10–11). This odd comment may be evidence that there is a growing conflict between Paul and the church, since Paul fears they will reject his representative. Paul adds that he has encouraged Apollos to visit the church, but Apollos is presently unwilling, though he may come later (16:12). After exhorting them to strength, faithfulness, and love (16:13–14), Paul commends several church members for their faithful service, including the household of Stephanas and the three-man delegation of Stephanas, Fortunatus, and Achaicus (16:15–18; see "Occasion," earlier in the chapter, pp. 108–9). Finally, he sends greetings from various churches and friends (16:19–20), adds a greeting in his own hand (16:21), and pronounces a curse on those who don't love the Lord and a prayer for the Lord's soon return (*Maranatha*, an Aramaic phrase meaning "Come, Lord!") (16:22). The letter ends with a benediction for the grace of the Lord Jesus and Paul's reiteration of his love for the church (16:23–24).

Old Testament Connections

Although 1 Corinthians is roughly the length of Romans, it has far fewer OT citations.[19] As a result Romans is often viewed as a theological letter with deep and foundational teaching derived from the Hebrew Scriptures, while 1 Corinthians is considered practical and pastoral, with Paul responding to church concerns in an ad hoc manner. Brian Rosner argues, however, that "the OT proves to be a major point of interest and a critical and formative source for the theology and ethics of the letter."[20]

Rosner notes that four OT books are particularly important for understanding 1 Corinthians and that allusions and citations from these four cluster around four main theological themes: temple worship (Malachi), divine wisdom (Isaiah), the grace of God (Deuteronomy), and the authority of Jesus Christ (Psalms).[21] For example, Paul alludes to Malachi three times in 1 Corinthians, and all three instances relate to the church as the new temple of God, the place where God's presence dwells. In 3:12–15, Paul alludes to Mal 2:2–3 in his discussion concerning the judgment of Christian leaders who are building God's temple, the church. In 10:21 he alludes to Mal 1:7, 12, where defiling the "Lord's table" refers to offering defiled food on the temple altar. Paul applies this to the Corinthians' defilement of the Lord's Supper by participating in pagan worship. In 1:2 Paul refers to the church as those who "in every place . . . call on the name of Jesus Christ," alluding to Mal 1:11 LXX, which speaks of a future time when Gentiles will worship God "in every place." This allusion suggests the Corinthians "are part of the fulfillment of God's eschatological plan to be

---

[19] The UBS Greek New Testament (5th ed.) lists sixty-four explicit OT quotations for Romans and only seventeen for 1 Corinthians.

[20] Brian S. Rosner, "Corinthians, First Letter to the," in *DNTUOT*, 127–33; quote from p. 127.

[21] Rosner, "Corinthians," 127–33.

worshiped among all the Gentiles."[22] This is not an ad hoc use of the Old Testament to respond to pressing demands in the church. It is rather a deeply integrated theology of the church as the new temple of God.

After tracing all four themes through the letter and finding similarly consistent theological threads, Rosner concludes:

> It is possible to read 1 Corinthians without pondering Paul's use of Malachi, Isaiah, Deuteronomy, and Psalms. However, to do so is to read the text only superficially. . . . The coherence of the letter, its big themes of wisdom, holiness, worship, edification, the glory of God, and the lordship of Christ, and its suffusion with the gospel of grace arising from Paul's mission and identity all stem from understanding the influence of these four books. Indeed, 1 Corinthians may be correctly described as "a hermeneutical event" . . . as a text best read in its inextricable and manifold relationship to the Scriptures of Israel.[23]

This lesson from 1 Corinthians may be applied to all of Paul's letters. Whether or not he is explicitly citing the OT, the themes, ideas, images, and allusions come from a mind thoroughly steeped in the Hebrew Scriptures.

Gospel Connections

Paul is universally recognized as the foremost theologian of the apostolic church. The letter to the Romans, for example, is one of the greatest theological treatises ever written. While we would never want to downplay Paul's theological acumen, not enough attention is given to Paul as pastor. In 1 Corinthians we see the heart and soul of Paul the pastor, as he deals with gritty, real-life, rubber-meets-the-road issues in the church at Corinth. The one issue that is most prominent is the call to unity, which takes up the first quarter of the letter. Following his introduction, Paul's first exhortation is to unity: "Now I urge you, brothers and sisters, in the name of our Lord Jesus Christ, that all of you agree in what you say, that there be no divisions among you, and that you be united with the same understanding and the same conviction" (1 Cor 1:10).

---

[22] Rosner, "Corinthians," 127. Cf. Roy E. Ciampa and Brian S. Rosner, "1 Corinthians," in *CNTUOT*, 696.

[23] Rosner, "Corinthians," 133. With "hermeneutical event" he is citing R. B. Hays, *Echoes of Scripture in the Letters of Paul* (New Haven, CT: Yale University Press, 1989), 35.

This call for unity is by no means unique to 1 Corinthians. It permeates Paul's letters. In Phil 2:2 he writes, "make my joy complete by thinking the same way, having the same love, united in spirit, intent on one purpose." In Eph 4:3 he says to make "every effort to keep the unity of the Spirit through the bond of peace." In Col 3:14 he says, "Above all, put on love, which is the perfect bond of unity." In Romans, after describing the infinite grace of God in providing our salvation, Paul calls believers to live out that grace in love and unity: "Love one another deeply as brothers and sisters. Take the lead in honoring one another. . . . Live in harmony with one another. . . . If possible, as far as it depends on you, live at peace with everyone" (Rom 12:10, 16, 18).

If unity is the goal, the means to unity is humility and self-sacrificial service—thinking of others first. Philippians 2:3 continues, "Do nothing out of selfish ambition or conceit, but in humility consider others as more important than yourselves." Romans 12:16: "Do not be proud; instead, associate with the humble. Do not be wise in your own estimation." Paul recognized that no matter how theologically informed church members were, it was the practice of love and self-sacrificial giving that was key for his churches to be transforming agents in the world.

Life Connections

Paul's call to unity among believers has profound implications for the church today. In my thirty-plus years of teaching as a seminary professor, I have seen many churches in trouble and pastors in crisis. But in all those years I don't think I have ever seen a church divided or destroyed because of false teaching *per se*. Now don't get me wrong. It is critical that we stay true to the Bible and faithful to our theological convictions. But I have found the most destructive force in the life of a church is not bad doctrine. It is internal division and dissension, resulting from pride, ego, and selfish ambition. Sometimes it is a church board against the pastor; sometimes pastor against another pastor; sometimes it is a disgruntled member against a leader. It can start as a small thing: a difference of opinion on worship style, or ministry focus, or financial priorities. But when feelings get hurt, anger ignites, and positions harden. A small thing can grow into a major crisis.

This is why Paul places such a strong emphasis on love and unity. He knew that disunity and division would cripple his churches. But that unity of spirit, mind, and purpose would make them the most powerful force in the world. So throughout his letters he constantly calls believers to love and unity, to placing the needs of others first, to building others up not breaking them down, and to seeking *first* the kingdom of God. Christian leadership is not about coercion or controlling others through the exercise of power; it is about empowering others to be all that God has called them to be.

Interactive Questions

1. When did Paul establish the church at Corinth? What were some of the challenges Christians faced in a city like Corinth?

2. When did Paul write 1 Corinthians, and what occasion prompted him to write?

3. How were the divisions at Corinth manifested? What does Paul present as the solution to these divisions (chaps. 1–4)?

4. What does Paul say the church needs to do in the case of a member living in an immoral relationship (5:1–13)? How might this passage relate to church discipline today?

5. How does Paul respond to believers who are involved in lawsuits with other believers (6:1–11)? How might these principles relate to conflicts in the church today?

6. How were some of the Corinthians justifying immoral behavior, like visiting prostitutes? How does Paul respond (6:12–20)?

7. What is Paul's view of marriage as expressed in chapter 7? His view of divorce? His view of singleness?

8. What guidelines does Paul give with reference to whether or not to eat food sacrificed to idols (chaps. 8–10)? How might his guidelines relate to areas of dispute (such as the use of alcohol or tobacco) in the church today?

9. What does Paul criticize about the church's behavior when taking the Lord's Supper? How does he respond (11:17–34)?

10. What was the Corinthians' fundamental problem with reference to spiritual gifts? What does Paul say is the purpose of the spiritual gifts and what guidelines does he give for their practice (chaps. 12–14)?

11. What false beliefs about the resurrection from the dead does Paul respond to in chapter 15? Why is the resurrection of Jesus so important for believers?

12. How might reading 1 Corinthians benefit Christians today?

Study Resources

Blomberg, Craig L. *1 Corinthians*. NIVAC. Grand Rapids: Zondervan, 1995.

Ciampa, Roy E., and Brian S. Rosner. *The First Letter to the Corinthians*. PNTC. Grand Rapids: Eerdmans, 2010.

Collins, Raymond F. *First Corinthians*. SP. Collegeville, MN: Liturgical Press, 1999.

Fee, Gordon D. *The First Epistle to the Corinthians*. Rev. ed. NICNT. Grand Rapids: Eerdmans, 2014.

Fitzmyer, Joseph A. *First Corinthians*. AYB. New Haven, CT: Yale University Press, 2008.

Gardner, Paul D. *1 Corinthians*. ZECNT. Grand Rapids: Zondervan, 2018.

Garland, David E. *1 Corinthians*. BECNT. Grand Rapids: Baker Books, 2003.

Johnson, Alan F. *1 Corinthians*. IVPNTC. Downers Grove, IL: InterVarsity, 2004.

Kovacs, Judith L. *1 Corinthians: Interpreted by Early Christian Commentators*. The Church's Bible. Grand Rapids: Eerdmans, 2005.

Morris, Leon. *1 Corinthians*. TNTC. Downers Grove, IL: InterVarsity, 1986.

Perkins, Pheme. *First Corinthians*. Paideia. Grand Rapids: Baker Academic, 2012.

Taylor, Mark E. *1 Corinthians*. NAC. Nashville: Broadman & Holman, 2014.

Thiselton, Anthony C. *The First Epistle to the Corinthians: A Commentary on the Greek Text*. NIGTC. Grand Rapids: Eerdmans, 2000.

Vang, Preben. *1 Corinthians*. TTCS. Grand Rapids: Baker Books, 2014.

Winter, Bruce W. *After Paul Left Corinth: The Influence of Secular Ethics and Social Change*. Grand Rapids: Eerdmans, 2001.

Witherington, Ben, III. *Conflict and Community in Corinth: A Socio-Rhetorical Commentary on 1 and 2 Corinthians*. Grand Rapids: Eerdmans, 1995.

6

2 Corinthians

Written from Macedonia, ca. 56–57 CE

Therefore, we are ambassadors for Christ, since God is making his appeal through us. We plead on Christ's behalf, "Be reconciled to God."

—2 Corinthians 5:20

Outline

I. Paul's Explanation of His Conduct and Apostolic Ministry (chaps. 1–7)
   - A. Introduction (1:1–11)
   - B. Paul's Integrity in Motives and Conduct (1:12–2:13)
   - C. The Apostolic Ministry Described (2:14–7:1)
   - D. Paul's Reconciliation with the Corinthians (7:2–16)

II. The Collection for the Christians in Jerusalem (chaps. 8–9)
   - A. Generosity Encouraged (8:1–15)
   - B. Titus and His Companions Sent to Corinth (8:16–9:5)
   - C. Results of Generous Giving (9:6–15)

III. Vindication of Paul's Apostolic Authority (chaps. 10–13)

A. Paul's Defense of His Apostolic Authority and Ministry (10:1–18)
B. Paul Forced into Foolish Boasting (11:1–12:13)
C. Paul's Planned Visit (12:14–13:10)
D. Conclusion (13:11–14)

Author, Occasion, Message

Author

The author identifies himself as the apostle Paul (1:1). As in the case of 1 Corinthians, Paul's authorship is almost universally accepted by scholars today.

Occasion

Sometime after writing 1 Corinthians, Paul heard reports that his previous letter had not resolved some issues at Corinth. Challenges to his authority were also increasing. Paul altered his original plans (described in 1 Cor 16:5–7) to visit Corinth after passing through Macedonia and instead decided to visit Corinth *twice*, first briefly on his way to Macedonia, and then for a longer period after his time in Macedonia. From Corinth he would return to Judea with his collection for the poor in Jerusalem (2 Cor 1:15–17). These revised plans changed again, however, when Paul's first visit ended in disappointment. Paul was publicly harassed and embarrassed by "false apostles" (11:13) attacking his authority and challenging his integrity (2:1; 5:13; 7:2; chaps. 10–13). His cancellation of his second visit and subsequent return to Ephesus also provoked charges of vacillation and fickleness (1:17).

Following this "painful visit" (2 Cor 2:1), Paul decided not to return to Corinth, but instead to write a letter, sending it to the church with Titus (2 Cor 2:3–4, 9; 7:8, 12). Paul then headed north from Ephesus to Troas to preach the gospel there. Although the Lord opened a door for successful ministry there, Paul had no peace of mind about the Corinthian situation, and Titus did not arrive from Corinth (2 Cor 2:12–13). So Paul crossed over to Macedonia, where he finally met Titus. Titus brought the good news that the Corinthians had repented and desired reconciliation (2 Cor 2:13; 7:5–16). Paul was overjoyed! From Macedonia he sat down to write the letter we call 2 Corinthians, following this letter with a personal visit to Corinth (2 Cor 12:14, 21; 13:1; Acts 20:1–4).

Paul wrote 2 Corinthians to express joy at the warm response the church had now given him (chaps. 1–7) and to remind them of their commitment to financially support the persecuted churches in Judea (chaps. 8–9). In the last part of the letter (chaps. 10–13), the tone changes dramatically from conciliation to confrontation, as Paul defends his apostolic authority and lashes out at his opponents. The reason for this change in tone is debated. The simplest explanation is that some in the church were still opposing Paul, so he now turns to defend himself against these. Another possibility is that Paul added this final section after receiving additional news from Corinth that some were still opposing him. Still others claim that chapters 10–13 constituted a later letter that Paul sent when he learned of the unrepentant minority. The most intriguing proposal is that chapters 10–13 were in fact *the severe and sorrowful letter* mentioned in 2 Cor 2:3–4, 9; 7:8, 12. If this were the case, a later scribe likely attached the letter as an appendix to 2 Corinthians, and it was subsequently incorporated into the text. While this proposal would go far in explaining the dramatic change in tone, it remains highly speculative. There is no evidence, textual or otherwise, that chapters 10–13 circulated independently and, apart from Paul's self-reference in 10:1 ("I, Paul"), there are none of the epistolary features one would expect at the beginning of a new letter (recipients, greeting, thanksgiving, etc.). While later scribes could have removed these features, there are also some content problems with this theory. For example, in chapters 10–13 Paul says he is intending to visit the Corinthians in the near future (12:14; 13:1). Yet when he wrote the sorrowful letter, he had no such intention, sending the letter *instead of* another painful visit (1:23).

Message

The theme of 2 Corinthians is the nature of Christian ministry, with all its joys and sorrows. Paul uses an array of metaphors to describe Christian leaders. They are Spirit-empowered pen and paper, writing Christ's letter on human hearts (3:1–3). They are simple clay jars with hidden treasure inside (4:7). Their bodies, beaten and bruised, are earthly tents longing for a heavenly dwelling (5:1–5). They are ambassadors of Christ with a ministry of reconciliation to the world (5:20).

SIDEBAR 6.1: PAUL'S CONTACTS AND CORRESPONDENCE WITH THE CHURCH AT CORINTH

Contact	Date (approx.)	Description	Scripture Reference(s)
First Visit	50–52	Paul establishes the church on his second missionary journey; stays approx. eighteen months.	Acts 18:1–18
Corinthians A	53–55	A now-lost letter written to respond to immorality in the Corinthian church	1 Cor 5:9
Corinthians B	55–56	= **1 Corinthians**; written from Ephesus on third missionary journey	1 Cor 16:8–9
Second Visit	55–57	Painful visit to Corinth from Ephesus	2 Cor 2:1
Corinthians C	56–57	Severe and sorrowful letter (lost letter) sent from Ephesus after Paul's painful visit to Corinth	2 Cor 2:3–4, 9; 7:8, 12); possibly 2 Cor 10–13
Corinthians D	56–57	= **2 Corinthians** written from Macedonia after Titus reports the church seeks reconciliation.	2 Cor 2:12–13; 7:5–16
Third Visit	57–58	Paul stays three months; writes the letter to the church in Rome	Acts 20:2; Rom 15:26; 2 Cor 12:14; 13:1
Corinthians E?	57–58	Hypothetical fifth letter, comprising 2 Corinthians 10–13	

The letter is the most autobiographical, personal, and emotional of Paul's letters, giving us a unique glimpse into his heart and soul. Paul is emerging from what has been one of the most painful periods of his ministry. The church he invested himself so deeply in had turned against him. His opponents had ruthlessly attacked his authority and his integrity. From Paul's response we can piece together some of their charges. They claimed he was fickle (2 Cor 1:17, 18, 23), proud and boastful (3:1;

5:12), worldly (10:2), unimpressive in appearance and speech (10:10; 11:6), unstable in thought (5:13; 11:16–19), not a true apostle (11:5; 12:11, 12), and dishonest (12:16–19). These attacks challenged not only Paul's authority as an apostle, but his very identity in Christ. Paul responds with a range of emotions: anger, indignation, sarcasm, sorrow, joy, and relief. Throughout this deeply personal response, Paul gives a brilliant and stirring description of the challenges, perils, and pitfalls of Christian ministry and the ultimate victory we have in Christ.

Interpretive Overview

Paul's Explanation of His Conduct and Apostolic Ministry (chaps. 1–7)

Introduction (1:1–11)

Paul begins the letter with his credentials: "Paul, an apostle of Christ Jesus, by God's will" (1:1). While he often begins letters with his apostolic identity, in this case it is particularly significant since his opponents were denying this very thing. After his usual greeting of "Grace to you and peace" (1:2), Paul praises the "God of all comfort," who "comforts us in all our affliction" so that we can "comfort" others through the comfort we ourselves receive from God (1:3–4). Words for comfort or encouragement (noun: *paraklēsis*; verb: *parakaleō*) occur ten times in verses 3–7 and arise directly from the occasion of the letter. Paul was in anguish, both from external trials and internal grief over his alienation from the Corinthians. But it is when he was in most peril that the "God of all comfort" stepped in to bring comfort through reconciliation (1:3–7). Paul then describes the external hardship he experienced in Asia, which was so severe that he and those with him were in fear for their lives. Their only hope was in "God who raises the dead." Through the prayers of many, God delivered them (1:8–11).

Paul's Integrity in Motives and Conduct (1:12–2:13)

After emphasizing God's gracious deliverance from his physical trials, Paul turns to the emotional trial of alienation from the Corinthians that sparked this letter. He first emphasizes that, by God's grace, he and his companions had always conducted themselves with "sincerity and purity," not with mere human wisdom. He always communicated clearly and with integrity with the Corinthians and hopes that, when they fully understand the circumstances, they will stand together with pride and support each other on the day of judgment (1:12–14). The confusion and lack of trust came about in part because of Paul's change of plans. His original plans were to visit Corinth twice, while going to and returning from Macedonia (1:15–16). That this itinerary changed does not mean he is spiritually fickle or unreliable, saying yes and no at the same time. The gospel message he preaches is by no means a vacillating one, but a wholly affirmative one: "Yes!" Indeed, all God's promises are a "yes" in Christ (= fully fulfilled), and our response is always in the affirmative: "Amen!" bringing glory to God. This certainty is confirmed in the fact that our salvation is sealed by the Holy Spirit, the down payment and guarantee of our salvation (1:17–22). Following this brief digression on the affirmation of the gospel, Paul returns to his explanation. The reason he did not return to Corinth after his first visit was to spare them another painful visit (1:23; 2:1). He sent a letter instead, written with tears and an anguished heart, in hopes that his next visit would be a reconciling one, not a painful one, revealing his great love for them (2:2–4).

At this point Paul digresses again, encouraging the church to forgive a brother who has wronged him (2:5–11). This person is likely the ringleader of those who opposed Paul.[1] After Paul's sorrowful letter, the majority had repented and then turned to discipline the offender. Paul says, "this punishment by the majority is sufficient for that person" (2:6). They should now "forgive and comfort him," reaffirming their love for him so that he is not "overwhelmed by excessive grief" (2:7). Paul's letter had tested their loyalty, and they had passed the test! But excessive punishment for this offender would create anger and bitterness, tools Satan could use to sow greater discord in the church (2:11).

Paul has mentioned the sorrowful letter he wrote (2:3–4) and now picks up the story from there. After sending the letter to Corinth with Titus, he came to Troas, where the Lord opened an opportunity for effective ministry (2:12). But he was very distraught: "I had no rest in my spirit because I did not find my brother Titus" (2:13). So instead of staying in Troas, "I said good-bye to them and left for Macedonia." At this point Paul breaks off the story and goes into what is the longest digression in all of his letters. The joy he experienced after meeting Titus in Macedonia was so great that he cannot contain himself, and he breaks into praise to God: "But thanks be to God, who always leads us in Christ's triumphal procession . . . !" (2:14). For the next five chapters (2:14–7:1) he digresses about the joys and challenges of Christian

---

[1] Earlier interpreters tended to identify this person as the incestuous man Paul calls the church to discipline in 1 Cor 5:1–5; but most commentators today identify him as the key figure who led the opposition against Paul during his painful visit to Corinth. For evidence, see G. Guthrie, *2 Corinthians*, BECNT (Grand Rapids: Baker, 2015), 139–40.

ministry. He doesn't resume his discussion of the circumstances of the letter until 7:2, when he says, "Make room for us in your hearts," and then in 7:5: "In fact, when we came into Macedonia . . ." This is where he left off in 2:13!

The Apostolic Ministry Described (2:14–7:1)

Paul begins by comparing the Christian ministry to a Roman triumph. A triumph was a great parade bestowed on a Roman general by the Roman senate to celebrate victory in battle. The honoree, called the triumphator, would ride in splendor in a richly decorated chariot, accompanied by soldiers, horsemen, musicians, incense carriers, the weapons of war, and captured plunder. Conquered soldiers and rulers would be led along in chains, often to be executed at the end of the procession as a sacrifice to the gods. Paul identifies Christ as the triumphator and the apostles as the incense bearers and then the incense itself, spreading the fragrance of Christ. To those who are being saved, this is the aroma of life, but to unbelievers it is the smell of death (2:14–16). This ministry is not for profit or self-promotion, as in the case of the false apostles, but is done with sincerity before God (2:17). The metaphor for ministry changes in 3:1–3 to that of a letter. The false apostles evidently carried letters of reference from leaders in Jerusalem to support their authority. Paul responds that he does not need such letters, since the Corinthians themselves are his letter, "written on our hearts, known and read by everyone." Drawing imagery from the promise of a new covenant in Jeremiah 31, Paul adds that these "letters" were not inscribed with ink, but with the Spirit of God, and were written not on tablets of stone (like the first covenant at Mount Sinai), but on human hearts (3:1–3; cf. Jer 31:31–34). Since these "letters" (transformed persons) were written by the Spirit of God, not by human effort, God's people can be confident of their competence as ministers of the new covenant. While the law written on stone only condemns, the transformation by the Spirit gives life (3:4–6).

Paul continues to develop his contrast between the first covenant at Mount Sinai and the new covenant of Jeremiah 31 inaugurated by Christ. The first covenant revealed God's glory, as evident from Moses's face that glowed after he descended from Mount Sinai. Yet that covenant only brought death by condemning sin. The new covenant is more glorious, since it provides true salvation by bestowing God's righteousness on believers. Paul compares the veil that Moses wore to the blindness many Jews experience when they read the OT law. But when they turn to the Lord, the veil is removed, and they see God's glory as the Spirit transforms them into the image of Christ (3:7–18; see Old Testament Connections in this chapter). The reality that, by

God's mercy, believers have been entrusted with this new covenant ministry means that they can confidently and courageously proclaim the truth. We never need to act deceitfully or distort God's Word, Paul says, but can speak with a clear conscience. To be sure, not everyone will receive the message. The gospel remains veiled to those whose minds have been blinded by Satan, "the god of this age" (4:4). But as Christian leaders, Paul says, our role is to get out of the way and let the message shine through. "For we are not proclaiming ourselves but Jesus Christ as Lord, and ourselves as your servants for Jesus's sake" (4:5). The creator God, who commanded light to shine out of darkness (Gen 1:3), has shined this light in our hearts so we could know God's glory as seen in the face of Jesus Christ (4:1–6).

Paul continues with an analogy. We are like clay pots—ordinary and easily broken—with God's great treasure inside. This metaphor illustrates that the power believers have comes entirely from God. It also demonstrates that no matter how beat up we get on the outside, even to the point of death, God will sustain us in the present and provide resurrection life in the future (4:7–15). For this reason, Paul says, believers can stand firm, because our "light and momentary troubles are achieving for us an eternal glory that far outweighs them all" (4:17 NIV). So our focus should not be on the temporary reality that we see, but the infinitely greater unseen and eternal reality that awaits us (4:16–18). Although this temporary earthly "tent" (our present body) is groaning and wasting away, we have a heavenly home (the resurrection body) from him that will clothe our spiritual nakedness. The Holy Spirit living in us is the guarantee of this body (5:1–5). Being confident of this reality, Paul asserts, we can "walk by faith, not by sight," striving always to please God. We are motivated by the fact that we will all stand before the judgment seat of Christ to give an account of what we did while in our earthly bodies (5:6–10).

The reality of this final judgment is one thing that motivates Paul to persuade others of the truth of the gospel. He is not trying to gain the good will of the Corinthians for his own benefit, but so that they can be equipped to answer their opponents. Because of his great passion for the Corinthians, Paul was evidently accused of being out of his mind. Paul responds that he is thinking perfectly clearly in his dealings with them. If he is out of his mind, it is because of his overwhelming passion for God. So Paul is compelled in his ministry not just by the fear of the Lord, but especially by his love of Christ, who gave his own life to bring life for all (5:11–15). As a result of what Christ has done, Paul sees everything and everyone differently. "In Christ" the new creation has come. God is reconciling the world to himself through Christ's sacrificial death. And, Paul asserts, God has invited us to be his ambassadors for this reconciling ministry. So Paul pleads with the Corinthians to be reconciled to God. The perfect and sinless one has taken their sin upon himself so that they might receive God's righteousness. At this momentous time—the day of salvation—God's grace has been poured out on them (5:16–21; 6:1–2).

Paul's reference to the ministry of reconciliation brings him back to his relationship with the Corinthians and the defense of his apostolic ministry. He has proven himself to be God's servant through the great suffering he has endured (6:3–5) and through the sincere love and the fruit of the Spirit he has demonstrated (6:6–7). In every up and down of life he has acted with integrity toward the Corinthians and, as their spiritual father, has kept his heart open to them. He urges them to open their heart to him (6:3–13).

Having defended himself, Paul now turns to indict his opponents. He refers to them as "unbelievers" and urges the church not to be "yoked together" with them in any way. This is because there should be no partnership between the righteous and the lawless, between light and darkness, and between Christ and Satan. The church is the temple of God, and there is no place for idols in God's temple. He refers to a series of OT passages calling God's people to be separated from evil and attached to God as Father (Lev 26:12; Isa 52:11; 2 Sam 7:14; Isa 43:6). By cleansing themselves from such impurity, they will fulfill God's call to holiness and separation from sin (6:14–18; 7:1).

Paul's Reconciliation with the Corinthians (7:2–16)

Although the church has reconciled with Paul verbally, he calls on them to complete this reconciliation by welcoming him: "Make room for us in your hearts" (7:2; cf. 6:11, 13). He has always sought their best interests, never wronging or exploiting them. His frank rebuke came from his love for them and pride in them. Now their reconciliation has brought great encouragement and overwhelming joy, despite their present trials (7:2–4).

At this point Paul returns to the story he left at 2:13, where he mentioned his journey into Macedonia in search of Titus. When he came into Macedonia, Paul says, he was facing both external threats and internal anxiety. But God brought enormous comfort with the arrival of Titus, who reported that the Corinthians had a deep sorrow for their actions toward him and a strong desire for reconciliation. So while Paul expresses sorrow that his letter caused them grief, he rejoices that this was a godly grief that resulted in repentance and a renewal of their relationship. This brought not only great comfort to Paul but also joy for Titus as the agent of reconciliation (7:5–16).

The Collection for the Christians in Jerusalem (chaps. 8–9)

Having described the joy of Christian service sparked by his reconciliation with the Corinthians, Paul now turns to the second major purpose of his letter, which is to prepare the church to support the impoverished churches of Judea.

GENEROSITY ENCOURAGED (8:1–15)

To prompt the Corinthians to give, Paul points to the example of the Macedonian churches (Philippi, Thessalonica, and Berea). Though they were experiencing persecution and were themselves poor, "their extreme poverty overflowed in a wealth of generosity" (8:2). Paul didn't need to coax the Macedonians to give. Rather "they begged us earnestly for the privilege of sharing in the ministry to the saints" (8:4). This is because their giving was not out of compulsion, nor was it a burden. It was a natural response to their relationship with the Lord (8:5). Just as the Corinthians excelled in so many other areas—faith, speech, knowledge, diligence, and love—so Paul expects that they will excel in generosity (8:7). They will give not because he commands it, but as evidence of their love (8:8). Their ultimate model is Jesus himself. Although (or perhaps "because") he had all the riches of the universe,[2] he became poor by entering lowly human existence, so that he could bring the riches of salvation to us (8:9). So, Paul calls on the church to finish the task they began the previous year (8:10–11). They do not need to give beyond their means, but rather what is right and fair, producing equality among believers. When God blesses us with an abundance, we should share it with those who are in need. They, in turn, will share it with us when we are in need (8:12–14).

TITUS AND HIS COMPANIONS SENT TO CORINTH (8:16–9:5)

Paul next turns to commend those coming to Corinth to collect the gift. He names Titus, his partner and coworker (8:16–17, 23; see "Occasion" under "Titus" in chap. 12, pp. 226–27) and two other "brothers," one who is praised among the churches for his gospel ministry (8:18–19) and another who has proven diligent in many circumstances and has great confidence in the Corinthians (8:22). Having these representatives from

---

[2] See John M. G. Barclay, "'Because He Was Rich He Became Poor': Translation, Exegesis and Hermeneutics in the Reading of 2 Cor 8.9," in Reimund Bieringer et al., eds., *Theologizing in the Corinthian Conflict: Studies in the Exegesis and Theology of 2 Corinthians*, BTS 16 (Leuven: Peeters, 2013), 331–44.

various churches will help to guarantee the integrity with which the collection is handled (8:19–20). Paul encourages the church to show these men proof of their love and the reason he boasts so much about the Corinthian church (8:24). Indeed, Paul is writing to them in preparation of this visit so that they will be ready. He knows that they have been eager to give, and he has boasted to the Macedonians about their zeal. By sending these men ahead, neither Paul nor the Corinthians will be caught unprepared and embarrassed (9:1–5).

Results of Generous Giving (9:6–15)

Paul concludes this section with several theological principles for generous giving. The first is that giving blesses the giver even more than the receiver. Those who sow sparingly will also reap sparingly, and those who sow generously will reap generously (9:6). Next, it is the attitude not the act that is important. God loves a cheerful giver. People should give not out of compulsion but from the overflow of a heart of gratitude toward God (9:7). Third, God's resources are unlimited, so no one can give more than God can provide. He will always meet our needs (9:8–11). Fourth, giving is simply the outgrowth of our gratitude toward God, giving thanks to the One who gave us the greatest gift of all, the gift of his Son (9:12–15)!

Vindication of Paul's Apostolic Authority (chaps. 10–13)

In the last part of the letter, Paul's tone changes dramatically, from joy and affection at the Corinthians' reconciliation to stern rebuke and continuing criticism, as he responds to those who are still opposing him (for various interpretations of this section, see "Occasion" earlier in this chapter).

Paul's Defense of His Apostolic Authority and Ministry (10:1–18)

Paul defends himself by responding to a number of charges against him. One of these was that he was timid in person but bold toward them when he was absent (10:1). They said, "His letters are weighty and powerful, but his physical presence is weak and his public speaking amounts to nothing" (10:10). Paul responds that his mild demeanor is not a reflection of weakness, but of Christlikeness—"the meekness and gentleness of Christ" (10:1). As a way to show the authority with which he acts, Paul adopts a metaphor of warfare. Although he lives in the flesh, he does not do battle in this physical realm, but in a spiritual one. He demolishes spiritual strongholds and every proud argument raised up against the knowledge of God. He takes every thought captive to obey Christ and was ready to punish those who disobeyed (10:2–6). He warns his opponents that when he is present this time, he will do exactly what he says in his letters (10:11). While Paul's opponents claimed authority by commending themselves, Paul's commendation came from the Lord. He is the Lord's servant and operates as such only in fields assigned to him (10:12–18).

Paul Forced into Foolish Boasting (11:1–12:13)

While only the Lord can provide true commendation, Paul asks the Corinthians to put up with a little "foolishness" as he commends himself to them. This is necessary since he has a godly jealousy for the Corinthians, not for himself, but for their true husband, which is Christ. His fear is that the false apostles who have infiltrated the church will deceive them, as Satan deceived Eve. They are preaching a different Jesus and a different gospel, and the Corinthians are falling for it. Paul asserts that he is in no way inferior to these so-called super-apostles. Though they were skillful speakers, Paul's knowledge of the gospel is superior (11:1–6).

Another charge made against Paul was that his willingness to preach the gospel free of charge meant his teaching was worthless (11:7–15).[3] Paul counters that he did this so as not to be a burden to them. In addition to working to support himself, he had received support from the Macedonian churches. In this sense, he had "robbed" other churches in showing his love for the Corinthians. By contrast, his opponents were false apostles and deceitful workers, disguising themselves as apostles of Christ in the same way that Satan disguises himself as an angel of light.

Paul here resorts to a bit of sarcasm, asking the Corinthians to bear a bit longer with his foolish boasting (11:16–21). After all, he says, you are so "wise" that you put up with fools, allowing these false apostles to enslave you, exploit you, take advantage of you, and slap you in the face. By contrast, we were much too "weak" to slap you around like that, treating you instead with love and gentleness.

Since these false apostles are willing to boast about their credentials, Paul says I will also dare to boast. What follows has sometimes been called Paul's "résumé" (11:22–29), presenting his Jewish credentials (11:22) and his service to Christ, illustrated by a remarkable list of hardships and suffering (11:23–29). Paul speaks not only of his physical suffering and threats (floggings, beatings, stoning, shipwrecks, hunger, bandits, etc.) but also the daily pressure of caring for the many churches

[3] Cf. 2:17; 1 Cor 9:7–15; 1 Thess 2.9; 2 Thess 3:8–9.

he has started. Paul boasts most of all in those things that show his weakness, since these demonstrate Christ's power at work within him. He notes as one example his escape from Damascus, when King Aretas sealed the city in an attempt to arrest him (11:30–33), an event also recounted in the book of Acts (9:23–25).

Paul continues boasting with reference to visions and revelations from the Lord (2 Cor 12:1–10). He speaks of himself in the third person ("I know a man in Christ . . .") about an event that occurred fourteen years earlier (around 42 CE). Although Paul himself is unsure whether it was a vision or a physical experience, he was lifted up to God's presence ("the third heaven" and "paradise"), where he heard and saw things so wonderful he cannot even express them in words. To keep Paul from becoming conceited about these extraordinary visions, God humbled him with what he calls a "thorn in the flesh." The nature of this "thorn" is uncertain. Paul calls it "a messenger of Satan to torment me," but we don't know whether it was a demonic presence; a human opponent; a physical, emotional, or psychological disability; or something else. But when Paul prayed repeatedly for the Lord to take it away, God's response was, "My grace is sufficient for you, for my power is perfected in weakness" (12:9). Paul therefore boasts most of all in his weaknesses and difficulties, because it is at those times that Christ's strength brings him through. He is strongest when he is living in complete dependence on God.

Paul is sorry that the Corinthians have forced him to boast in this way by questioning his authority and apostleship. Even though he is "nothing," he is in no way inferior to the "super-apostles" who were challenging him (12:11). The Corinthians have seen the evidence of his apostleship through his signs, wonders, and miracles (12:12). With some sarcasm he says the only way he wronged them was by failing to charge them for his ministry, and he begs their forgiveness for this (12:13)!

Paul's Planned Visit (12:14–13:10)

Paul concludes his defense of this ministry by speaking of his upcoming visit, the third time he will be with them. As their spiritual parent, his goal was never to burden them or to ask anything of them, but to show them his love (12:14–15). Though wrongly accused of deceiving them, he never took advantage of them, nor did any of those (like Titus) that he sent to them (12:16–18). Even his defense of his own actions is not for his own good, but to build them up. With great vulnerability, Paul speaks of his fear that when he comes, there will be conflict and arguments again. He fears that he will again be humiliated in their presence and will grieve over those who have not yet repented of their sins (12:19–21).

For these Paul has a final warning. Just as the law required two or three witnesses for a conviction (Deut 19:15), this will be a fair and open examination (13:1). But with Christ's authority, he will not be lenient to those who are convicted of sin. Although Christ was crucified in weakness, he now lives by the power of God. In the same way, God's power will be demonstrated even through Paul's "weakness" (13:2–4). It is necessary, therefore, for each of the Corinthians to examine themselves to see if they are in fact in the faith and if Christ is living within them. His prayer is that they will pass the test and do what is right, acknowledging Paul's apostleship. His primary goal, however, is not for his own success, but for the truth to prevail and for the Corinthians to grow into fully mature believers (13:5–9). His hope is that these things will be settled with this letter rather than when he arrives, so that his time with them will build them up rather than breaking them down (13:10).

CONCLUSION (13:11–14)

Paul closes the letter with several commands, with greetings, and with a benediction. The commands are to be mature, to be encouraged, to be united, and to be at peace (with one another). If taken to heart, these exhortations would serve as the answer to all the problems at Corinth, and "the God of love and peace will be with you" (13:11). Paul then encourages the Corinthians to greet one another with a kiss—a sign of family affection—and sends greetings from all the believers who are with him (13:12). He ends with a remarkably Trinitarian benediction: "The grace of the Lord Jesus Christ, and the love of God, and the fellowship of the Holy Spirit be with you all" (13:13).

Old Testament Connections

One of Paul's most unusual and creative uses of the Old Testament occurs in 2 Cor 3:7–18, where the apostle alludes to events in Exod 34:29–35 to (1) demonstrate the superiority of the new covenant to the old and to (2) point to the "veil" that is presently blinding many Jews to the truth of the gospel.

In its original context, Exod 34:29–35 describes how, when Moses came down from Mount Sinai with the two (replacement) tablets of the Ten Commandments, his face was glowing because he had been in the presence of Yahweh. Moses was unaware of this glory (a sign of humility), but his brother Aaron and the other Israelites were afraid to come near until Moses spoke words of assurance to them. Moses then delivered the tablets that God had inscribed (34:29–32). Moses would wear a veil whenever he was with the people, except when he delivered Yahweh's commands, and would also remove the veil when he entered God's presence (29:33–35). This shows that for Moses to be unveiled in Yahweh's presence was not disrespectful or dangerous; it was a sign of reverence and transparency. So in its original context, Exod 34:29–35 teaches the awesome glory of God and the high status of Moses among the Israelites.

While Paul expands on the meaning of this passage, he does not necessarily contradict it. In the context of 2 Corinthians, Paul is speaking of the privilege God has given him and others to be ministers of the new covenant. He notes that while "the letter kills . . . the Spirit gives life" (2 Cor 3:6), meaning that while the old covenant law could only condemn sin, the new covenant (Jer 31:31–34), inaugurated through Christ's death and resurrection, provides reconciliation with God and the presence of his life-giving Spirit.

Paul first shows the new covenant's superiority with a lesser-to-greater argument. If the old covenant (which could only condemn) brought such great glory, how much greater glory comes with the new covenant, which provides true righteousness and the life-giving Spirit (2 Cor 3:7–9). Furthermore, the old covenant brought only a transitory glory that faded, while the new covenant brings an eternal glory that lasts forever (3:10–11).

Second, Paul indicates that Moses wore the veil not to protect the Israelites (which is also true in Exodus), but to hide the fading glory on his face from them (not mentioned in Exodus). The veil then becomes something that hides the truth (3:12–13). This, Paul says, applies to the Israelites of his day. Whenever Moses is read in the synagogues, a veil lies over their hearts, blinding them to the truth (3:14–15). When a person turns to Christ, however, the veil is lifted, and the glory of the Lord is revealed as the Spirit transforms that person into the image of Christ (3:16–18). One can see something of Paul's scriptural hermeneutic in this example. The OT text is not replaced, but is illuminated, expanded, and informed by the coming of Jesus and the dawn of God's promised salvation.[4]

Gospel Connections

As we have seen, one of the key themes of 2 Corinthians is a call for Christian generosity (chaps. 8–9). Paul encourages the Corinthians to give generously to the churches

---

[4] For Paul's use of Scripture throughout 2 Corinthians, see P. Balla, "2 Corinthians," in *CNTUOT*, 753–83; Jared Compton, "Corinthians, Second Letter to the," in *DNTUOT*, 133–39; Paul Han, *Swimming in the Sea of Scripture: Paul's Use of the Old Testament in 2 Corinthians 4:7–13:13*, LNTS 519 (London: Bloomsbury T&T Clark, 2014).

in Judea that are suffering from famine and persecution. Not surprisingly, the principles set out here similarly appear in the teaching of Jesus.

(1) Paul stresses that in God's economy, the more you give, the more you receive. Those who sow generously will reap generously (2 Cor 9:6). Jesus taught the same thing in Luke 6:38: "Give, and it will be given to you; a good measure—pressed down, shaken together, and running over—will be poured into your lap. For with the measure you use, it will be measured back to you." God blesses those who give, because giving reflects his very nature. He loves all people and sends the sun to shine and the rain to fall even on his enemies. The command to love our enemies is a reflection of his character and our identity as children of God (Matt 5:43–48).

(2) Paul also teaches that it is the attitude of giving, not the amount, that is important. The Macedonian believers gave out of their poverty (2 Cor 8:1–5). This recalls Jesus's comments concerning the widow in the temple. Although she gave only a tiny fraction of what the wealthy were giving, her offering was far greater than theirs, "For all these people have put in gifts out of their surplus, but she out of her poverty has put in all she had to live on" (Luke 21:4; cf. Mark 12:43–44).

(3) Our attitude in giving is critical, because our gift is the natural response for what God has given to us. Christ was infinitely rich and became poor for our sake (2 Cor 8:9). Our response to this "indescribable gift" (9:15) should be to show similar grace toward others. Jesus teaches something similar in the parable of the unmerciful servant. Though forgiven an impossibly large debt by his master, a slave refuses to forgive his fellow slave a tiny debt. He has no conception of the value of the gift he has been given (Matt 8:21–35). This is also why Jesus tells his followers to give their offering in secret, rather than openly for the praise of others (Matt 6:1–4). If we expect to be rewarded for our paltry gift, we have no conception of the infinite gift of grace that we have been given.

(4) When we begin to comprehend the value of what we have been given, our own giving becomes a joyful privilege, not a painful duty. This is why Paul says, "God loves a cheerful giver" (2 Cor 9:7). In Acts 20:35, Paul quotes an otherwise unknown saying of Jesus in his discourse to the elders at Ephesus, reminding them of the words of the Lord Jesus, "It is more blessed to give than to receive."[5]

---

[5] This saying is part of what are called *agrapha* ("unwritten things"), meaning authentic sayings of Jesus that do not appear in the four Gospels.

Life Connections

Perhaps no passage in the Bible sums up our role as believers as well as 2 Cor 5:17–19:

> Therefore, if anyone is in Christ, he is a new creation; the old has passed away, and see, the new has come! Everything is from God, who has reconciled us to himself through Christ and has given us the ministry of reconciliation. That is, in Christ, God was reconciling the world to himself, not counting their trespasses against them, and he has committed the message of reconciliation to us.

"In Christ" we are already part of the new creation—living in the new heaven and the new earth. As Christ's ambassadors, his agents of reconciliation, we are all of Jesus some people will ever see. What a remarkable privilege, and an even greater responsibility.

Interactive Questions

1. What events occurred between the writing of 1 Corinthians and 2 Corinthians that prompted Paul to write this letter? Explain Paul's painful visit and sorrowful letter.

2. What issues does Paul deal with in each of the three main sections of 2 Corinthians (chaps. 1–7; 8–9; 10–13)?

3. Identify some of the images Paul uses to describe his apostolic ministry in chapters 2–7.

4. Identify some of the principles related to giving that Paul identifies in chapters 8–9.

5. In what way does the tone of the letter change in chapters 10–13? To whom is Paul likely speaking in these chapters?

6. What are some of the arguments Paul uses against his opponents in these chapters?

7. How does Paul defend himself against the false apostles in 11:22–29?

8. Why does Paul say he was given a "thorn in the flesh," and how did God respond when Paul prayed for it to be taken away? What lesson did Paul learn from this?

9. How might reading 2 Corinthians benefit Christians today?

Study Resources

Barnett, Paul. *The Second Epistle to the Corinthians*. NICNT. Grand Rapids: Eerdmans, 1997.

Belleville, Linda L. *2 Corinthians*. IVPNTC. Downers Grove, IL: InterVarsity, 1996.

Diehl, Judith A. *2 Corinthians*. SGBC. Grand Rapids: Zondervan, 2020.

Furnish, Victor Paul. *II Corinthians*. AYB. New Haven, CT: Yale University Press, 1984.

Garland, David E. *2 Corinthians*. NAC. Nashville: Broadman & Holman, 1999.

Guthrie, George H. *2 Corinthians*. BECNT. Grand Rapids: Baker Books, 2015.

Hafemann, Scott J. *2 Corinthians*. NIVAC. Grand Rapids: Zondervan, 2000.

Harris, Murray J. *The Second Epistle to the Corinthians: A Commentary on the Greek Text*. NIGTC. Grand Rapids: Eerdmans, 2005.

Hubbard, Moyer V. *2 Corinthians*. TTCS. Grand Rapids: Baker, 2017.

Kruse, Colin G. *2 Corinthians*. TNTC. Downers Grove, IL: IVP Academic, 2015.

Lambrecht, Jan. *Second Corinthians*. SP. Collegeville: Liturgical Press, 2007.

Martin, Ralph T. *2 Corinthians*. Rev. ed. WBC. Grand Rapids: Zondervan, 2014.

Pascuzzi, Maria. *First and Second Corinthians*. New Collegeville Bible Commentary. Collegeville: Liturgical Press, 2005.

Seifrid, Mark A. *The Second Letter to the Corinthians*. PNTC. Grand Rapids: Eerdmans, 2014.

Thrall, Margaret E. *2 Corinthians*. 2 vols. ICC. Edinburgh: T&T Clark, 1994.

Witherington, Ben, III. *Conflict and Community in Corinth: A Socio-Rhetorical Commentary on 1 and 2 Corinthians*. Grand Rapids: Eerdmans, 1995.

7

Romans

Written from Corinth, ca. 57–58 CE

> But now, apart from the law, the righteousness of God has been revealed, attested by the Law and the Prophets. The righteousness of God is through faith in Jesus Christ to all who believe, since there is no distinction.
>
> —Romans 3:21–22

Outline

I. Introduction (1:1–17)
   A. Author, Recipients, and Greeting (1:1–7)
   B. Thanksgiving, Prayer, and Desire to Come (1:8–15)
   C. Theme: The Righteousness of God (1:16–17)
II. Humanity's Need of Righteousness (1:18–3:20)
   A. The Guilt of the Wicked (1:18–32)
   B. The Guilt of the Self-Righteous (2:1–16)
   C. The Guilt of the Jew Who Claims Righteousness (2:17–3:8)
   D. Conclusion: The Guilt of all Humanity (3:9–20)

III. God's Provision of Righteousness (3:21–5:21)
    A. Justification by Faith (3:21–31)
    B. The Example of Abraham (4:1–25)
    C. The Blessings of Righteousness (5:1–11)
    D. The Basis of These Blessings: Christ Reverses Adam's Fall (5:12–21)
IV. Living out the Life of Righteousness (6:1–8:39)
    A. Freedom from Sin (6:1–23)
    B. Freedom from the Law (7:1–25)
    C. Life in the Spirit (8:1–39)
V. Israel's Role in Righteousness (9:1–11:39)
    A. The Tragedy of Israel's Unbelief (9:1–5)
    B. God's Sovereign Choice (9:6–29)
    C. Human Responsibility: Faith (9:30–10:21)
    D. God's Purpose for Israel (11:1–36)
VI. Application: The Working Out of Righteousness (12:1–15:13)
    A. A Living Sacrifice Producing a Renewed Mind (12:1–2)
    B. Renewal with Reference to Self and Others (12:3–21)
    C. Renewal with Reference to Civil Authorities (13:1–7)
    D. Christian Love for All People: "Living in the Light" (13:8–14)
    E. Christian Liberty Controlled by Christian Love (14:1–15:13)
VII. Conclusion: Personal Messages and Benediction (15:14–16:27)
    A. Paul's Ministry to the Gentiles (15:14–22)
    B. Paul's Plans (15:23–33)
    C. Commendations, Greetings, and Warnings (16:1–24)
    D. Doxology (16:25–27)

Author, Occasion, Message

Author

The author identifies himself as Paul the apostle (1:1), and this attribution is accepted by virtually all scholars. The letter was evidently dictated to a secretary named Tertius (see 16:22).

Occasion

Romans was written from Corinth during Paul's third missionary journey (Acts 20:2–3), about 56–57 CE. While in Corinth, Paul was completing a collection of money for the poor Christians in Judea (1 Cor 16:1–4; 2 Cor 8–9). His plans were to return to Jerusalem, distribute the money, then go first to Rome and then on to Spain. Paul's philosophy of ministry was to preach in places where the gospel had not yet been heard (Rom 15:20). Having evangelized vast regions from Nabatea to Greece, Paul set his sights on Spain, the westernmost part of the Roman Empire. On the way to Spain, he hoped to fulfill his ambition of visiting the thriving church in Rome to share his spiritual gifts with them and to gain their support for his outreach to Spain (1:8–15; 15:22–29).

These plans were altered by Paul's arrest in Jerusalem. As a prisoner, however, he appealed to Caesar and so was transferred to Rome, where he was able to fulfill his vision of preaching the gospel there (Acts 28).

SIDEBAR 7.1: THE CHURCH IN ROME

The letter we call Romans is addressed "to all who are in Rome, loved by God, called as saints" (1:7). Rome was a large city, and this description refers not to a single congregation, but to a collection of house churches located in the city. The greetings in Romans 16 appear to identify at least five different congregations (16:5, 10, 11, 14, 15).

While both Peter and Paul were likely martyred in Rome, it is unlikely that either founded the church there. When Paul wrote, he had not yet been to Rome (15:23–29), but the church had been established for years, with a strong reputation throughout the Christian world (1:8–13). The church may have been started by Jews from Rome on pilgrimage to Jerusalem, who responded to Peter's preaching on the day of Pentecost (Acts 2:10, 36–41).

When Paul wrote, the church was predominantly Gentile (1:5–6, 13–15; 11:13, 15:15–16), although there were certainly Jews among them (2:17–24; 4:1). This Gentile majority likely resulted from the expulsion of Jews from Rome under the Roman emperor Claudius around 49 CE (Acts 18:1–3; see Ancient Connections 2.8). With many Jewish Christian leaders expelled, Gentile Christians filled the leadership gaps. Although many Jews eventually made their way back to Rome, the vacuum they had left permanently changed the makeup of the church. Parts of Paul's letter, especially chapter 14, are meant to encourage unity among these various factions.

Message

As noted previously, Paul wants to visit the church in Rome, share his spiritual gifts with them, and gain their support for his outreach into Spain. With this goal of partnership in mind, he provides the church with *a summary of his gospel message*. This makes Romans somewhat different from the letters of Paul we have surveyed up to this point. While those have tended to address specific questions, problems, and concerns in the church, Romans reads more like an essay on "the gospel according to Paul." Central to the first half of the letter is the theme of the "righteousness of God" (1:16–17). All humanity is sinful and stands condemned before a righteous and perfect God (1:18–3:20). Salvation comes not through human works or through identification with Israel as God's covenant people, but by God's grace received through faith in Christ's atoning death on the cross. On the basis of Christ's sacrifice, God justifies, or "declares righteous" those who put their faith in him (3:21–5:21). Believers now live that life of righteousness through the power of the Holy Spirit who lives in them (6:1–8:39).

In addition to summarizing and defending his gospel, Paul has other purposes for writing. In light of the widespread rejection of the gospel among the Jews, Paul writes about the role of Israel in God's plan, the reasons for the nation's failures, and God's sovereignty in all of this (chaps. 9–11). In light of continuing tension between Jewish and Gentile factions in the church, he calls them to unity, especially over the issues that often divided Jews and Gentiles (chaps. 14–15) (see sidebar 7.1). He also calls the church to be good and obedient citizens of the empire, living in peace with others and expressing Christ's unconditional love (chaps. 12–13).[1]

Interpretive Overview

Introduction (1:1–17)

AUTHOR, RECIPIENTS, AND GREETING (1:1–7)

Paul's introduction contains a remarkable amount of theological depth, confirming that Paul is using this letter to present his gospel to the church in Rome. He identifies himself as a "slave" or "servant" (*doulos*) of Christ Jesus, meaning one whose total

[1] See Scot McKnight, *Reading Romans Backwards: A Gospel of Peace in the Midst of Empire* (Waco, TX: Baylor University Press, 2019), who claims that the issues addressed in Romans 12–15 are in fact the driving force behind the theological discussions in chapters 1–11.

devotion belongs to Christ. He has been called to be an apostle (messenger, emissary) whose message is the "gospel/good news of God." This good news is the fulfillment of God's promises given to Israel by the prophets in the Holy Scriptures. The content of the gospel concerns God's Son, who as "a descendant of David" is in the royal line to fulfill God's promise to David to establish an eternal reign of justice and righteousness (2 Sam 7:14, 17; Isa 11:1–10; Jer 23:5–6; Ezek 34:23–24). This claim was vindicated when Jesus, the Son of God *in humility* during his earthly life, became the Son of God *in power* by being raised from the dead through the power of the Holy Spirit (1:3–4).[2] Through him, Paul says, we have received *grace* (the free gift of salvation) and *apostleship* (a commission to proclaim this grace to others) to bring the Gentiles to a place of faith in God and obedience to his will (1:5–6). The recipients of the letter are "all in Rome who are loved by God and called to be his holy people" (1:7 NIV).

Thanksgiving, Prayer, and Desire to Come (1:8–15)

After identifying himself and his gospel, Paul expresses his thanksgiving for the church. He has heard of their reputation throughout the Roman world and so constantly prays for them, hoping to come and visit them soon. His goal in coming is to strengthen them with his spiritual gifts and to be encouraged by their faith (1:8–12). While he has been prevented from coming to Rome in the past, it is only right for him to do so now, since God has commissioned him to proclaim the gospel to the Gentiles everywhere (1:13–15).

Theme: The Righteousness of God (1:16–17)

Paul's mention of his commission to preach the gospel/good news (1:15) causes him to elaborate on the nature of this gospel. Though the message of a crucified Messiah may appear strange and shameful to many, Paul is not ashamed because the message represents God's power to save people, Jews and Gentiles alike. This is because the gospel reveals *the righteousness of God*, a phrase that for Paul means both God's perfection in his character and actions, and also God's bestowal of that perfection on believers on the basis of Christ's death on the cross. That this righteousness is "from faith

---

[2] Many scholars think Paul's summary of the gospel in verses 3b–4 is taken from an early Christian hymn or creed that the Christians in Rome would have been familiar with. By reciting the creed, Paul shows that they share a common gospel. For more on early Christian creeds and hymns, see "Gospel Connections" in chapter 12.

to faith" (1:17) probably means salvation is "by faith from first to last" (NIV), that is, completely by faith.[3] To defend this point, Paul quotes Hab 2:4: "The righteous will live by faith."[4]

Humanity's Need of Righteousness (1:18–3:20)

After introducing his theme as the revelation of God's righteousness, Paul turns to the question of why humanity needs to be made right with God. He shows step-by-step that *all people* are sinful and so stand guilty before a righteous and perfect God. Neither human effort nor membership in the covenant people of Israel can earn salvation.

THE GUILT OF THE WICKED (1:18–32)

Paul begins by stating that God's righteous wrath, his just punishment for sin, is being poured out against human beings because they have intentionally rejected him. Although God has revealed himself through his creation, human beings have suppressed this truth, exchanging the glory of the immortal God with worthless idols. This continual rejection results in the deterioration of their hearts and minds, until they collapse into self-deception. "Claiming to be wise, they became fools" (1:22). The result was utter depravity. Humanity went its own way and "exchanged" God's truth with error (1:23, 25, 26) so that God "delivered them over" (1:24, 26, 28) to the natural result of their actions. They replaced God's glory with idols; so God gave them over to sexual impurity, degrading their bodies (1:21–24). They replaced God's truth with a lie, worshiping created things instead of the Creator; so God gave them over to disgraceful passions, resulting in all manner of sin (1:25–27). They replaced knowledge of God with their own wisdom, so God gave them over to a corrupt mind. The result is that they see good as evil and evil as good (1:28–31).

---

[3] For other ways this phrase has been interpreted, see C. E. B. Cranfield, *A Critical and Exegetical Commentary on the Epistle to the Romans*, 2 vols., ICC (Edinburgh: T&T Clark, 1975) 1:99–100; T. R. Schreiner, *Romans*, BECNT (Grand Rapids: Baker, 2018), 73–74.

[4] Some translate Hab 2:4 as "The one who is righteous by faith will live" (CSB note), which aligns closely with Paul's theology in Romans.

The Guilt of the Self-Righteous (2:1–16)

Paul next turns from the obviously wicked to those who think they are good enough to merit God's favor. Some commentators consider this section to be the beginning of the argument against Jews who claimed to be righteous; it continues in 2:17–3:8. Others take it as an argument against Gentile moralists, those who considered themselves to have a high moral standing. In either case, Paul is continuing to develop his argument that *all* people stand condemned before a perfect and righteous God. The Jews who have the law will be condemned by the law. The Gentiles who do not have the law will be condemned by their own conscience, since they have an inner moral compass telling them right from wrong.

The Guilt of the Jew Who Claims Righteousness (2:17–3:8)

Whether or not Paul had the Jews in mind in 2:1–16, he now turns explicitly to them. He demonstrates that even the Jews, God's chosen people, fell short of God's righteous standards. Though they have been given the privilege of revealing God's Word to the world, they fail to live up to its standards (2:17–24). The Jews believed that they were saved on the basis of their special status as the covenant people of God. But Paul says God is the God of truth and an impartial judge, so all will be judged according to their actions. Physical circumcision means nothing unless it is accompanied with a "circumcision . . . of the heart" that results in obedience (2:25–29).

Paul then responds to several possible objections. The first is, If physical circumcision has no value, then what good is it to be a Jew? Paul responds that it is a great benefit, since Jews were given the precious Word of God (3:1–2). The second objection is, Does the unbelief of some Jews reveal God's unfaithfulness to his covenant people? Paul responds, "Absolutely not!" (Greek: *mē genoito*, "May it never be!"). Paul uses this strong Greek expression ten times in Romans, usually when he is responding to an imaginary debater.[5] His point here is that God's faithfulness is basic, an essential attribute. Without it he would not be God. Even if everyone else is called a liar, God will be found to be true (quoting Ps 51:4) (3:3–4). The third objection is, If our unrighteousness highlights God's righteousness, we are helping God and so should not be punished! Paul again says, "Absolutely not!" or "How absurd!" (*mē genoito*).

[5] Rom 3:4, 6, 31; 6:2, 15; 7:7, 13; 9:14; 11:1, 11. Only four other uses in his letters: 1 Cor 6:15; Gal 2:17; 3:21; 6:14.

If this were so, how could God judge the world? There would be no justice if sin were left unpunished (3:5–8).

ANCIENT CONNECTIONS 7.1: SALVATION BY CIRCUMCISION?

Some Jews claimed that their circumcision (which meant identification as God's covenant people) assured their salvation. One rabbi (R. Levi) is quoted as saying, "In the future, Abraham will sit at the entrance of Gehenna and will not allow any circumcised person of Israel to descend into it" (Gen. Rab. 48:8; ca. 400 CE).[6]

Conclusion: The Guilt of all Humanity (3:9–20)

Paul's conclusion is that no one has an advantage over another, since all are guilty before God (3:9). This point is reinforced with a long stream of OT quotes highlighting the depravity of humanity (3:10–18).[7] Paul concludes that "no one will be justified in his sight by the works of the law" (3:20). The gavel falls and the judge pronounces, "Guilty on all counts!"

God's Provision of Righteousness (3:21–5:21)

Justification by Faith (3:21–31)

Paul has demonstrated that both Jews and Gentiles are sinners and unable to save themselves. All fall short of God's righteousness and so cannot stand in his glorious presence. That's the bad news. The good news is that "now, apart from the law," but in continuity with prophetic Scripture, God has launched a plan that both satisfies his perfect justice and also rescues humanity from the punishment their sin deserves. We are "justified freely by his grace through the redemption that is in Christ Jesus" (3:24). Every word in this sentence is important. "Justify" is a forensic or legal term meaning "to declare righteous" or "to acquit." It is the pronouncement by the judge

[6] Accessed July 16, 2024, at https://www.sefaria.org/Bereshit_Rabbah.48.8?lang=bi.

[7] Ps 14:1–3 (= Ps 53:1–3) (vv. 10–12); Ps 5:9 (v. 13a); Ps 140:3 (v. 13b); Ps 10:7 (v. 14); Isa 59:7, 8 (vv. 15–17); Ps 36:1 (v. 18).

of "not guilty." In some contexts, the basis of this declaration is one's own innocence or goodness, in which case the word means "vindicated" or "proven righteous" (see Jas 2:24; Rom 3:4 [of God]). But here the acquittal is not by human merit, but "freely by his grace, through the redemption that is in Christ Jesus" (3:24). Redemption means to buy back or set free a slave or kidnap victim, as God set Israel free from slavery in Egypt (Exod 15:13; Pss 77:15; 78:35) and from exile in Babylon (Isa 41:14; 43:1). Paul will use this slave market analogy again in chapter 6. The price Christ paid for our freedom was his death on the cross. In this way, God is both "just" and the "justifier" (3:26). The sin was paid for, but it was Christ, not humanity, who received its punishment. Believers are saved by God's grace alone on the basis of Christ's atoning death on the cross (3:21–26).[8] As a result, no one can boast about their salvation. God saves Jews and Gentiles alike in the same way—by faith in Christ (3:27–31).

The Example of Abraham (4:1–25)

To prove his point, Paul calls the most important witness in Judaism to the stand: Abraham, the father of the Jewish race (see Gal 3:1–29). He quotes Gen 15:6 to show that Abraham was saved by faith: "Abraham believed God, and it was credited to him for righteousness" (4:3; cf. 4:9, 22–23). There are only two options as to how Abraham was declared righteous. Either he earned it as payment for his work, or it was given to him as a gift (4:1–5). Paul draws on King David as corroborating testimony, citing Ps 32:1–2 as a celebration of God's free forgiveness of sins (4:6–8). Further proof that Abraham was saved by faith is the timing of events. Genesis 15:6 occurred *before* Abraham's circumcision, showing that he is the father of all who believe, whether circumcised or uncircumcised (4:9–12). The fulfillment of God's promise to Abraham that he would be the father of many nations (4:16–18; cf. Gen 17:5) did not therefore come by keeping the law, but by the righteousness that comes by faith. The law only brings wrath, not salvation, because it only points out sin but cannot deal with its penalty. Only God, who created all things and who brought life from Abraham's dead body and Sarah's dead womb, could bring life to us through the resurrection of his Son (4:13–25).

---

[8] The term "sacrifice of atonement" (v. 25, NIV), could also be translated "mercy seat" (CSB; see Heb 9:5). The mercy seat was the atonement cover on the ark of the covenant, where blood was sprinkled on the Day of Atonement (Exod 25:17–22; Lev 16:14–15). On the cross Jesus became the place where atonement was achieved, setting us free from the penalty and the power of sin.

The Blessings of Righteousness (5:1–11)

Paul here describes some of the blessings believers receive through justification. We have peace with God through our Lord Jesus Christ, access into his presence, and joy in the hope of future glory. This hope, in turn, provides endurance to face present sufferings. Notice the progression: *Affliction* produces *endurance*, which produces *character*, which produces even greater *hope* (5:1–4). This hope is confirmed by God's love experienced through the reconciling work of Christ and the indwelling presence of God's Spirit (5:5–11).

The Basis of These Blessings: Christ Reverses Adam's Fall (5:12–21)

Paul next turns to the basis for justification, which is that Jesus reversed the results of Adam's fall. Though all became sinners through Adam's one sin, all can be made righteous through Christ's one righteous act. Adam's disobedience brought death, but Christ's obedience brings life. The passage is difficult to outline at this point because Paul does not complete the thought that he begins in 5:12. He begins, "Therefore, just as sin entered the world through one man, and death through sin . . ." We expect Paul to conclude, ". . . so also salvation was achieved by one man." But instead, he elaborates on this first point from verses 12b–17. He then begins his sentence again in verse 18, this time finishing his thought: "So then, as through one trespass there is condemnation for everyone, so also through one righteous act there is justification leading to life for everyone."

SIDEBAR 7.2: THE TYPOLOGICAL RELATIONSHIP BETWEEN ADAM AND CHRIST

Rom 5:12–21

Adam's Trespass	Christ's Gift
Sin reigned	Grace reigns
By one man, sin entered the world	By one man sin was defeated
By one act of sin, all became sinners	By one act of obedience, many are made righteous

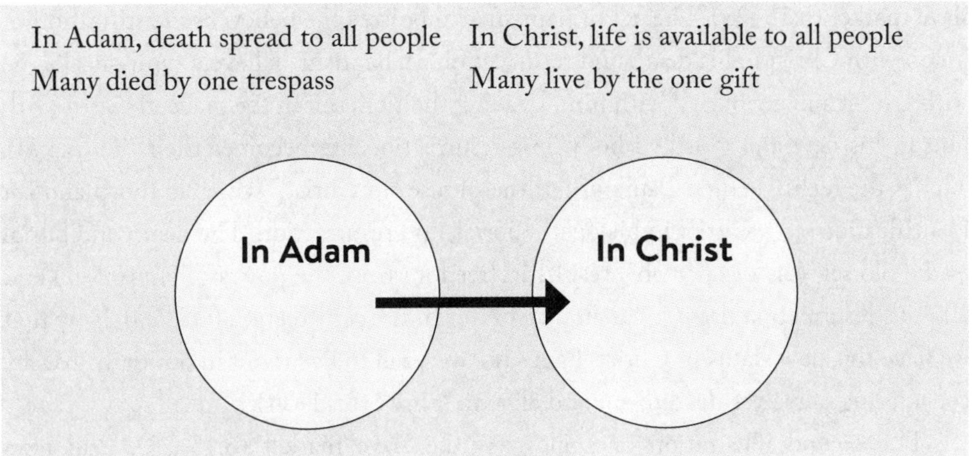

Living out the Life of Righteousness (6:1–8:39)

Having demonstrated how Jesus's death and resurrection reversed the curse that Adam's sin brought, Paul now turns to how this new life of righteousness is experienced by believers. Having been freed from bondage to sin (chap. 6), the law (chap. 7), and death, they are set free to live a new life through the power of the Spirit (chap. 8). They are no longer slaves, but children of God, eagerly awaiting their ultimate victory and glorification.

Freedom from Sin (6:1–23)

Paul points out that believers are not only free from the penalty of sin (chap. 5); they are also free from its power. Paul begins with the hypothetical question, "Should we continue in sin so that grace may multiply?" (6:1). In other words, if we are saved by grace alone, can't we live as we please? The question arises out of Paul's statement in 5:20, "But where sin multiplied, grace multiplied even more." Paul responds "Absolutely not! [*mē genoito*] How can we who died to sin still live in it?" (6:2). To view grace as an excuse to sin is a misunderstanding of the believer's new position in Christ. They have been set free from sin's bondage. Why would they submit once again to its power?

Paul gives two analogies to illustrate this freedom from the power of sin, the first related to the act of baptism (6:3–14) and the second drawn from the Greco-Roman slave market (6:15–23). The act of baptism symbolizes the believer's identification or union with Christ in his death and resurrection. In baptism, believers symbolically die with Christ and are buried with him. Leaving their old self in the grave, they rise with him in his new and glorified body. His resurrection life becomes their life (6:3–4). This is the reality behind Paul's use of the phrase "in Christ," which is shorthand for identification with Christ in his death, burial, and resurrection. The death and burial of the old self (or "old person") results in freedom from the power of sin (6:5–7) and Christ's resurrection provides assurance of our future resurrection (6:8–10). Now that we have this new status in Christ, Paul says, we need to live it out in our daily lives by considering ourselves dead to sin and alive to Christ (6:11–14).

The second illustration or analogy is the slave market (6:15–23). Paul here responds to the question: "Should we sin because we are not under the law but under grace?" (6:15). Doesn't salvation by God's free grace remove all moral constraints? The question is similar to the previous one (v. 1). There, however, Paul asked whether we should continue to sin "so that" grace may multiply, that is, to reveal more of God's grace. Here, it is whether we should sin "because" grace abounds, that is, because our salvation has been assured (we are spiritually bulletproof). Paul's emphatic response begins the same way, "Absolutely not!" (*mē genoito*), followed by the explanation: "Don't you know . . ." Before we were slaves to sin, meaning we were unable to stop sinning, but now we have been set free from sin's power. Our new master is not sin but righteousness (6:18). A transfer of ownership means a transfer of allegiance. In 6:16–23, Paul describes the progress and result of the two slaveries. Slavery to sin results in greater and greater lawlessness, ultimately resulting in death. Slavery (or obedience) to righteousness results in ever increasing holiness, or "sanctification," resulting in eternal life.

Freedom from the Law (7:1–25)

In chapter 6, Paul describes how believers are set free from the power of sin. Now in chapter 7 he describes how they are free from the power of the law. Paul begins by drawing an analogy to marriage. The marriage covenant has authority over a person only as long as they live. In the same way, since we as believers have died in relation to the law, we are free from its authority. Our new allegiance is to Christ, through whom we "bear fruit" for God (7:1–4). Verses 5–6 elaborate on two kinds of fruit, one produced by the Spirit, and one produced by the "flesh" (*sarx*). This contrast will lead to a detailed contrast in chapter 8 between life in the Spirit and life in the flesh.

First, however, Paul answers several potential objections concerning the nature of the law and sin. The first is, If sin and the law both hold us in bondage (7:4–6), is the law itself sinful? (7:7). Paul responds with his rhetorical "Absolutely not!" (*mē genoito*). The law is holy, just, and good. It was intended to bring life. But by pointing out our sin, it resulted in death (7:7–12). The second clarification is, Did the law, which is supposedly good, actually cause death? (7:13). Again, the response is "Absolutely not!" It is *sin* that produced death. The law only reveals how bad sin is. This awareness of the destructive power of sin and how weak we are to oppose it results in a great inner conflict. Paul affirms that the law is "spiritual" (meaning it reflects God's character), but I am "fleshly" (living in my fallen state), and so consistently give in to the power of sin (7:14). However, when I live this way, I hate myself and my actions, and so acknowledge what is right (7:15–16). I desire to do good, but sin constantly exerts its power over me (7:17–20). This constant conflict between the law and sin results in absolute frustration (7:21–24). Only by God's grace can I be released from sin's control (7:25). Since Paul speaks in the first person ("I") throughout this section, there is a major debate as to whether Paul is here describing his experience as an unbeliever or as a believer.[9] This is a very difficult question, but in either case, the point is that in our fallen human nature (in Adam/in the "flesh"), we are powerless against sin. Victory comes only through the internal transformation accomplished by Christ and in the power of the indwelling Spirit which Christ provides. Paul concludes: "What a wretched man I am! Who will rescue me from this body of death? Thanks be to God through Jesus Christ our Lord!" (7:24–25).

Life in the Spirit (8:1–39)

Having described the frustration and utter failure of trying to keep the law in the power of the flesh (7:14–25), in chapter 8 Paul describes the alternative—living life in the realm and power of God's Spirit. Believers avoid the judgment their sin deserves because the Spirit has set them free from the power of sin and death. What the law could not do because of our fallen nature, God accomplished through the death of his Son, who paid the penalty for our sin and so fulfilled the requirements of the law (8:1–4).

Now that believers exist in the realm of the Spirit, they must actively live out that life by setting their minds on the things of the Spirit rather than the things of the

[9] For detailed discussion, see Douglas J. Moo, *The Epistle to the Romans*, NICNT (Grand Rapids: Eerdmans, 1996), 441–67.

flesh. The mind set on the flesh is hostile to God, resulting in death. The mind set on the Spirit has peace with God, resulting in spiritual life for our mortal bodies and eternal life for our immortal bodies in the future (8:5–13). Those led by God's Spirit are adopted children of God, and as God's children they are heirs of God and coheirs with Christ. A willingness to suffer for Christ in the present will result in glorification with him in the future (8:14–17).

Picking up this theme of glorification, Paul contrasts our present mortality and suffering with the future glory that comes to those who are in Christ. The Holy Spirit is the "firstfruits"—the present evidence of the future harvest—of this glory. Though we, together with all of creation, experience pain and suffering in the present, the Spirit gives us strength today and hope for the future. Our restoration is assured because of God's absolute faithfulness to his purpose in saving us. All those he foreknew, he also predestined; and those he predestined, he called; and those he called, he justified; and those he justified, he glorified (8:18–30). This inevitability of our salvation leads Paul to rejoice with a series of rhetorical questions emphasizing the certainty of our salvation accomplished by Christ. We are more than conquerors through the one who loved us. Absolutely *nothing* in all of creation can separate us from the love of God that is in Jesus Christ our Lord (8:31–39).

Israel's Role in Righteousness (9:1–11:39)

For eight chapters Paul has been describing the gospel message. Though we were sinners condemned to death, God justified us by his grace through faith in Christ's sacrificial death on the cross. Having died and risen "in Christ," we now have the Spirit of God living in us, empowering us to live lives pleasing to God. Now in chapters 9–11 Paul turns to a pressing question that still needs to be answered: If God's promises have come to fulfillment in Christ, how can it be that a majority of the people of Israel have rejected the gospel? Have God's promise to them failed?

The Tragedy of Israel's Unbelief (9:1–5)

Paul begins by expressing his personal anguish and sorrow over Israel's rejection of God's salvation. These are his own people, and his love for them is so great he would exchange his own salvation for theirs! He describes the amazing position of privilege that Israel was given as God's chosen people: adoption as God's children, God's divine presence in the tabernacle, the covenants, the law, the temple worship, the promises for the Messiah (9:1–5).

God's Sovereign Choice (9:6–29)

So have God's promises failed because of Israel's unbelief? Paul responds with a resounding "No!" Not everyone who is called an "Israelite" is a child of the promise. God's sovereign plan has been working itself out through those he has chosen (like Jacob over Esau), and even through those who opposed him (like Pharaoh). To those who object that this is not fair, Paul simply says the clay has no right to ask the potter, "Why did you make me like this?" The potter knows best. God's mercy is just that—compassion and grace poured out on undeserving people. We as lowly human beings and recipients of this grace have no right to question or challenge how the sovereign God is accomplishing his purpose in creation (9:6–29).

Human Responsibility: Faith (9:30–10:21)

While God acts sovereignly to accomplish his purpose, this does not remove Israel from responsibility. Israel missed out on the promises because they failed to receive the righteousness that comes through faith in Christ. They sought to establish their own righteousness through the works of the law. They stumbled over the stumbling stone, which was their own self-righteousness (Isa 8:14; 28:16). Since salvation is based on faith alone, there is no difference between Jew and Gentile. Salvation comes to all who call on the name of the Lord (9:30–10:13).

Paul next recounts the process by which the gospel is received or rejected. Preachers are sent; the gospel is proclaimed; people hear; they respond in faith or rejection. Israel heard and understood the message, but a majority rejected it because they were obstinate and disobedient. By contrast, many Gentiles, who were not God's people and were not seeking God, heard the message and believed (10:14–21).

God's Purpose for Israel (11:1–36)

Having shown that Israel had the opportunity to respond because the gospel was proclaimed throughout the whole world, Paul now shows that, in fact, many in Israel *did* receive God's promised blessings. Paul himself is an example of this—an Israelite from the tribe of Benjamin. As in the days of Elijah, a remnant has been saved, chosen by God's grace. Israel is now divided between a righteous remnant and an unbelieving and stubborn majority (11:1–10).

Asking the rhetorical question, Did Israel stumble so as to fall beyond recovery? Paul answers with a strong "Absolutely not!" (*mē genoito*). Their rejection of the gospel meant the good news had gone to the Gentiles, which in turn provoked envy among Israelites. Like leaven spreads in dough, the faith of the remnant could spread to the rest. Paul develops an analogy of an olive tree. Natural branches (the Jews) had been broken off so that wild branches (the Gentiles) could be grafted in. This must not provoke pride in the Gentiles, however, since this was all by God's grace. Gentiles, too, must continue in faith lest they be broken off by unbelief and replaced by the natural branches (11:11–24).

While a remnant of Israel believed, Paul notes the rest of Israel "experienced a hardening in part until the full number of Gentiles has come in, and in this way all Israel will be saved" (11:25 NIV). A major debate revolves around who Paul is referring to when he speaks of "all Israel" being saved. Does he mean (1) all believers (= the "true Israel"), the total number of believers, both Jews and Gentiles, who will be saved through Christ's work; (2) all elect Jews who will be saved throughout the present age (equivalent to the "fullness" of Israel in 11:12; cf. "the fullness of the Gentiles" in 11:25); or, (3) presently unbelieving Jews who will turn to Christ in large numbers at or just before the Second Coming. While Paul's references to both Jews and Gentiles being children of Abraham by faith (4:16; cf. 2:28–29; 9:6–8) would tend to favor the first view, Paul's reference to this "Israel" presently being enemies of God (11:28) would seem to support the third view. Paul hopes and expects that his people will turn to Christ in the end.

Paul concludes his discussion of God's sovereignty in Israel's salvation with a doxology, drawing language from Isa 40:13 and Job 41:11. He praises God for his unfathomable wisdom and knowledge. As the sovereign creator, sustainer, and ultimate goal of all things, he deserves all glory and honor and praise for all eternity (11:33–36).

Application: The Working Out of Righteousness (12:1–15:13)

Paul spent the first half of this letter (Romans 1–8) explaining God's provision of salvation for all humanity through Christ's sacrificial death on the cross. Believers now have a new relationship with God in Christ, empowered by the Holy Spirit. Then Paul showed that, despite the rejection of the gospel by many in Israel, God's promises have not failed (Romans 9–11). He now turns to the appropriate response and practical outworking of this great salvation.

A Living Sacrifice Producing a Renewed Mind (12:1–2)

In response to God's merciful salvation, Paul calls on believers to offer themselves to God as a "living sacrifice." This is imagery from the OT sacrificial system, where the life of an animal was taken as an offering to God. In the same way, Paul says, we must give our whole life to God, not as a corpse, but as a "living" sacrifice, one that is "holy and pleasing to God." This act of spiritual service to God is the appropriate, or "fitting" (*logikos*),[10] response to what God has done for us (12:1). Since they are wholly God's possession, believers must not be shaped into conformity to the world's values and priorities, but must be transformed by the renewing of their minds. This mind renewed by the power of the Holy Spirit enables believers to discern God's will and to make good decisions that please God.

Renewal with Reference to Self and Others (12:3–21)

The transformation accomplished through the renewal of our minds should result, first of all, in an appropriate and sensible view of ourselves. We should not think too highly or too lowly (12:3). This works itself out in the life of the church by each individual exercising their unique spiritual gifts for the benefit of the whole church, the body of Christ (12:4–8). Most importantly, it should result in God's love shining through us for the benefit of others. Paul launches into a description of Christian ethics, comparable to the great love chapter in 1 Corinthians 13, concerning what it means to love and serve one another self-sacrificially (12:9–21).

Renewal with Reference to Civil Authorities (13:1–7)

After emphasizing love and service as the appropriate attitude toward fellow believers, Paul addresses the Christian's responsibility to those outside the church, starting with governing authorities. He affirms that these authorities have been established by God with the duty of enforcing justice and punishing evildoers, and so the Christian's responsibility is to submit to the government, pay taxes, and live as law-abiding

---

[10] The meaning of this term is greatly debated. Among the many suggestions are "reasonable," "rational," or "spiritual." See Cranfield, *Critical and Exegetical Commentary*, 2:602–5; Moo, *Epistle to the Romans*, 751–54.

citizens. Paul's remarks are no doubt contextualized for his time and place, where good relations with Rome provided greater freedom to proclaim the gospel. Elsewhere in Scripture there are clearly times when obedience to God is in conflict with an evil government. In such cases, "we must obey God rather than people" (Acts 5:29; cf. Exod 2:15–18; Dan 3:1–30).

Christian Love for All People: "Living in the Light" (13:8–14)

More Christian ethics follow. Paul says the only debt we should owe others is to love them. The fundamental command to "Love your neighbor as yourself" (Lev 19:18) fulfills the whole law, since it encompasses the commands against things like adultery, murder, stealing, and covetousness (13:8–10). The need to live this way is particularly urgent in light of the eschatological place we find ourselves, between the inauguration of God's salvation through Christ and its final consummation. Paul says, "The night is nearly over, and the day is near, so let us discard the deeds of darkness and put on the armor of light" (13:12).

Christian Liberty Controlled by Christian Love (14:1–15:13)

Paul turns next from Christian ethics in general to the particular situation of the church in Rome. He addresses two groups, which he refers to as the "strong" and the "weak." The strong are primarily Gentile Christians who are asserting that obedience to legalistic rules is not what makes you righteous. Salvation does not depend on what you eat or drink (keeping Jewish dietary laws) or on which day you worship (Jewish Sabbath observance). The weak are those Jewish (and perhaps some Gentile) Christians, who view these rules as important and necessary for their spiritual success. Paul mediates by affirming Christian liberty (he identifies himself with the "strong"; 15:1) but calling the church to promote unity by lifting others up instead of breaking them down. Those who are strong in faith and able to exercise their freedom in Christ must not treat the weak with contempt nor put them in situations that would cause them to fall into sin. Paul writes, "Do not destroy, by what you eat, someone for whom Christ died" (14:15). This is because, "The kingdom of God is not eating and drinking, but righteousness, peace, and joy in the Holy Spirit" (14:17). While it may be true that "everything is clean," we must not tear down God's work over secondary issues like food (14:20). The strong should therefore be willing to give up their freedom for the sake of their brother or sister in Christ. The weak, on the other hand, are not to judge or despise the strong in areas that are morally neutral. Loving others, building up the body of Christ, and living in unity should be their goal. This was the example of Christ, who was willing to sacrifice all for the good of others (15:3). By living this way, the church will "glorify the God and Father of our Lord Jesus Christ with one mind and one voice" (15:6).

Conclusion: Personal Messages and Benediction (15:14–16:27)

Paul's Ministry to the Gentiles (15:14–22)

As Paul begins to wrap up his letter, he commends the Roman Christians for their strong faith and exhorts them to move on to greater maturity. He has the authority to address them in this way because of the unique commission God has given him as apostle to the Gentiles and because he has been faithful to that commission. His goal has always been to preach the gospel where Christ has not been named, so that he would not be building on someone else's foundation (15:14–22).

Paul's Plans (15:23–33)

Paul's vision to preach where the gospel has not yet been heard is the reason he has not yet visited Rome, since the church had been established there for many years. But now that he has evangelized so much in the East, he hopes to visit them and to enlist their support for his missionary outreach to Spain. Meanwhile, however, he is headed to Jerusalem with a collection of money for the struggling church there. He asks the church in Rome to pray for a positive response in Jerusalem, for protection against his enemies there, and for safe travels as he comes to visit them.

Commendations, Greetings, and Warnings (16:1–24)

Paul concludes his letter with a variety of things: (1) commendations for Phoebe, a deacon in the church in Cenchreae (near Corinth, where Paul is), who is likely carrying the letter to the church, and (2) Paul's greetings to members of the church in Rome, including references to at least five house churches. It is amazing to see the diversity and vitality of the church in Rome and the many contacts and networks Paul has established there. He also includes (3) final instructions, warning the church against those who cause divisions and false teachers (16:17–20), and (4) greetings from Paul's associates, including Tertius, who is the secretary transcribing the letter (16:21–23).

Doxology (16:25–27)

Paul's doxology beautifully summarizes the message of Romans. The good news of Jesus the Messiah that Paul proclaims is the fulfillment of God's promises through the prophets and has as its goal that all nations might come to the obedience that comes from faith.

Old Testament Connections

As Paul's *magnum opus*, it is not surprising that the letter to the Romans contains more quotations and allusions to the OT than any of his other letters. The UBS Greek New Testament (5th ed.) lists sixty-one OT citations, more than three times as many as in any other Pauline letter.[11] Forty-two of these are marked by introductory formulas that identify them as coming from Scripture.[12] It would take a volume many times the size of this one to examine all of these. Instead, we will note one passage that shows the foundational nature of Scripture with reference to Paul's gospel (Rom 1:1–3) and another that affirms the OT's abiding value for new covenant believers (Rom 15:4).

After introducing himself as a servant of Christ Jesus and an apostle set apart for the gospel of God (1:1), Paul asserts that this gospel is not a novel idea but was rather "promised [by God] beforehand through his prophets in the Holy Scriptures" (1:2). Paul's gospel is legitimized by the fact that it is a continuation and climax of God's plan of salvation as promised through his prophets. The OT, in turn, provides the foundation and presupposition for all that follows. Paul continues with the content of the gospel of God; it concerns "his Son, Jesus Christ our Lord, who was a descendant of David according to the flesh and was appointed to be the powerful Son of God according to the Spirit of holiness by the resurrection of the dead" (1:3–4). This statement connects Jesus to traditional Jewish hopes for the Messiah. In 2 Samuel 7 God made a covenant with David, promising to raise up his descendant after him who would have a father-son relationship with God and through whom God would establish an eternal throne and kingdom (2 Sam 7:5–16). While this promise found its initial and partial fulfillment in Solomon, the promise of an eternal kingdom was

---

[11] C. G. Kruse suggests more than sixty-eight citations and ninety-one illusions or verbal parallels from the OT and Apocrypha, depending on how they are identified. "Paul's Use of Scripture in Romans," in *Paul and Scripture*, ed. S. E. Porter and C. D. Land, Pauline Studies 10 (Leiden: Brill, 2019), 77–92, esp. 77.

[12] David G. Peterson, "Romans, Letter to the," in *DNTUOT*, 711, citing Christopher D. Stanley, *Arguing with Scripture* (Edinburgh: T&T Clark, 2004), 42.

picked up by later prophets and applied to the eschatological king from the line of David—the Messiah—who would be endowed with the Spirit of the Lord and would establish an eternal kingdom of peace, justice, and righteousness (Isa 9:1–7; 11:1–16; Jer 23:5–6).[13] Paul links the fulfillment of this promise to the declaration of Jesus's divine sonship (alluding to Ps 2:7) at his resurrection from the dead.

From this starting point firmly grounded in Scripture, Paul defends several major gospel themes in Romans with support from the OT. These include, among others, the condemnation of all humanity because of their sin (Rom 3:10–18), justification by faith apart from the law (4:3, 9, 18, 22), God's sovereignty in salvation (9:7, 12–13, 15, 17; 11:34–35), Israel's present state of unbelief (9:33; 10:19, 21; 11:8–10), the remnant of Israel that is saved (9:27, 29; 11:3, 4), and the inclusion of the Gentiles in God's plan (9:25–26; 10:11, 20).

Near the end of the letter, Paul provides a paradigmatic statement about the continuing relevance of Scripture: "For whatever was written in the past was written for our instruction, so that we may have hope through endurance and through the encouragement from the Scriptures" (Rom 15:4). Placed in the context of Paul's call for sacrificial service among believers as a means of promoting unity, and the example of Christ in this regard, this passage is a reminder that the OT Scriptures are more than prophetic predictions. They are a source of continuing encouragement and guidance for believers today.

Gospel Connections

Paul's letters to the church in Rome and to the Galatians have much in common, since both focus on the theme of justification by faith. Both letters stress that salvation comes by God's grace alone, apart from the works of the law. In both, Paul identifies Abraham, the father of the Jewish faith, as the model of saving faith, citing Gen 15:6 as scriptural proof (Rom 4:3, 9, 22; Gal 3:6–9). In both, Paul quotes Hab 2:4 to show that "the righteous will live by faith" (Rom 1:17; Gal 3:11). In both, he contrasts slavery to sin with freedom in Christ (Gal 5:1; Rom 6:6, 16–22). In both, he emphasizes the power of God's Spirit to provide victory over the "flesh" (Rom 8; Gal 5:16–25).[14]

Despite these and other common themes, the tone of the two letters is remarkably different. While Romans is a systematic and logical defense of the gospel, Galatians

---

[13] For details sees M. L. Strauss, "Messiah," in *DNTUOT*, 515–17.

[14] See, for example, quotations of Lev 18:5 to show the impossibility of salvation by works (Rom 10:5; Gal 3:12) and Lev 19:18 as the summation of the law (Rom 13:9; Gal 5:14).

has a strong emotional appeal. In Romans, Paul is the lawyer methodically presenting his case. He anticipates and then answers the arguments of his opponents. In Galatians Paul is much more emotionally engaged. He expresses shock and outrage, amazed that the Galatians are so quickly abandoning the true gospel for a counterfeit. He pronounces a curse on anyone who would preach a different gospel. He calls the Galatians "foolish" and asks sarcastically, "Who has cast a spell on you?" (3:1). He chides those who would require Gentiles to be circumcised, encouraging them to go all the way and castrate themselves! (5:12). He is willing to criticize even respected leaders like Peter and Barnabas when he sees hypocrisy in their actions (3:11–14). If Romans reveals the mind of Paul, Galatians reveals his heart.

The differences relate to the different occasions and purposes. Galatians is written in the heat of battle, a life-and-death struggle with eternal consequences for Paul's spiritual children. This is a battle Paul cannot lose. Romans, by contrast, is Paul's formal letter of introduction to the Roman church, a diplomatic masterpiece seeking to show they share a common set of beliefs. Different circumstances demand a different approach.

Life Connections

Since the beginning of time, hatred, conflict, and warfare have been a perpetual part of human existence. When we are opposed or attacked, our "natural" (fallen) inclination is to hit back. This results in an endless cycle of revenge and retaliation. Look at every long-standing conflict in the world today and this is its nature. Yet in the midst of Romans 12—the transition from the theological to the "practical" part of Romans—Paul identifies the key to breaking this endless cycle. He writes, "Do not repay anyone evil for evil. . . . Do not be conquered by evil, but conquer evil with good" (12:17, 21). This revolutionary teaching goes beyond passive resistance or turning the other cheek. It is active resistance, responding to evil with good, responding to hatred with love. Paul, of course, received this teaching from Jesus, who told his followers, "Love your enemies and pray for those who persecute you." If someone sued you for your shirt, you should give him your coat as well. If a soldier conscripted you to carry his bags for a mile, you should carry them for two (Matt 5:38–48). This is not about justice. It is about self-sacrifice for the sake of reconciliation. It is also about being "children of your Father in heaven." When humanity rejected God, God did not reject them. He responded with love and self-sacrifice, sending his own Son to die in our place. What God has done for us, he now calls us to do for others, initiating reconciliation through self-sacrificial love and service.

Interactive Questions

1. Where was Paul when he wrote Romans and what were his plans? Where did he want to take the gospel?

2. What happened to the Jews of Rome that altered the leadership of the church there?

3. What is the central message of Romans? Why is Paul writing this letter?

4. What does "the righteousness of God" mean for Paul in Romans?

5. Why are human beings guilty before God? How have they responded to God's self-revelation in creation?

6. What does justification mean and what is the basis for our justification?

7. How does Paul use Abraham to confirm that we are justified by faith?

8. What is the point of Paul's comparison between Jesus and Adam in chapter 5?

9. What analogies does Paul draw in chapters 6 and 7 to demonstrate our freedom from sin and the law?

10. How does Paul respond in chapters 9–11 to the accusation that God's promises to Israel have failed?

11. In chapter 12 how does Paul say we should respond to God's great mercy in saving us?

12. According to chapter 13, how should Christians respond to civil authorities?

13. Who are the weaker and stronger brothers or sisters in chapters 14–15? What principles does Paul give here about how we should treat one another?

14. How might reading Romans benefit Christians today?

Study Resources

Bird, Michael F. *Romans*. SGBC. Grand Rapids: Zondervan, 2016.

Bruce, F. F. *Romans*. TNTC. Downers Grove, IL: InterVarsity, 1988.

Cranfield, C. E. B. *A Critical and Exegetical Commentary on the Epistle to the Romans*. 2 vols. 6th ed. ICC. Edinburgh: T&T Clark, 1975, 1979.

Dunn, J. D. G. *Romans*. 2 vols. WBC. Grand Rapids: Zondervan, 1988, 2015.
Fitzmyer, Joseph A. *Romans*. AYB. New Haven, CT: Yale University Press, 1993.
Gorman, Michael J. *Romans: A Theological and Pastoral Commentary*. Grand Rapids: Eerdmans, 2022.
Jewett, Robert. *Romans*. Hermeneia. Philadelphia: Fortress, 2006.
Käsemann, Ernst. *Commentary on Romans*. Grand Rapids: Eerdmans, 1994.
McKnight, Scot. *Reading Romans Backwards: A Gospel of Peace in the Midst of Empire*. Waco, TX: Baylor University Press, 2019.
Moo, Douglas J. *The Epistle to the Romans*. NICNT. Grand Rapids: Eerdmans, 1996.
———. *Romans*. NIVAC. Grand Rapids: Zondervan, 2000.
Kruse, Colin. *Paul's Letter to the Romans*. PNTC. Grand Rapids: Eerdmans, 2012.
Mounce, Robert, *Romans*. NAC. Nashville: Broadman & Holman, 1995.
Osborne, Grant R. *Romans*. IVPNTC. Downers Grove, IL: InterVarsity, 2004.
Pate, C. Marvin. *Romans*. TTCS. Grand Rapids: Baker Books, 2013.
Schreiner, Thomas R. *Romans*. 2nd ed. BECNT. Grand Rapids: Baker Books, 2018.
Witherington, Ben, III. *Paul's Letter to the Romans: A Socio-Rhetorical Commentary*. Grand Rapids: Eerdmans, 2004.
Wu, Jackson. *Reading Romans with Eastern Eyes: Honor and Shame in Paul's Message and Mission*. Downers Grove, IL: IVP Academic, 2019.

PRISON LETTERS

Ephesians

Philippians

Colossians

Philemon

8

Ephesians

Probably written from Rome, ca. 60–62 CE

> Blessed is the God and Father of our Lord Jesus Christ, who has blessed us with every spiritual blessing in the heavens in Christ. For he chose us in him, before the foundation of the world, to be holy and blameless in love before him.
>
> —Ephesians 1:3–4

Outline

I. Introduction (1:1–2)
II. God's Purpose in the Church (1:3–3:21)
III. Practical Ways to Fulfill God's Purpose in the Church (4:1–6:20)
IV. Conclusion (6:21–24)

Author, Occasion, Message

Author

The authorship of Ephesians by Paul has been challenged more than any of Paul's letters except the Pastoral Epistles. While few deny that Ephesians represents a masterful summary of Paul's theology (see "Message" p. 182), many consider it to be written by a disciple of Paul as a memorial to his legacy. Arguments against Pauline authorship are primarily theological and stylistic. Some scholars claim that Ephesians has a more developed theology on some issues than typically seen in Paul's writings. For example, in Ephesians the word "church" refers to the universal church made up of all believers (1:22; 3:10, 21; 5:23, 24, 25, 27, 29, 32), while Paul routinely uses the word for individual congregations (e.g., "the church in Cenchreae," Rom 16:1; cf. 16:5; 1 Cor 1:2; 4:15–16, etc.). Similarly, the undisputed Pauline letters have a strong future eschatology, where the believer's hope is in the Parousia, the return of Christ. Ephesians has a greater focus on realized eschatology, with salvation as a present possession. Stylistically, Ephesians also has some significant differences from Paul's undisputed letters. The author uses long complex sentences with multiple subordinate clauses. Paul generally writes in a briefer, more staccato fashion.

These differences, however, can be overstated. Though Paul doesn't refer specifically to the universal church elsewhere, he comes very close, for example speaking of all believers as members of the one body of Christ (1 Cor 12:4–31; cf. Gal 1:13). Similarly, even if the primary emphasis in Ephesians is on realized eschatology (see 1:3; 2:6), the letter envisions the consummation of that salvation (see Eph 1:14; 2:7; 4:30; 5:6; 6:8, 13).[1] These small differences are as likely to come from Paul's own theological reflection as from developments by his disciples. As H. J. Cadbury said, "Which is more likely—that an imitator of Paul in the first century composed a writing ninety-five percent in accordance with Paul's style or that Paul himself wrote a letter diverging five or ten percent from his usual style?"[2] Small differences in vocabulary and style could also be due to input from Paul's associates or his use of a different secretary.

---

[1] D. A. Carson and Douglas J. Moo, *An Introduction to the New Testament*, 2nd ed. (Grand Rapids: Zondervan, 2005), 483; Andrew Lincoln, *Ephesians*, WBC (Nashville: Thomas Nelson, 1990), lxxxix–xc.

[2] H. J. Cadbury, "The Dilemma of Ephesians," *NTS* 5 (1958–59): 101, cited by Carson and Moo, *Introduction*, 481.

On the positive side, the strong and widespread acceptance of Ephesians as Paul's in the early church points to Pauline authorship.[3] While a few evangelical scholars today reject the authorship by Paul,[4] the great majority affirm it.[5]

Occasion

Assuming that the letter was written by Paul during his first Roman imprisonment (see sidebar 9.1), the most significant issue concerning the occasion of Ephesians is its destination and audience. Many scholars have argued that Ephesians was originally a circular letter meant to be passed among the churches in Asia Minor.

(1) The words "at Ephesus" are absent from 1:1 in some of our earliest manuscripts and other early witnesses.[6]

(2) There are no personal greetings at the end of the letter. This is particularly surprising since, as noted above, Paul ministered in Ephesus for three years on his third missionary journey (Acts 19) and was extremely close to the church and its leadership (Acts 20:17–38).

(3) Paul writes that he has "heard" of the readers' faith (1:15) and they have "heard" of his ministry (3:2). This is a very odd statement if written exclusively to Ephesus, since Paul knew first-hand the faith of the Ephesians.

(4) There seems to be no treatment of *specific* church problems. When Paul is writing to an individual church, he usually addresses issues specific to that church.

(5) In Colossians 4:16, Paul tells the Colossians to read the letter coming from Laodicea. This could be Ephesians arriving as a circular letter.

(6) Tertullian claimed that the heretic Marcion of Sinope identified Ephesians as "the letter to the Laodiceans" in his work *Apostolikon* (Tertullian, *Against Marcion* 5.11).

This evidence is compelling, and it seems likely that this letter was intended not only for Ephesus, but also to circulate among various churches in Asia Minor.

---

[3] See Clinton E. Arnold, *Ephesians*, ZECNT (Grand Rapids: Zondervan), 47.

[4] See, for example, J. D. G. Dunn, *The Theology of Paul the Apostle* (Grand Rapids: Eerdmans, 1998), 13n39; Ralph Martin, *Ephesians, Colossians, and Philemon*, IBC (Louisville: John Knox, 1991), 4; Lincoln, *Ephesians*, lx–lxxiii; Paul J. Achtemeier, Joel B. Green, and Marianne Meye Thompson, *Introducing the New Testament* (Grand Rapids: Eerdmans, 2001), 480–86.

[5] Arnold, *Ephesians*, 46n98 provides an impressive list.

[6] The words are absent from p^{46} B א 6 1739. Early church fathers who were aware of this reading include Origen, Basil, Jerome, and Tertullian. See Arnold, *Ephesians*, 25–26.

Message

Ephesians is a remarkably concise summary of Paul's gospel, emphasizing God's sovereign plan for reconciling fallen humanity to himself through the person and work of Christ and reconciling human beings—both Jews and Gentiles—to one another in the church, the body in Christ. This saving work of God through Christ also has cosmic dimensions, representing the victory of God and his church over Satan and the spiritual forces of evil.

Interpretive Overview

Introduction (1:1–2)

Paul's introduction and greeting is typical of his other letters. As noted in the introduction above, the absence of the words "at Ephesus" in 1:1 likely indicates that the letter was intended as a circular letter to be passed among the churches of Asia Minor. This would account for the lack of personal greetings and discussion of specific church problems.

God's Purpose in the Church (1:3–3:21)

The letter can be divided in two nearly equal parts. The first half (chaps. 1–3) is primarily doctrinal, describing the nature of the church as the people of God. The second half (chaps. 4–6) describes the practical application of these truths.

Delaying his typical thanksgiving and prayer for the church, Paul launches into a remarkably compressed hymn of praise to God for the salvation he has provided and the spiritual blessings believers have received in Christ. Verses 3–14 are one sentence in Greek! God's sovereign purpose was fulfilled when he chose believers as his own before creation, predestined them for adoption as his children, redeemed them through his death, forgave their sins by his grace, and sealed them with the promised Holy Spirit, the downpayment of their inheritance in Christ. All of this should result in unending praise to God for his glorious presence and grace.

Paul next turns from praise to God to thanksgiving and prayer for the faith and love these believers have demonstrated (1:15–23). He prays especially that God would give them spiritual wisdom and insight to comprehend the glorious salvation he has just described. This salvation was accomplished through the immeasurable greatness of God's power, which he demonstrated by raising Jesus from the dead and exalting him to the highest position at God's right hand. Believers share in this position because the church is "his body, the fullness of the one who fills all things in every way" (1:23).

Having mentioned the church as the body of Christ, Paul now describes the nature of the church (2:1–10). Previously his readers were spiritually dead, living in a way consistent with the evil world system and Satan, its ruler. As disobedient children of the "flesh" (*sarx* = fallen humanity), they were destined to experience God's just and righteous wrath against sin. But in a display of God's great love and mercy, he raised them from the dead with Christ and seated them with him in God's presence. This salvation was not a result of any merit or action on their part but resulted solely from God's grace. Having been recreated and transformed in Christ Jesus, believers live out this new status by doing good works which God has prepared for them.

How does this salvation of individuals relate to God's people as a community? In the past God worked through his covenant people Israel. Uncircumcised Gentiles were on the outside, without hope and without God. But all along the purpose of God's law and his covenants was to accomplish salvation through the death of Jesus the Messiah. Now, through their identification with Christ, Jews and Gentiles have been brought together in peace and reconciliation as one people. Gentiles are no longer foreigners and strangers, but fellow citizens and members of God's household, sharing in the one Spirit of God. This new community, the church, is God's new and holy temple, built on the foundation of the apostles and prophets with Jesus Christ as its cornerstone (2:11–22).

How does Paul himself fit into this new community? The salvation of the Gentiles was a mystery in the past but was made known to Paul and the other apostles by the Spirit. This mystery was that "the Gentiles are coheirs, members of the same body, and partners in the promise in Christ Jesus through the gospel" (3:6). Paul, who views himself as the least of God's people, was given the extraordinary privilege to proclaim this message of God's eternal purpose accomplished in Christ (3:11). This understanding of God's purpose being fulfilled should inspire Paul's readers to boldness and confidence and should be a source of encouragement when facing suffering (3:1–13).

Paul concludes the first half of the letter with a prayer, offered to the Father of every family on earth—Jews and Gentiles alike. He prays that his readers would be strengthened by the Holy Spirit, that they would experience the living presence of Christ in their hearts, that love would be the foundation of all their relationships, and that they would better understand the incomprehensible love God has shown us in Christ. While this seems like a tall order for lowly human beings, Paul concludes with a doxology praising the God who is able to do anything "above and beyond all that we ask or think" because of the power of the Holy Spirit at work within us (3:14–21).

Practical Ways to Fulfill God's Purpose in the Church (4:1–6:20)

Paul has been describing God's divine plan in Christ that brought restoration to his creation and reconciliation between Jews and Gentiles. Now he turns to the practical application these great truths should have for the people of God.

Paul first calls his readers to live a life worthy of the calling they have received. This means demonstrating humility, gentleness, patience, and love, bringing unity and peace to the body of Christ. This unity is possible because they are all in this together. There is one body—the church—united by the one Spirit and with a common allegiance to the one Lord, one faith, one baptism, and one God and Father of all. Ironically, this unity finds its strength in diversity. When Christ ascended to heaven, he poured out a variety of spiritual gifts on his people. The purpose of these gifts is not for self-promotion, but other-promotion, "to equip the saints for the work of ministry, to build up the body of Christ" (4:12). And when the body is built up, it will grow into full maturity, producing spiritual adults who can discern truth from error and reach their full potential in Christ (4:1–16).

Paul next drills down to more specifics on what godly living looks like (4:17–5:20). Their former life in the Gentile world was one of promiscuity and impurity. They must now take off that old self as if it were a dirty set of clothes and put on a new self created in God's likeness. This means speaking the truth to others, not letting anger turn to sin, not stealing but working honestly, not using foul language, building others up instead of breaking them down, being kind and compassionate, being willing to forgive others just as they are forgiven in Christ (4:17–32).

They can do this by imitating God their Father and living a life of self-sacrifice, as Christ did. This means avoiding sexual immorality, greed, obscenity, crude jokes, and idolatry (5:1–5). They did these things when they lived in darkness, but now they are God's children—children of light. Living in the light means demonstrating goodness, righteousness, and truth, doing what is pleasing to the Lord (5:6–14). It means demonstrating godly wisdom, making the most of the time God has given. It means not drinking excessively, which damages oneself and others. Instead of being filled with alcohol, they should be filled with the Holy Spirit. True joy comes not from getting drunk, but from worshiping together in joyful song, giving thanks to God for everything, and an attitude of mutual submission toward others (5:15–21).

Paul next unpacks what this mutual submission should look like in the context of the Greco-Roman household (5:22–6:9). Wives are to submit to their husbands and husbands should love their wives with the same kind of self-sacrificial love that Jesus demonstrated when he gave his life for the church. Children are to obey their parents, and parents are not to exasperate their children. Slaves should obey their masters as they would serve Christ; and masters are to treat their slaves in a way that pleases the Lord (see sidebar 11.1: Why Does Paul Not Condemn Slavery?).

Finally, Paul reminds his readers that they are not just involved in a physical struggle but in a spiritual one. He describes the spiritual weapons used in this conflict metaphorically, using imagery of a fully outfitted Roman soldier (6:10–17). Believers must stand ready for battle, with truth like a belt around their waist, righteousness like a breastplate protecting vital organs, sandals laced up and ready to run everywhere to proclaim the gospel, a shield symbolizing faith that protects against Satan's attacks, the helmet of salvation and the sword of the Spirit, which is the word of God. All of these spiritual weapons are animated through prayer, which keeps us dependent on God and connected with fellow believers. Paul requests prayer for himself, not for physical protection, but for boldness to keep proclaiming the good news of salvation, for which he is an ambassador in chains (6:18–20).

Conclusion (6:21–24)

Paul concludes the letter with just one personal reference, commending to the readers Tychicus (cf. Col 4:7; 2 Tim 4:12; Titus 3:12), "our dearly loved brother and faithful servant" (6:21), who will report on Paul's condition and encourage them. If the letter is a circular one (see "Occasion" on p. 181), Tychicus may have been accompanying it from church to church. Paul ends with a theologically rich benediction pronouncing peace, love, faith, and grace from God the Father and the Lord Jesus Christ.

Old Testament Connections

One of the most controversial OT citations in the Pauline corpus is in Eph 4:8, where Paul cites Psalm 68 (67 LXX) with reference to Christ's ascension.[7] In Eph 4:1–6 Paul has been calling the church to love and unity in light of what God has done through Christ by bringing diverse peoples together in one body. This unity is maintained through diversity, as each believer uses their spiritual gifts to build up the church (4:7–16). In verse 8 Paul refers to Christ's distribution of spiritual gifts with an OT quotation from Ps 68:18. Compare the original psalm with Paul's citation:

---

[7] For a good survey of recent research, see S. M. Ehorn, "The Use of Psalm 68(67).19 in Ephesians 4.8: A History of Research," *CBR* 12 (2013): 96–120.

Ps 68:18 NIV	Eph 4:8 NIV
When you ascended on high you took many captives; you **received** gifts from people (MT 68:19; 67:19 LXX)	When he ascended on high He took many captives; and **gave** gifts to his people

While the original psalm referred to tribute ("gifts") *received* by Yahweh from his vanquished enemies, Paul apparently changes this to spiritual gifts *given* by Christ at his ascension.

Various attempts have been made to explain Paul's alteration of the text. Some say Paul simply misquotes the psalm to make it say what he wants it to say. Others suggest that Paul is using a textual tradition different from either the Greek Septuagint (LXX) or Hebrew Masoretic Text (MT). Some Jewish traditions interpreted the "you" of the psalm to be not Yahweh, but Moses, who received the Torah at Mount Sinai and gave it to the people. The Aramaic Targum on Ps 68:18 reads "You ascended to the firmament, Prophet Moses; you led captive captivity; you learned the words of Torah; you *gave* them as gifts to the sons of men."[8] Perhaps Paul is building a typology contrasting the law of Moses with the Christ event.[9] One problem with this is that there is little evidence that this interpretation goes back to the time of Paul.[10]

Perhaps the most convincing explanation for Paul's change is that he has the whole of Psalm 68 in view. In its original context, Psalm 68 presents Yahweh as the Divine Warrior who reveals his power, defeats his enemies, and strengthens the people of God. As Lunde and Dunne explain: "The psalmist moves from the LORD's deliverance in the exodus (vv. 4–8), to his provision of the land through his mighty victories (vv. 9–14), to his choice of Zion as the mountain of his enthronement (vv. 15–17). Then, after his description of this enthronement (v. 18), the writer turns to survey both the LORD's present (vv. 19–20) and future provisions (vv. 21–23, 28–31)."[11]

---

[8] Cited by Frank S. Thielman, "Ephesians," in *CNTUOT*, 821.

[9] Cf. W. Hall Harris, *Descent of Christ. Ephesians 4:7–11 and Traditional Hebrew Imagery* (Grand Rapids: Baker, 1996).

[10] Arnold, *Ephesians*, 249–50.

[11] Jonathan M. Lunde and John A. Dunne, "Paul's Creative & Contextual Use of Psalm 68 in Ephesians 4:8," *WTJ* 74, no. 1 (2012): 99–117, quote from p. 107. Cf. T. G. Gombis, "Cosmic Lordship and Divine Gift-Giving," *NovT* 47 (2005): 367–80; S. Baugh, "Ephesians," in *DNTUOT*, 212–16; Joshua M. Greever, "Typological Expectation of Psalm 68 and Its Application in Ephesians 4:8," *TynBul* 71, no. 2 (2020): 253–79.

Paul thus sees a "remarkable typology that exists between the actions of Yahweh in the whole psalm and those accomplished by Christ in his work on the cross, resurrection, and ascension."[12] If Paul has the whole psalm in view, the change from "receiving" to "giving" is not a misquotation, but a summary of Yahweh's actions at the psalm's climax. This has profound implications for Paul's divine Christology, since, as elsewhere in Paul, Jesus is portrayed as fulfilling the role of Yahweh himself.

Gospel Connections

One of the central themes of Ephesians is the church, its nature and purpose. While Paul normally uses the term "church" (*ekklēsia*) to refer to a local congregation or house church (e.g., Rom 16:1, 4, 5; 1 Cor 1:2; 4:17; 2 Cor 8:18, etc.), in Ephesians the term always refers to the universal church made up of all believers (1:22; 3:10, 21; 5:23, 24, 25, 27, 29, 32). Some scholars point to this difference as evidence against the Pauline authorship of Ephesians. But this is unnecessary. Paul occasionally uses the term more broadly of all believers (1 Cor 15:9; Gal 1:13; Phil 3:6), especially in his later letters (Col 1:18, 24; 1 Tim 3:5, 15). It is not surprising that Paul would use the term this way in a letter meant to circulate to various churches and one that is so focused on the transforming work of Christ in all believers.

Life Connections

As we noted previously, Ephesians is divided roughly into two halves, the first dealing more with theology (chaps. 1–3) and the second with practice (chaps. 4–6). The two halves are in fact two sides of the same coin. The salvation we have received freely "by grace through faith" makes us "his workmanship, created in Christ Jesus for good works" (2:8–10). The Christian life is simply living in light of the new person that we have become. We have "take[n] off" the old self and have "put on the new self, the one created according to God's likeness" (4:22–24). We show grace to others because we have received grace from God (2:8; 4:29). We forgive one another, "just as God also forgave you" (4:32). We sacrificially love and submit to one another, "just as Christ loved the church and gave himself for her to make her holy" (5:25–26).

---

[12] Lunde and Dunne, "Paul's Creative and Contextual Use," 115–16.

Interactive Questions

1. Why has the Pauline authorship of Ephesians been questioned by some scholars?

2. Why do many scholars think that Ephesians was originally meant to be a circular letter passed from church to church in Asia Minor? Note various bits of evidence for this.

3. What is the theme of the hymn of praise that begins the letter?

4. How do the last three chapters of Ephesians relate to the first three chapters?

5. How does Paul describe the spiritual conflict in which believers are engaged?

6. Does Paul take Psalm 68 (67 LXX) out of context? What are some explanations for this passage?

7. How might reading Ephesians benefit Christians today?

Study Resources

Arnold, Clinton E. *Ephesians*. ZECNT. Grand Rapids: Zondervan, 2010.

Barth, Marcus. *Ephesians*. 2 vols. AYB. New York: Doubleday, 1974.

Best, Ernest. *A Critical and Exegetical Commentary on Ephesians*. ICC. Edinburgh: T&T Clark, 2004.

Bruce, F. F. *The Epistles to the Colossians, to Philemon, and to the Ephesians*. 2nd ed. NICNT. Grand Rapids: Eerdmans, 1984.

Campbell, Constantine R. *The Letter to the Ephesians*. PNTC. Grand Rapids: Eerdmans, 2023.

Cohick, Lynn. *The Letter to the Ephesians*. NICNT. Grand Rapids: Eerdmans, 2020.

Gombis, Timothy G. *The Drama of Ephesians: Participating in the Triumph of God*. Downers Grove, IL: IVP Academic, 2010.

Hoehner, Harold. *Ephesians: An Exegetical Commentary*. Grand Rapids: Baker, 2003.

Lincoln, Andrew T. *Ephesians*. WBC. Nashville: Thomas Nelson, 1990.

Perkins, Pheme. *Ephesians*. ANTC. Nashville: Abingdon, 1997.

Snodgrass, Klyne. *Ephesians*. NIVAC. Grand Rapids: Zondervan, 1996.

Thielman, Frank. *Ephesians*. BECNT. Grand Rapids: Baker, 2010.

9

Philippians

Probably written from Rome, ca. 62 CE

I give thanks to my God for every remembrance of you, always praying with joy for all of you in my every prayer, because of your partnership in the gospel from the first day until now.

—Philippians 1:3–5

Outline

I. Introduction (1:1–11)
II. Paul's Circumstances (1:12–26)
III. Paul's Exhortation to Steadfast Faith and Unity (1:27–2:18)
IV. Information about Paul's Coworkers (2:19–30)
V. Warning against False Teachers (3:1–4:1)
VI. More Exhortations and Encouragements (4:2–9)
VII. Final Thanksgiving for the Gifts Received and Conclusion (4:10–23)

Author, Occasion, Message

Author

The letter is from "Paul and Timothy" (1:1), but the contents and the first-person singular confirm that Paul is the primary author. The authenticity of the letter is affirmed by virtually all scholars.

Occasion

The city of Philippi was located in central Macedonia, sixteen kilometers inland from the port of Neapolis (modern Kavala). It was named after Philip II of Macedon, father of Alexander the Great, who had captured the city from the Thracians in the fourth century BCE. The city rose to special prominence under Caesar Augustus, who made it a Roman colony and settled many veterans of war there. As a Roman colony, Philippi had the legal status of Roman territory in Italy and special privileges, such as exemption from tribute and various taxes. Being a slice of Rome in Macedonia was a source of great pride for its citizens.

The church at Philippi was established by Paul, Silas and Timothy on Paul's second missionary journey (Acts 15:36–18:22). Luke reports that after being directed away from Asia and Bithynia by the Spirit, Paul received a vision to cross the Aegean Sea to Macedonia (Acts 16:6–9), where churches were established in Philippi, Thessalonica, and Berea. As we have seen in our study of Acts, the church began in the home of a woman named Lydia and was forged in the context of persecution (Acts 16:16–40).

Paul's subsequent relationship with the church at Philippi was a close one. The church was a true partner in ministry (Phil 1:5; 4:14) and had repeatedly supported Paul financially (4:15–16). Shortly before this letter was written, the church had sent another gift with a church member named Epaphroditus, who was to assist Paul during his imprisonment. Epaphroditus, however, had fallen ill and almost died, causing great concern both for Paul and for the Philippians (2:25–30; 4:14–18).

Paul writes for a variety of reasons: (1) He is sending Epaphroditus back to the Philippians with commendations for his faithful service (2:25–30). (2) He wants to thank the church for their faithful support, past and present (4:10, 14–15). (3) He wants to alleviate the church's concerns about his imprisonment and assure them that God is at work even through these difficult circumstances (1:12–30). (4) He wants to notify them of his plans to send Timothy shortly (2:23) and of his own desire to visit them (1:25–26; 2:24). (5) He wants to spur them on to greater love and unity in the face of a growing threat of conflict within the church (2:2–4; 4:2). (6) He wants to warn them of certain external threats to the church, especially from Judaizers (3:2–4). In terms of its genre, the letter has been compared to Greco-Roman letters of friendship.[1] In modern terms, the letter may be compared to a news-filled missionary support letter, written to dear friends and partners in ministry.

Philippians was written by Paul from prison (1:7, 12–26). This was most likely during Paul's first Roman imprisonment, ca. 60–62 CE (see sidebar 9.1, The Provenance of the Prison Epistles).

Message

The central theme of Philippians is the joy of knowing Christ. Terms of joy and rejoicing occur throughout the letter (1:4, 18, 25; 2:2, 17, 18, 28, 29; 3:1; 4:1, 4, 10). "Rejoice in the Lord always," Paul writes, "I will say it again: Rejoice!" (4:4). The greatest joy in life is to live for Christ. Paul says, "For me, to live is Christ and to die is gain" (1:21). His ultimate goal is "to know him and the power of his resurrection and the fellowship of his sufferings, being conformed to his death" (3:10). Joy in life comes through Christian fellowship, which Paul defines as partnership in the gospel, to "live your life worthy of the gospel of Christ . . . standing firm in one spirit, in one accord, contending together for the faith of the gospel" (1:27). He seeks to model this life for other believers and calls on the Philippians to follow his example (3:17).

SIDEBAR 9.1: THE PROVENANCE OF THE PRISON EPISTLES

The four "Prison Epistles"—Ephesians, Philippians, Colossians, and Philemon—are so-called because in each Paul indicates that he is presently in prison (Eph 3:1; 4:1; Phil 1:7, 12–26; Col 4:10; Phlm 1).[2] The four have traditionally been viewed as written during Paul's house arrest in Rome described by Luke at the end of Acts (28:30; ca. 60–62 CE). Support for this location comes especially from Philippians, where Paul mentions his testimony before the "whole palace guard" (1:13 NIV), presumably Caesar's personal guard in Rome, and greetings sent from "those who belong to Caesar's household" (4:22).

---

[1] See M. Silva, *Philippians*, BECNT (Grand Rapids: Baker, 2005), 19–20; G. D. Fee, *Paul's Letter to the Philippians*, NICNT (Grand Rapids: Eerdmans, 1995), 2–7. Fee claims the letter combines features of a letter of friendship with a letter of moral exhortation.

[2] For details of Roman imprisonment see Brian Rapske, *The Book of Acts and Paul in Roman Custody* (Grand Rapids: Eerdmans,1994).

But a Roman provenance also has its detractors. Some have claimed that the distance between Rome and Philippi was too great to account for the various trips back and forth implied in the letter.[3] Paul speaks of many imprisonments during his ministry (2 Cor 11:23), so other locations have been proposed, the two most common being Caesarea Maritima and Ephesus, in Asia Minor. Acts describes a two-year imprisonment in Caesarea before Paul was sent to Rome (Acts 23:33; 24:27), and Paul himself mentions severe trials in Asia that may have involved imprisonment (1 Cor 15:32; 2 Cor 1:8–10; cf. 1 Cor 4:9–13; 4:8–12; 6:4–11; Acts 20:18, 19). While the "praetorium" often refers to Caesar's elite troops in Rome, the Greek term (*praitōrion*) was also used of military headquarters throughout the Roman provinces (see Herod's praetorium in Acts 23:35; cf. Mark 15:16). Members of Caesar's household, meaning servants, attendants, and extended family, could be found in various governmental posts throughout the empire.

Despite these uncertainties, in our judgment Rome remains the most likely place of writing, at least for Philippians. (1) Early Christian tradition favors Rome. (2) Together, the references to both the praetorium and Caesar's household tip the balance in favor of Rome. (3) By most accountings, there was more than enough time during Paul's two-year (or longer) incarceration for the various journeys back-and-forth between Philippi and Rome.[4]

It is possible, of course, that Ephesians, Colossians, and Philemon were written during a different imprisonment. Ephesus, in Asia, seems an unlikely location for Colossians or Philemon, however, since Luke was with Paul when he wrote those letters (Col 3:14; Phlm 24), but Paul's Ephesian ministry (Acts 19:1–41) is not one of the "we" sections of Acts. This leaves open the possibility of Rome or Caesarea Maritima (Luke was with Paul in both locations), or another unknown imprisonment. In the absence of better evidence, we will assume the traditional Roman provenance for all four prison letters.

---

[3] These include (1) news of Paul's imprisonment reaches the Philippians; (2) they send Epaphroditus to help Paul (2:25); (3) news of Epaphroditus's illness travels back to Philippi (2:26); (4) news of their concern goes back to Paul (2:26); (5) Paul sends Epaphroditus with the letter (2:25). See G. S. Duncan, *St. Paul's Ephesian Ministry: A Reconstruction* (London: Hodder & Stoughton. 1929), 80–82.

[4] See Silva, *Philippians*, 5.

Interpretive Overview

Introduction (1:1–11)

Paul identifies himself as the author and includes Timothy, who is well-known to the Philippians (see 2:19–24). He and Timothy are "servants" or "slaves" (*douloi*) of Christ Jesus. Paul doesn't bother to identify himself as an apostle, perhaps because his apostolic authority is not being challenged at Philippi. He writes to all the "saints" (CSB), or "God's holy people" (NIV), in Philippi, including their leaders, the overseers (*episkopoi*) and deacons (*diakonoi*). Names of church offices do not appear to have been standardized by this early date, and "overseers" is likely equivalent to "elders," referring to the spiritual leaders of the church (cf. Acts 14:23; 1 Tim 3:1–7; Titus 1:5–9). "Deacons" (or "servants"; cf. 1 Tim 3:8–13; Rom 16:1) likely performed more administrative and supportive roles (1:1–2).

Paul thanks God for the Philippians and prays for them every time he thinks about them. He is particularly grateful for their partnership in the gospel, which began on the day they received the good news and has continued through all the ups and downs of his ministry. Paul's words are full of joy, gratitude, and affection for the Philippians, and he anticipates their continued spiritual growth until Christ returns (1:3–11).

Paul's Circumstances (1:12–26)

Paul turns from his thanksgiving for the Philippians' faith and friendship to his own circumstances. The church was greatly concerned when they heard of his arrest and incarceration, and so Paul wants to assure and encourage them that God is at work. His imprisonment has actually served to advance the gospel, providing opportunities to share his faith with the whole imperial guard (presumably as they have rotated through their shifts guarding him). This, in turn, has given other believers confidence and boldness to share their faith. While most of these are genuine and sincere, some are jealous of Paul and acting out of selfish motives. But "what does it matter?" (1:18), Paul says, all that is important is that Christ is proclaimed (1:12–20).

In the end, Paul says, it doesn't matter whether he lives or dies. In fact, he is torn in his own desires. On the one hand, dying and being with Christ would be better. But by remaining alive, he can continue to encourage the Philippians in their faith. In light of this, Paul expects to be released and to return to them (1:21–26).

Paul's Exhortation to Steadfast Faith and Unity (1:27–2:18)

Whether he comes to them or not, Paul's message for them is the same. They should live lives worthy of the gospel and in line with their true heavenly citizenship. This means standing firm in their faith, united with other believers, and fearless against their enemies. This kind of courage is a sure sign that God is with them, confirming their salvation and their enemies' destruction. The suffering they are enduring in this struggle is actually a privilege and a gift from God, to suffer as Christ did. It also confirms that they are involved in the same great spiritual conflict as Paul and other believers (1:27–30).

Success in this spiritual battle will come only if believers stay united (2:1–11). The *basis* for this unity, Paul says, are the things we share in Christ. He expresses these in four conditional clauses: "If . . . there is any encouragement in Christ, if any consolation of love, if any fellowship with the Spirit, if any affection and mercy" (2:1). Since you have these spiritual blessings, Paul says, then complete or fulfill my joy by staying united. He defines the *meaning* of unity with four phrases: "thinking the same way, having the same love, united in spirit, intent on one purpose" (2:2).

But how do we maintain unity in the church when we have so many differences of opinion and perspective? Paul says the *means* to unity is humility: "Do nothing out of selfish ambition or conceit, but in humility consider others as more important than yourselves. Everyone should look not to his own interests, but rather to the interests of others" (2:3–4). The key to unity is to set aside personal pride and ambition and to adopt a servant's attitude that lifts others up rather than breaking them down.

Finally, the *model* for this kind of humility is Jesus himself. So, Paul says, "Adopt the same attitude as that of Christ Jesus" (2:5). What follows in verses 6–11 is an extraordinary description of Jesus's humility, when he became a human being and suffered on our behalf. This passage has a clear poetic structure and there is considerable debate as to whether Paul wrote it himself or whether he is citing an early Christian hymn or confession.[5] What is not in question is that this is the most profound description of the *incarnation*—God taking on human form—in the whole NT. Although Jesus existed in the form of God (meaning, all that God was, he was), he did not consider equality with God a thing to be exploited, or used to his

---

[5] On the origin and interpretation of this passage, see Ralph P. Martin, *A Hymn of Christ: Philippians 2:5–11 in Recent Interpretation and in the Setting of Early Christian Worship* (Downers Grove, IL: InterVarsity, 1997). For more on early Christian hymns, see "Gospel Connections" in chap. 12.

advantage.[6] Instead, he "emptied" himself by setting aside his divine privileges and taking on the form of a servant, a lowly human being.[7] The service he rendered was the most excruciating and humiliating sacrifice of all, death by crucifixion (2:6–8). But after sacrifice came vindication. Because of Jesus's extraordinary act of self-sacrifice, God exalted him to the highest possible position and gave him a name that is above every name.[8] At the name of Jesus, every created being in the universe will one day bow down before him and acknowledge "that Jesus Christ is Lord, to the glory of God the Father" (2:9–11).

In light of Jesus's divine status and sacrifice for the Philippians ("Therefore . . ."; v. 12), Paul says, they should continue to live a life of obedience as they "work out [their] salvation with fear and trembling" (v. 12). "Work out" doesn't mean to earn their salvation, and Paul quickly adds that it is "God who is working in you . . . according to his good purpose" (v. 13). Working out their salvation means not grumbling or fighting among themselves, living as children of God who bring light to a dark world, and holding firm to the gospel message that brings life. By living this way, Paul says, even if his life is poured out like a drink offering that disappears into the ground,[9] when he stands before Christ on judgment day, he will rejoice that what he did for Christ will endure (2:12–18).

Information about Paul's Coworkers (2:19–30)

From his exhortations to faith and unity Paul turns to two examples of those who model these attributes. First is Timothy, who was perhaps Paul's closest associate and a spiritual son (2:22). Although Paul has been delayed in returning to the Philippians because of his imprisonment, he hopes to send Timothy shortly as his representative. This is appropriate since Timothy, more than anyone else, genuinely cares for the Philippians and always has their best interests in mind (2:19–24).

---

[6] The noun *harpagmos* used here can mean something to be "seized," "held on to," or "exploited."

[7] The Greek verb translated "emptied" is *kenoō*, so this act of "emptying" is often called the Kenosis.

[8] Paul does not identify what this "name" is. It may be "Jesus," as the next line suggests. Or Paul may be thinking of YHWH (Yahweh), God's covenant name, which is translated as *kyrios* ("Lord") in the Greek Old Testament (LXX). Paul uses *kyrios* in v. 11 when he says "every tongue will confess that Jesus Christ is *Lord*." The primary point, however, is that one's name indicates one's status and Jesus's status is the highest of them all.

[9] Cf. Gen 35:14; Exod 29:40; Lev 23:13; Num 6:15, 17; 15:5; 28:7, 14; 2 Sam 23:16; 2 Chr 29:35; 2 Tim 4:6.

While Paul hopes to send Timothy shortly, he is now sending Epaphroditus, his spiritual brother, coworker, and fellow soldier. The Philippians had sent Epaphroditus as their messenger to assist Paul, but Epaphroditus became ill and nearly died. God was merciful, however, sparing his life and also sparing Paul and the Philippians the deep sorrow his death would have caused. Paul encourages the church to welcome and honor him and others like him for his sacrifice and suffering (2:25–30).[10]

Warning against False Teachers (3:1–4:1)

After commending faithful servants like Timothy and Epaphroditus, Paul warns the church against *unfaithful* ones, false teachers he calls "dogs," "evil workers," and "those who mutilate the flesh." Paul is almost certainly referring to Judaizers, Jewish Christians who insisted that Gentiles needed to be circumcised and keep the law of Moses to be saved (see pp. 49–50, 74–89). Mutilation is Paul's derogatory term for circumcision, since the ritual—when considered an act that earns salvation—does no spiritual good, but merely maims (cf. Gal 5:12). True "circumcision," meaning the spiritual mark that identifies the true covenant people of God, is faith in Christ and the reception of the Holy Spirit (3:1–3).

Paul acknowledges that he was once someone who put confidence in the "flesh," meaning his identity as a law-observant Jew. But he now realizes that this status is worthless compared to the "surpassing value of knowing Christ Jesus my Lord" (3:8). True righteousness does not come through the law, but through faith in Christ. His only goal now, is "to know him and the power of his resurrection and the fellowship of his sufferings, being conformed to his death" (3:4–11).

Paul recognizes that this goal of knowing Christ is not something he has fully achieved. Putting past failures behind him, he presses forward to pursue "the prize promised by God's heavenly call in Christ Jesus" (3:14). He encourages the Philippians to follow his example rather than the example of those who focus on their own accomplishments. As true believers, our citizenship is not here on earth, but in heaven, and we eagerly await our Savior from there. When he returns, he will transform our lowly bodies into the same kind of glorious body that Christ received at his resurrection. In light of this hope and expectation, Paul encourages his dearly loved brothers and sisters at Philippi—his "joy and crown"—to "stand firm in the Lord" (3:12–4:1).

---

[10] Some scholars suggest Paul says to welcome and honor Epaphroditus because some in the church, unaware of Epaphoditus's illness, had criticized him for remaining so long in Rome.

More Exhortations and Encouragements (4:2–9)

Before concluding his letter, Paul provides several additional pieces of encouragement and exhortation. He first returns to the theme of unity, calling two women who are in conflict, Euodia and Syntyche, to be reconciled (4:2–3). These women must have had significant ministry roles in the church, since he refers to them as "coworkers" who have "contended for the gospel at my side" (4:3). Returning to a central theme of the letter, he calls the church to rejoice and to put aside worry and anxiety (4:4–7). This can be accomplished through an attitude of prayer and trust in God, bringing our needs to him and allowing his surpassing peace to "guard [our] hearts and minds in Christ Jesus" (4:7). Finally, he again calls the church to imitate his example as they dwell on those things that are truly virtuous: what is true, honorable, just, pure, lovely, commendable, morally excellent, and praiseworthy (4:8–9).

Final Thanksgiving for the Gifts Received and Conclusion (4:10–23)

In closing, Paul again praises God and thanks the Philippians for the gifts he has received, which demonstrated their love and concern for him.[11] While grateful, he adds that he does not actually need these things because God supplies everything he needs and has taught him to be content in whatever circumstances he is in. Yet the Philippians have done well, consistently showing themselves to be true partners in ministry from the earliest days. Having received their gift through Epaphroditus, he is "fully supplied." In return, Paul says, "my God will supply all your needs, according to his riches in glory in Christ Jesus" (4:19). Paul concludes by sending greetings from all his coworkers and all the believers with him, "especially those who belong to Caesar's household" (4:22). This reminder of Paul's present situation confirms again that, whatever the trials or circumstances, God is in control, accomplishing his sovereign purposes.

Old Testament Connections

Philippians, like Colossians, 1–2 Thessalonians, and Philemon, has no explicit OT citations. This is likely due in part to the fact that the church at Philippi was almost entirely made up of Gentiles, who were less steeped in the Hebrew Scriptures. It may

[11] See Stephen E. Fowl, "Know Your Context: Giving and Receiving Money in Philippians," *Int* 56 (2002): 45–58.

also result from Paul's especially close relationship with the church. He tends to cite Scripture most when in an apologetic mode: defending the gospel, expressing his authority as an apostle, or affirming the legitimacy of the Gentile mission.

This does not mean that Philippians has no connections to the OT. Paul himself is steeped in Scripture and frequently uses biblical language and imagery. For example, he describes the gift sent by the Philippians as a "fragrant offering, an acceptable sacrifice, pleasing to God" (4:18), recalling OT passages that describe Israel's sacrifices as a sweet-smelling aroma to God (e.g., Exod 29:18, 25, 41; Num 28:2; Ezek 20:41).[12]

Some scholars see echoes of Paul's Adam/Christ analogy in the Christ hymn of 2:6–11 (cf. Rom 5:12–21; 1 Cor 15:20–28). That Jesus was "in the form of God" (Phil 2:6) before his incarnation may correspond to Adam's creation "in the image of God" (Gen 1:26; cf. Col 1:15). While Adam sought to be equal with God (Gen 3:4, 22), Christ did not consider his equality with God something to be used to his advantage (Phil 2:6). Instead of exalting himself, as Adam did, Jesus "emptied" (Phil 2:7) himself and took on the form of a servant.[13] Parallels have also been drawn between the Christ hymn and the suffering servant of Isa 52:13–53:12. Jesus's willingness to take on the form of a servant and to become obedient to the point of death (Phil 2:7–8) recalls the role of the Servant, who "poured out his life unto death" (Isa 53:12 NIV).[14]

As elsewhere, Paul exhibits a very high Christology by identifying OT passages that refer to Yahweh with Jesus himself. The "day of the Lord," the time of God's eschatological judgment, becomes in Philippians "the day of Christ (Jesus)" (1:8, 10; 2:16). Similarly, the conclusion of the Christ hymn, where "every knee will bow . . . and every tongue will confess . . ." (Phil 2:10–11), clearly echoes Isa 45:23, where Yahweh says, "Before me every knee will bow; by me every tongue will swear" (NIV).[15]

---

[12] M. Silva, "Philippians," in *CNTUOT*, 838; M. S. Harmon, "Philippians, Letter to the," in *DNTUOT*, 602–3.

[13] M. D. Hooker, "Philippians 2:6–11," in *Jesus und Paulus. Festschrift für Werner Georg Kümmel zum 70. Geburtstag*, eds. E. E. Ellis and E. Grässer (Göttingen: Vandenhoeck & Ruprecht, 1978), 151–164; Hooker, "Adam *Redivivus*: Philippians 2 Once More," in *The Old Testament in the New: Essays in Honour of J. L. North*, ed. S. Moyise, JSNTSup 189 (Sheffield: Sheffield Academic, 2000) 220–34; Martin, *A Hymn of Christ*, 106–19.

[14] Martin, *A Hymn of Christ*, 183–90.

[15] Silva, "Philippians," 837–38.

Gospel Connections

The themes of joy and rejoicing appear throughout Philippians. Paul uses the noun "joy" (*chara*) and its cognate verbs "rejoice" (*chairō*) and "rejoice with" (*sygchairō)* a total of sixteen times in this short letter! Paul prays with joy whenever he thinks about what God has done in the lives of the Philippians (1:4). He rejoices that the gospel is being preached in Rome, even when it is done with wrong motives (1:18). He can rejoice even at the possibility of his impending death, since that will mean to be with Christ (2:17–18; cf. 1:23). He knows that the Philippians will rejoice when they see their faithful friend Epaphroditus again (2:28) and will welcome him with great joy (2:29). Paul rejoiced in the Lord greatly when he saw the generous gift they sent (4:10).

It is sometimes said that Christian joy is not the absence of sorrow but the presence of God.[16] This letter bears this out. Though Paul is languishing in prison and uncertain about his future, he is not full of fear or dread or anxiety. He is full of joy, because God is present with him and is at work in the lives of his Philippian brothers and sisters. They are his "joy and crown" (4:1). This is why he can say "Rejoice in the Lord always, I will say it again: Rejoice!" (4:4)

Life Connections

One term that is very common in Christian circles is "fellowship." Many people are even aware that the Greek word translated "fellowship" is *koinōnia*. But what is *koinōnia*/fellowship? As a child growing up in a church, fellowship meant one thing to me: food! When the pastor announced that we were going to have a time of fellowship, it meant we were going to eat. We even had a room at our church called "Fellowship Hall," set up with tables and chairs, and right next to the kitchen. And there were different levels of fellowship. The most basic level was "punch and cookies" fellowship. The highest level was the "potluck," a feast where everyone brought food to share.

In reality, the Greek word *koinōnia* has nothing inherently to do with food. It means to share something in common or to work together for a common goal. It is sometimes translated as "participation" or "partnership." This is its meaning in Phil 1:5,

---

[16] This quote is attributed to Janet Erskine Stuart by Elisabeth Elliot in *Suffering Is Never for Nothing* (Nashville: B&H Books, 2019), 14. But I cannot find it in Stuart's writings.

where Paul thanks God for the Philippians because of their "partnership [*koinōnia*] in the gospel from the first day until now." He says this about them because they "are all partners with [him] in grace, both in [his] imprisonment and in the defense and confirmation of the gospel" (1:7). Through their support and encouragement of his ministry, they had become true partners with him. His success was their success, and their success was his. This is the essence of Christian fellowship, recognizing that we are not competing with one another. We are partnering together for the common cause of the gospel.

Interactive Questions

1. When and under what circumstances was the church at Philippi founded?

2. What was Paul's relationship with the church like? In what ways had they supported him?

3. What are the various reasons that Paul wrote the letter?

4. What is the central theme of Philippians?

5. In what ways does Paul say the gospel is advancing despite his imprisonment?

6. What does Paul encourage the Philippians to do in chapter 2:1–11? What role does the hymn to Christ (2:6–11) play in this encouragement to them?

7. In what ways does Paul commend Timothy and Epaphroditus? How does this echo what is said about Christ in 2:5–11?

8. What group does Paul warn against in chapter 3?

9. Paul thanks the Philippines for their gift but then says he doesn't actually need it. Why not?

10. How might reading Philippians benefit Christians today?

Study Resources

Brown, Jeannine K. *Philippians*. TNTC. Downers Grove, IL: IVP Academic, 2022.
Cohick, Lynn H. *Philippians*. SGBC. Grand Rapids: Zondervan, 2013.
Fee, Gordon D. *Paul's Letter to the Philippians*. NICNT. Grand Rapids: Eerdmans, 1995.

Guthrie, George. *Philippians*. ZECNT. Grand Rapids: Zondervan, 2023.

Hawthorne, Gerald F., and Ralph P. Martin. *Philippians*. 2nd ed. WBC. Grand Rapids: Zondervan, 2004.

Osiek, Carolyn. *Philippians*. ANTC. Nashville: Abingdon, 2000.

Silva, Moisés. *Philippians*. 2nd ed. BECNT. Grand Rapids: Baker, 2005.

Thielman, Frank. *Philippians*. NIVAC. Grand Rapids: Zondervan, 1995.

Thurston, Bonnie B., and Judith Ryan. *Philippians*. SP. Collegeville: Liturgical Press, 2003.

10

Colossians

Probably written from Rome ca. 60–62 CE

For God was pleased to have all his fullness dwell in [Christ],
and through him to reconcile everything to himself,
whether things on earth or things in heaven,
by making peace through his blood, shed on the cross.
—Colossians 1:19–20

Outline of Colossians

I. Introduction (1:1–14)
II. The Supremacy of Christ in His Person and Work (1:15–23)
III. Paul's Ministry for the Sake of the Church (1:24–2:7)
IV. Paul's Warning: The Supremacy of Christ over the Heresy (2:8–23)
V. Paul's Exhortations: Living in Light of the Supremacy of Christ (3:1–4:6)
VI. Final Greetings (4:7–18)

Author, Occasion, Message

Author

While Colossians is one of the "disputed" letters of Paul (together with Ephesians, 2 Thessalonians, 1–2 Timothy, and Titus), it is the least disputed of these, with many scholars affirming Pauline authorship.[1] As with the other debated letters, some point especially to differences in language, style, and theology. For example, the presentation of the cosmic Christ in Colossians (1:15–20; 2:9–10) is said to be an advance on Paul's Christology elsewhere. Yet Paul presents a very high Christology elsewhere (e.g., 1 Cor 8:6; Phil 2:6, 10–11) and the minor advances found in Colossians can be attributed to the unique situation addressed in Colossians (see "Occasion," below). Other arguments revolve around the letter's striking similarities to Ephesians, which opponents claim shows that Colossians came from the same post-Pauline circles as Ephesians. But these similarities could just as easily be explained as both coming from Paul, or as the pseudonymous author of Ephesians borrowing from Paul's (authentic) letter to the Colossians.

Occasion

The city of Colossae was located in Phrygia, on the banks of the river Lycus, about 100 miles east of Ephesus. Paul seems not yet to have visited the church, since he speaks of having "heard" of their faith (1:4, 8–9) and of those who have not seen him in person (2:1). The church was likely established by Paul's disciple Epaphras, a native of Colossae (see 1:7–8; 4:12–13; cf. Phlm 23). This was probably during Paul's time in Ephesus on his third missionary journey, when "all the residents of Asia, both Jews and Greeks, heard the word of the Lord" (Acts 19:10).

At the time of writing Colossians, Epaphras is with Paul (4:12), presumably in Rome during Paul's first Roman imprisonment (see sidebar 9.1, The Provenance of the Prison Epistles). In his letter to Philemon, Paul refers to Epaphras as a "fellow prisoner" (v. 23), though whether Epaphras's imprisonment with Paul was voluntary or compulsory is uncertain. Tychicus, another of Paul's associates, is carrying the letter and bringing news to the church about Paul and Epaphras (4:7–8).

---

[1] See D. A. Carson and Douglas J. Moo, *An Introduction to the New Testament*, 2nd ed. (Grand Rapids: Zondervan, 2005), 517–21.

Message

Epaphras may have come to Rome to get Paul's advice about a growing problem in the church, since much of the letter appears to be Paul's response to false teaching. The exact nature of this teaching is uncertain, but Paul alludes to various features:

- claims to higher wisdom and knowledge (2:2–3, 23)
- empty philosophical speculation based on human tradition and the "elements of the world" rather than on Christ (2:8, 20)
- circumcision rites (2:11)
- Jewish dietary and Sabbath observances (2:16)
- the worship of angels (2:18)
- appealing to spiritual powers and authorities (2:10, 15, 20)
- false humility (2:23)
- severe asceticism and self-abasement (2:21–23)

There has been much scholarly debate on the background to this heresy. Some of the terms used to describe it—"wisdom," "knowledge," "philosophy," "fullness," and "elements of the world"—suggest Greek or early gnostic thought (see Ancient Connections 10.1: Gnosticism). Others—circumcision, festivals and Sabbath days—point to Jewish influence. Because of these diverse components, some scholars question whether there was a single "Colossian heresy." Paul may be warning against a variety of false beliefs.[2] Most scholars, however, continue to believe Paul is responding to a specific belief system threatening to undermine the church. Religion in Asia Minor at this time was quite syncretistic, blending Jewish and Greek traditions with belief in folk religion and magic.[3] For Paul the central problem with the heresy is that it devalued Christ by stressing a spirituality based on esoteric wisdom, legalistic practices, Jewish rituals, and appealing to angelic beings or spiritual intermediaries. Paul responds by emphasizing the supremacy of Christ. He is the creator and sustainer of all things, the image of the invisible God. All God's "fullness" dwells in him. He has dominion over all spiritual rulers and authorities. He alone is the Savior who brought reconciliation between God and humanity.

---

[2] See Morna D. Hooker, "Were There False Teachers in Colossae?," in *Christ and Spirit in the New Testament: : Studies in Honour of Charles Francis Digby Moule*, ed. Barnabas Lindars and Stephen S. Smallley (Cambridge: Cambridge University Press, 1973), 315–31.

[3] See Clinton E. Arnold, *The Colossian Syncretism,* WUNT 77 (Tübingen: Mohr Siebeck, 1995).

ANCIENT CONNECTIONS 10.1: GNOSTICISM

Gnosticism is the name given to a religious tradition that arose in the Mediterranean region in the late first and early second centuries CE. Although its precise origins are unknown, Gnosticism appears to have arisen in the context of the dualistic worldview found in Platonic philosophy. Plato considered the physical world to be an illusion and true reality to be the world of ideas. Gnostics drew a similar distinction between the corrupt and illusory physical world and the true world of pure spirit.

The gnostic foundation myth concerned the supreme god, or *plērōma* ("fullness"), who was wholly transcendent and pure spirit. Emanating from this god were many *aeons*, or lesser spirit beings. One of these (sometimes called the demiurge) created the fallen material world. In contrast to Judaism and Christianity, where God's physical creation is good and human beings bear the image of God, Gnosticism saw the material world as evil and the physical body as something to escape.

Gnōsis means "knowledge," and gnostics believed salvation or enlightenment came through secret knowledge of their true spiritual identity and heavenly origin. Jesus Christ became in Gnosticism one *aeon*, or emanation, sent to teach humans about their true nature. Most gnostics rejected the doctrine of the incarnation (that God became a human being in the person of Jesus Christ), the saving significance of his death on the cross, and his bodily resurrection from the dead.

While we don't see full-blown Gnosticism in the New Testament period, some NT writings, especially 1 Corinthians, Colossians, Gospel of John, and 1 John, respond to ideas and beliefs that came to be associated with Gnosticism. These beliefs are sometimes called "early" or "incipient" Gnosticism. By the second century, Gnosticism had become the greatest theological challenge to the early church. Early church fathers, like Justin Martyr (ca.100–168), Irenaeus (ca. 130–202), Clement of Alexandria (ca. 150–216), Tertullian (ca. 155–230), and Origen (ca. 182–251), wrote against gnostics and their beliefs. Until the twentieth century, most of our knowledge about Gnosticism came from these opponents. The Nag Hammadi Codices, discovered in 1945 in Egypt, are a collection of early gnostic writings that provide primary-source accounts of their beliefs. Some important gnostic works include the Gospel of Thomas, the Apocryphon of James, the Gospel of Philip, and the Gospel of Truth.

For further study, see Kurt Rudolph, "Gnosticism," in *ABD* 2:1033–40; Kurt Rudolph, *Gnosis: The Nature and History of Gnosticism* (San Francisco: Harper and Row, 1984); Birger A. Pearson, *Ancient Gnosticism: Traditions and Literature* (Minneapolis: Fortress, 2007); James M. Robinson, ed., *The Nag Hammadi Library*, 3rd rev. ed. (San Francisco: HarperSanFrancisco, 1990).

Interpretive Overview

Introduction (1:1–14)

Paul identifies himself as "an apostle of Christ Jesus by God's will" together with "Timothy our brother." The recipients are "the saints in Christ at Colossae." Paul thanks God for the three great Christian virtues, faith in Christ Jesus, love for all God's people, and hope that provides assurance of heaven. This hope comes from the gospel they received, which is bearing fruit throughout the world. This gospel was brought to them by Epaphras, who has informed Paul about their faith and love. Paul consistently prays for them, asking God to give them spiritual wisdom and insight. This will enable them to live a life that is pleasing to God, to bear spiritual fruit, and to persevere until they receive their promised inheritance. This inheritance is in fact already theirs, since they have been rescued from the realm of darkness and transferred into the kingdom of God's Son, who redeemed them and forgave their sins.

The Supremacy of Christ in His Person and Work (1:15–23)

With this mention of the salvation we have in Christ, Paul launches into one of the most exalted descriptions of the person and work of Christ in the NT. He is the image of the invisible God, meaning he perfectly reveals who God is (1:15). He is supreme over all creation; everything that exists was created by him, through him, and for him. He existed before anything else and holds it all together (1:16–17). He is the head of the church, and his resurrection was the beginning of the end-time resurrection. Through his sacrificial death on the cross, he achieved peace, reconciling everything in heaven and on earth to himself (1:18–20). While previously we were alienated from God, now we have been reconciled to God through faith in Christ (1:21–23).

Paul's Ministry for the Sake of the Church (1:24–2:7)

It is this gospel message that Paul now proclaims. He finds great joy even in suffering, since this suffering completes "what is lacking in Christ's afflictions" (1:24). This does not mean that Jesus's death on the cross was insufficient, but that this salvation was incomplete until the good news was proclaimed to the ends of the earth. Paul's commission to make known to the Gentiles the great mystery of "Christ in you, the hope of glory" completes the work of Christ (1:25–27). This is why Paul strives so hard to see believers like those in Colossae and Laodicea achieve spiritual maturity and full knowledge of Christ, because in Christ "are hidden all the treasures of wisdom and knowledge" (1:28–2:3). Paul's goal for them is that just as they were firmly rooted when they received Christ Jesus, so they would continue to grow stronger so that they would not be deceived by false teachers (2:4–7).

Paul's Warning: The Supremacy of Christ over the Heresy (2:8–23)

Paul's mention of attempts to deceive the Colossians (2:4) brings him to the heart of his message. He warns them against being taken captive "through philosophy . . . based on human tradition" (2:8). The opponents were evidently claiming that Christ's person and work were not sufficient. Salvation also demanded special knowledge and certain rituals and practices. Paul counters that "the entire fullness of God's nature dwells bodily in Christ" (2:9). The believer's identification with Christ in his death, burial, and resurrection results in the forgiveness of sins and new life in him. The debt owed has been completely cancelled and nailed to his cross (2:10–14). Christ's absolute triumph over all spiritual rulers and authorities means that dependence on any human rules and regulations—such as what to eat, or what days or festivals to keep, or rituals to perform—are a mere shadow of the reality that is Christ (2:15–19). Dying with Christ means dying to the spiritual powers of this world and to the regulations and rituals meant to placate them. They are all destined to perish. While these things might have a superficial appearance of spiritual wisdom, they have no ultimate value (2:20–23).

Paul's Exhortations: Living in Light of the Supremacy of Christ (3:1–4:6)

Having described the superiority of Christ to any human-made religion, Paul next turns to the practical application of this spiritual truth. Through their identification with Christ in his life, death, and resurrection, believers have died with him and have been raised and exalted with him to God's right hand. His resurrection life is now theirs. This new spiritual status must be lived out by putting to death the evil and sinful thoughts and behaviors that characterized their old fallen life. As the new creation, the image of God is being renewed in believers and human divisions such as those between Jews and Gentiles, and slave and free, are eliminated (3:1–11).

As God's chosen, holy, and dearly loved people, believers take off their old selves and put on the qualities of the new creation, including compassion, kindness, humility, gentleness, and patience. They forgive others as God forgave them. They love, as God loved them. The peace he brought should rule their hearts, uniting them with others in worship and song. And everything they say and do should be in the name of the Lord Jesus (3:12–17).

As he did in Ephesians, Paul applies the general truths of our status in Christ to relationships in the Greco-Roman household. These relate to husbands and wives, parents and children, and masters and slaves (3:18–4:1).

In a series of final instructions, Paul encourages the Colossians to be devoted to prayer and thanksgiving. He asks especially that they pray for opportunities for him to further proclaim the good news of salvation. He encourages them to act wisely towards outsiders. God is constantly bringing people into their lives, and Christians should make the most of these opportunities to share the gospel (4:2–6).

ANCIENT CONNECTIONS 10.2: VICE AND VIRTUE LISTS

Readers are sometimes puzzled when they come across lists of good and bad behaviors in the New Testament letters. For example, Col 3:5–8 lists a series of vices that believers should "put away," including sexual immorality, impurity, lust, evil desire, and greed. This is followed in Col 3:12–14 by a list of virtues to "put on": compassion, kindness, humility, gentleness, and patience. Similarly, in Gal 5:19–23 the vices, called the "works of the flesh," are set in contrast with the virtues, which are the "fruit of the Spirit." Similar lists of vices and virtues are found throughout the NT letters: Rom 1:29–31; 1 Cor 6:9–10; 2 Cor 6:3–10; 12:20–21; Eph 4:1–3, 31–32; 6:10–17; Phil 4:4–9; 1 Tim 1:8–11; 2 Tim 3:1–5; 1 Pet 2:1; 4:3–4; 2 Pet 1:5–7.

While such lists may seem a bit odd today, they were a common feature in the moral discourse of the Greco-Roman world.[4] For example, the biographer

[4] See John T. Fitzgerald, "Virtue/Vice Lists," in *ABD* 6:857–59.

and philosopher Diogenes Laertius (3rd c. CE) writes, "Amongst the virtues some are primary, some are subordinate to these. The following are the primary: wisdom, courage, justice, temperance. Particular virtues are magnanimity, continence, endurance, presence of mind, good counsel." Among vices he notes that "folly, cowardice, injustice, profligacy are accounted primary; but incontinence, stupidity, ill-advisedness are subordinate" (Diogenes Laertius, *Lives of Eminent Philosophers: Zeno* 7.92–93, 110–12).

Paul's lists of vices and virtues have similarities to these Greco-Roman lists, but they are also distinctly Christian. While Greco-Roman vice lists commonly describe the low moral character of the uneducated and ignoble masses, in Paul they portray those who live in the flesh, that is, according to the values of this present fallen world. Virtues, by contrast, do not describe those of the upper or noble classes, as in much Greco-Roman literature, but rather those sinners who have been sanctified in Christ and are now led and guided by the Holy Spirit (cf. 1 Cor 6:9–11).

Final Greetings (4:7–18)

Paul concludes his letter with a series of greetings and personal notes. Many of these have parallels to the letter of Philemon, indicating that these two letters are coming to Colossae together. Tychicus, who is likely the letter-carrier, and Onesimus, Philemon's runaway slave (see "Occasion" and "Message" in chap. 11, pp. 216–17), will report to them on Paul's situation. Paul sends greetings from a number of his associates, providing interesting bits of information. It is here, for example, that we learn that John Mark was Barnabas's cousin (4:10) and that Luke was a physician and a Gentile (4:11, 14). We also learn that Epaphras, who likely founded the churches in Colossae, Laodicea, and Hierapolis, is with Paul in Rome (4:12–13). We also learn that this letter is to be sent to Laodicea and that another letter (possibly Ephesians) is coming from Laodicea (see "Occasion" in chap. 8, p. 181). This illustrates the manner in which Paul's letters were copied and circulated. A somewhat cryptic personal message about completing a ministry task is given to a man name Archippus, who may be the son of Philemon (see "Occasion" and "Message" in chap. 11, pp. 216–17). Paul ends by taking pen in hand and writing a final greeting and signature with his own hand (4:18).

Old Testament Connections

There are no explicit citations from the Old Testament in either Colossians or Philemon. As noted above, however, the false teaching that had sprung up in Colossae had Jewish legalism as a key component. Paul therefore counters the heresy by pointing to the supremacy of Christ. He is the fulfillment of the OT law and the consummation of Judaism. This is emphasized in many ways in Colossians. Whereas under the old covenant God's wisdom was expressed in Torah, in the new covenant Christ is the personification of divine wisdom. "In him are hidden all the treasures of wisdom and knowledge" (2:3; cf. 1:15–20). In the OT, God's presence and divine glory dwelt in the Jerusalem Temple. In the age of salvation, Christ is the new and greater temple, the place where God's presence dwells. "For God was pleased to have all his fullness dwell in him" (1:19; cf. 2:9). Under the old covenant, festivals, new moons, Sabbath days, and dietary laws were to be kept. But these things were a mere "shadow of what was to come." In the new age of salvation, their "substance" and reality are found in Christ (2:16–17). The first exodus resulted in Israel's redemption and their inheritance in the land of Israel. The eschatological new exodus accomplished through Christ's life, death, and resurrection results in the redemption of his church and our inheritance of an eternal kingdom. "He has rescued us from the domain of darkness and transferred us into the kingdom of the Son he loves" (1:12–14).[5]

Gospel Connections

The central theme of Colossians is the supremacy of Christ, his status and authority over all things in heaven and on earth. While the deity of Christ is taught in many passages throughout the NT, it is perhaps most clearly expressed in three great passages: John 1:1–18; Heb 1:1–4; and Col 1:15–20. And these three say remarkably similar things about Christ. All three, for example, point to Jesus as God's self-revelation. The Prologue of John (1:1–18) begins with the statement that the "Word" (*logos*) was both "with God" and "was God" (John 1:1). He is a unique person distinct

---

[5] For these and other examples, see Christopher A. Beetham, *Echoes of Scripture in the Letter of Paul to the Colossians* (Leiden: Brill, 2008), esp. 251; G. K. Beale, "Colossians and Philemon, Letters to the," in *DNTUOT*, 110–114; Gordon D. Fee, "Old Testament Intertexuality in Colossians," in *History and Exegesis: New Testament Essays in Honor of Dr. E. Earle Ellis for his 80th birthday*, ed. Sang-Won Son (New York: T&T Clark, 2006), 201–21.

from the Father but is himself fully God. The Prologue concludes by asserting that while no one has ever seen God, the Son "who is himself God and is at the Father's side—he has revealed him" (John 1:18). Colossians 1:15 similarly says that Jesus is "the image [*eikōn*] of the invisible God." As in John 1:18, Jesus makes the invisible God visible and transcendent one knowable. Hebrews 1:3 says something very similar by identifying Jesus as "the radiance of God's glory and the exact expression of his nature." Both the terms "image" (*eikōn*) of Col 1:15 and "exact expression" (*charaktēr*) of Heb 1:3 carry the sense of a true and accurate representation of God. Paul reiterates this same point in Col 1:19 and 2:9, when he says that all the "fullness" (*plērōma*) of God dwells in the Son. As Jesus says in John 14:9, "The one who has seen me has seen the Father."

In addition to describing Jesus as God's perfect self-revelation, all three passages identify the Son as the creator of the universe. John 1:3 says, "All things were created through him, and apart from him not one thing was created that has been created" (John 1:3; cf. 1:10). Hebrews 1:2 asserts that God "made the universe through him" and Col 1:16 that "everything was created by him, in heaven and on earth, the visible and the invisible, whether thrones or dominions or rulers or authorities—all things have been created through him and for him." Colossians and Hebrews describe him as not only creator, but sustainer of all things: "By him all things hold together" (Col 1:17); "sustaining all things by his powerful word" (Heb 1:3).

Third, all three passages describe Jesus as the savior of the world, whose death overcame sin's destructive power and reconciled human beings to God. In Hebrews this is expressed as the purification from sins through Christ's once-for-all sacrifice as our great high priest (Heb 1:3; 7:27). In Colossians, the Son reconciles all things in heaven and on earth to himself through his blood shed on the cross (Col 1:20). And in John 1:12–14, the Word brings grace and truth and so restores humanity to its status as children of God.

The fact that this remarkably high Christology comes in the writings of three different authors coming from three different communities in the early church confirms that Christ's deity was not a fringe belief or a novelty developed by later Christians under pagan influence. It was rather a core belief widely accepted and affirmed throughout the first century church.

Life Connections

There is a saying in English: "Don't be so heavenly minded that you're no earthly good." This is usually meant to be a criticism of those who focus on their internal spiritual life to such an extent that they never do anything practical to help others. But Paul takes a totally different perspective in his letter to the Colossians. He explicitly says to be heavenly minded: "So if you have been raised with Christ, seek the things above, where Christ is, seated at the right hand of God. Set your minds on things above, not on earthly things" (Col 3:1–2). By identifying with Christ in his life, death, resurrection, and ascension, we take on his resurrection life. The result can be a radically changed life: "Therefore, as God's chosen ones, holy and dearly loved, put on compassion, kindness, humility, gentleness, and patience, bearing with one another and forgiving one another if anyone has a grievance against another. Just as the Lord has forgiven you, so you are also to forgive. Above all, put on love, which is the perfect bond of unity" (Col 3:12–14). Living with a heavenly mindset does not mean a "do-nothing" spirituality. It means the restoration of the image of God in our lives, which then overflows in attitudes and actions that produce enormous earthly good.

Interactive Questions

1. Who was Epaphras and when was the church in Colossae likely started?

2. What were the main features of the "Colossian heresy"?

3. Why is it so difficult to specifically identify the heresy?

4. How does Paul respond to this false teaching? What do we learn here about who Jesus is and what he accomplished for us?

5. What does Paul mean when he says that he is completing "what is lacking" in Christ's suffering for the church? What could possibly be lacking in Christ's work?

6. In what way is the letter to the Colossians closely linked with the letter to Philemon?

7. How might reading Colossians benefit Christians today?

Study Resources

Beale, G. K. *Colossians and Philemon*. BECNT. Grand Rapids: Baker, 2019.

Bruce, F.F. *The Epistles to the Colossians, to Philemon, and to the Ephesians*. NICNT. 2nd rev. ed. Grand Rapids: Eerdmans, 1984.

Dunn, James D. G. *The Epistles to the Colossians and to Philemon*. NIGTC. Grand Rapids: Eerdmans, 1996.

Garland, David. *Colossians, Philemon*. NIVAC. Grand Rapids: Zondervan, 1998.

McKnight, Scot. *The Letter to the Colossians*. NICNT. Grand Rapids: Eerdmans, 2018.
Pao, David W. *Colossians and Philemon*. ZECNT. Grand Rapids: Zondervan, 2012.
Thompson, Marianne Meye. *Colossians & Philemon*. THNTC. Grand Rapids: Eerdmans, 2005.
Wright, N. T. *Colossians and Philemon*. TNTC. Grand Rapids: Eerdmans, 1989.

11

Philemon

Probably written from Rome ca. 60–62 CE

I, Paul, as an elderly man and now also as a prisoner of
Christ Jesus, appeal to you for my son, Onesimus.
—Philemon 9b–10a

Outline

I. Introduction (1–3)
II. Thanksgiving and Prayer (4–7)
III. Appeal on behalf of Onesimus (8–21)
IV. Conclusion (22–25)

Author, Occasion, Message

Author

The author claims to be "Paul, a prisoner of Christ Jesus," and the authenticity of this authorship is almost universally accepted by scholars.

Occasion

The letter to Philemon is the shortest of Paul's letters in the NT. It is closely related to Colossians and was almost certainly carried with it: (1) In Col 4:7–9, Onesimus, the subject of this letter, is said to be accompanying Tychicus to Colossae. (2) Epaphras, the founder of the church in Colossae, heads the greetings in Philemon 23. (3) Mark, Aristarchus, Demas, and Luke are all referred to as Paul's associates in both letters (Col 4:10, 14; Phlm 24). Archippus, one of the addressees in Philemon (probably Philemon's son) is sent a special message in Col 4:17.

The traditional understanding of the letter is this: Paul writes to Philemon, a leader in the church at Colossae, concerning his slave Onesimus. Onesimus had run away, perhaps absconding with some of his master's money (see v. 18), and eventually ended up in Rome. There he met the apostle Paul, who led him to faith in Christ (v. 10). Realizing that he must right his wrong, Onesimus is returning to Philemon. Paul therefore writes this letter of intercession and reconciliation for Onesimus, appealing to Philemon "our dear friend and coworker" (v. 1) to forgive Onesimus and welcome him back as a new brother in Christ.

There are some alternate interpretations of this occasion. (1) Paul may be in prison in Ephesus rather than in Rome, a location much closer to Colossae.[1] (2) Onesimus may not have met Paul by accident in Rome. He may have intentionally sought him out there, knowing Paul's relationship to his master. (3) A most innovative and elaborate proposal was made by John Knox, following suggestions made by E. J. Goodspeed. Knox claimed that Archippus, not Philemon, was the owner of Onesimus. Paul is writing to Philemon, the overseer of the Lycus Valley churches who lives in Laodicea, and is asking Philemon to intervene with Archippus to release Onesimus to pursue Christian ministry. The letter mentioned in Col 4:16 that is coming from Laodicea is therefore Philemon, which was preserved in the canon because it was the charter of freedom for Onesimus, who later became bishop of the influential church in Ephesus.[2] Though fascinating and creative, this explanation has not found wide acceptance among scholars.

---

[1] See R. E. Brown, *An Introduction to the New Testament* (New York: Doubleday, 1997), 507–8; N. T. Wright, *The Epistles of Paul to the Colossians and to Philemon*, TNTC (Grand Rapids: Eerdmans, 1986), 37–39, 165, 169; Wright, *Paul and the Faithfulness of God* (Minneapolis: Fortress, 2013), 1:7–8.

[2] John Knox, *Philemon among the Letters of Paul* (New York: Abingdon, 1935).

Message

At first sight this shortest of Paul's letters may seem out of place in the New Testament. Why should such a brief, personal, and situational letter be included in the great foundational documents of Christianity? Yet the message of Philemon is revolutionary, representing the very heart of gospel.[3] In the Greco-Roman world, slaves were mere property, to be used, abused, or discarded at the whim of their masters. The light of the gospel shines into this dark world and brings the hope of redemption and reconciliation. What is considered property should be seen as a person bearing the image of God. In Christ, the slave becomes "the Lord's freedman" (1 Cor 7:22), "no longer a slave but a son" (Gal 4:7), "God's children . . . heirs of God and coheirs with Christ" (Rom 8:16–17). Paul refers to Onesimus as "my son" and "my very own heart" and as Philemon's "dearly loved brother" (Phlm 10, 16). Dividing lines, social divisions, and prejudices that seem woven into the fabric of society are destined to be shattered in light of the transforming power of the kingdom of God, where "There is no Jew or Greek, slave or free, male and female; since you are all one in Christ Jesus" (Gal 3:28).

Interpretive Overview

Introduction (1–3)

Paul identifies the letter as coming from himself and "Timothy our brother," but he is clearly the primary author. Paul's status as "a prisoner" indicates his present house arrest, but he does not say a prisoner of Rome, but "of Christ Jesus," indicating his true allegiance. The letter is addressed to "Philemon our dear friend and coworker, to Apphia our sister, to Archippus our fellow soldier, and to the church that meets in your home." Apphia is probably Philemon's wife and Archippus his son. While the letter would likely have been read before the whole church, Paul's use of the singular pronouns "I" and "you" throughout shows that the letter primarily concerns Philemon and himself.

---

[3] This is why N. T. Wright places his chapter on Philemon at the beginning of his two-volume magnum opus on the apostle, *Paul and the Faithfulness of God* (Minneapolis: Fortress, 2013). See chap. 1, "Return of the Runaway?," 3–74.

Thanksgiving and Prayer (4–7)

Paul follows his greeting with thanksgiving and prayer, a common feature in Paul's letters. He thanks God for Philemon's faith in Christ and love for other believers. His prayer is that what they share in the faith would give Philemon a deeper understanding of the true partnership (*koinōnia*) that believers have in Christ. This is already evident in Philemon's love for others, which has refreshed the hearts of God's people.

Appeal on behalf of Onesimus (8–21)

Paul next turns to his explicit appeal. While he has authority (as an apostle) to command Philemon to do what is right with reference to Onesimus, he instead makes his request to Philemon on the basis of Christian love. As an "old man" he appeals to Philemon for his "son," whom he (spiritually) gave birth to while in prison. In a play on words with Onesimus's name, which means "useful," Paul points out that while Onesimus was once useless to Philemon, he has now become useful to both Philemon and to Paul. In fact, by sending Onesimus back, Paul feels like he is sending his own heart away. He would have preferred to keep Onesimus to aid him in his ministry. But it is right for Paul to send him back, to show the reconciling power of the gospel. While Philemon briefly lost a slave, he has gained back a brother in Christ (vv. 8–16).

Since Onesimus is now a partner in ministry, Paul appeals to Philemon to welcome him as he would welcome Paul himself. If Onesimus owes Philemon anything, Paul will pay it back himself—but then noting that Philemon actually owes Paul his very life (presumably he led Philemon to Christ). As Philemon had previously refreshed the hearts of other believers (v. 7), so Paul asks him to refresh his heart. Finally, he expresses confidence that Philemon will do not only what he asks, but even more (vv. 17–21). Some commentators think the "even more" is a request to give Onesimus his freedom and perhaps to send him back to work with Paul.[4]

Conclusion (22–25)

Before wrapping up the letter, Paul expresses his hope through their prayers for his release and restoration to them, asking Philemon to prepare a guest room for him.

---

[4] See, for example, James D. G. Dunn, *The Epistles to the Colossians and to Philemon*, NIGTC (Grand Rapids: Eerdmans, 1996), 345nn6–7. On the radical nature of Paul's request in light of the social conventions of the day (and implications for Paul's theology), see Wright, *Paul and the Faithfulness of God*, 1:3–74.

Paul then concludes with greetings from Epaphras, who is with Paul in prison, as well as Mark, Aristarchus, Demas, and Luke (23–24; cf. Col 4:9–17), and a benediction that "the grace of the Lord Jesus be with your spirit" (v. 25).

SIDEBAR 11.1: WHY DOES PAUL NOT CONDEMN SLAVERY?

It is disturbing to many modern readers that the Bible does not condemn slavery and in many cases allows and even condones it (Lev 25:39–55; Deut 23:15–16). Throughout history biblical statements have been used to justify and defend this evil practice. While Paul encourages masters to treat their slaves fairly and with compassion, he does not explicitly call for their emancipation nor the abolishment of the institution of slavery. He instead tells slaves to obey and submit to their masters (Eph 6:5–9; Col 3:22–4:1; 1 Tim 6:1–2; cf. 1 Pet 2:18–20).

How are we to explain this? While we can certainly wish that Paul would have written more forcefully against slavery, it is important to recognize the societal limitations he was under. The Roman economy was built on the backs of slaves. By some estimates, as much as 20 to 30 percent of the Roman population were slaves. Maintaining this institution was viewed as essential to the political, cultural, and economic survival of Roman civilization. Opposition to slavery was considered treason and a threat to the social order. Nor was this an abstract threat. There had been three major slave revolts in the Roman Republic, in the second and first centuries BCE, resulting in horrific casualties.[5] For Paul to speak out explicitly against slavery would likely have resulted in his immediate arrest and execution as an insurrectionist.

Not only were there societal limits on Paul, but there were also vocational ones. From Paul's perspective, the end times were dawning, and the time was short (1 Cor 7:29; 10:11). He had been commissioned by Christ to preach the gospel to all nations.[6] In his view, the best way to accomplish this was by boldly preaching the gospel, while at the same time living as a law-abiding citizen and obeying the authorities that existed (Rom 13:1–7; 1 Thess 4:11). While later Christians would be called by God to preach emancipation, Paul's vocation was to preach the gospel.

---

[5] Known as the Servile Wars (135–132; 104–100; and 73–71 BCE).

[6] Rom 1:5, 13–16; 11:13; 15:16; Gal 1:16; 2:2; 2:7–10; Eph 3:1, 6, 8; 1 Tim 2:7; 2 Tim 4:17; Acts 9:15; 22:21; 26:17.

At the same time, there are clear indications that Paul opposed slavery and sought ways to undermine it. He calls himself a "slave of Christ" (Rom 1:1) and says that slaves and their owners serve the same master (1 Cor 7:22–23; Eph 6:9; Col 4:1). He asserts that "in Christ" there was no slave or free (Gal 3:28) and insists that slaves have the same dignity as their masters (Col 3:22–24). He encourages Philemon to welcome Onesimus back "no longer as a slave, but more than a slave—as a dearly loved brother," implying that he should set Onesimus free. He implies the same thing when he says he is confident "you will do even more than I say" (Phlm 16, 21). While he calls slaves to be content in whatever position God has placed them, he encourages them to gain their freedom if they are able (1 Cor 7:21). While called by God to a different task and limited by the cultural norms in which he lived, Paul was an abolitionist at heart.

Interactive Questions

1. What is the traditional understanding of the occasion of Philemon? Who is Onesimus? Who is Philemon? What is Paul's purpose in writing?

2. What radically different proposal did John Knox make about the occasion of the letter?

3. In what ways does Paul appeal to Philemon?

4. What does Paul want Philemon to do?

5. Should Paul have spoken more strongly in condemnation of slavery? Why or why not?

Study Resources

See "Study Resources" in chap. 10 (pp. 213–14).

PASTORAL LETTERS

1 Timothy

Titus

2 Timothy

12

1 Timothy, Titus, 2 Timothy

> I have fought the good fight, I have finished the race, I have kept the faith. There is reserved for me the crown of righteousness, which the Lord, the righteous Judge, will give me on that day, and not only to me, but to all those who have loved his appearing.
>
> —2 Timothy 4:7–8

The two letters to Timothy and one to Titus are called the "Pastoral Epistles" because they concern the pastoral care and oversight of churches and qualifications for leaders.

Author, Recipients, Occasion

Author

Paul's authorship of the Pastoral Epistles has been questioned more than any of his other letters. Most scholars who view them as non-Pauline assume that they were not written to deceive, but rather to honor the apostle's legacy (see "Pseudepigraphy and the Letters of Paul," pp. 16–17 in chap. 1). The challenges to Pauline authorship are primarily related to chronology, language, and theology. (1) Chronologically, Acts ends with Paul in prison in Rome, and there is no account given of his release and subsequent travels. Since the journeys described in the Pastorals don't fit well into the Acts narrative, some argue that these letters were written by a later writer who fabricated the historical references. (2) In terms of vocabulary and style, critics of Pauline authorship claim there are a high number of non-Pauline words in the Pastorals, and the Greek style differs from Paul's elsewhere.[1] (3) There are also various claimed theological differences between the Pastorals and the authentic Pauline letters. For example, the attitude toward the OT law is more positive in the Pastorals, where the author says, "we know that the law is good, provided one uses it legitimately" (1 Tim 1:8). Church organization is also more institutional than in Paul's day, with formalized offices like elders, bishops, and deacons. Finally, in the Pastorals, the gospel message is less the dynamic power of salvation (Rom 1:16–17; 1 Cor 1:18) and has become "sound doctrine," a collection of beliefs to be protected and preserved (1 Tim 1:10–11; 6:20; 2 Tim 1:12, 14; 4:3; Titus 1:9; 2:1).

None of these claims point conclusively to a post-Pauline context. (1) In terms of chronology, there are strong indications that Paul expected to be released from his (first) Roman imprisonment (Phil 1:25; 2:24). Judging from the initial hearings described in Acts, the charge against him would likely have been viewed by the Roman authorities as a religious debate within Judaism rather than a criminal offense warranting capital punishment (Acts 24:12–13; 25:10–11, 25; 26:30–31). If Paul was released, the journeys described in the Pastorals make good sense. (2) Differences in style and vocabulary are notoriously difficult to assess, especially with such a small database. The differences could be attributed to the unique content of the Pastorals and/or the use of a secretary, who left a strong imprint on the style of the Pastorals.[2] (3) While we do see some theological development in the Pastorals, these differences are not enough to be convincingly judged as non-Pauline. (a) For example, the perspective on the law is not substantially different from elsewhere in Paul. Consider Rom 7:12, where Paul assesses the law as "holy and just and good"—though it was never intended to bring salvation. Positively, all of Paul's main theological themes occur in the Pastorals. (b) Nor is church leadership that much more formalized than elsewhere in Paul. We see, for example, deacons in the undisputed letters (Phil 1:1;

[1] See especially the classic study by P. N. Harrison, *The Problem of the Pastoral Epistles* (London: Oxford University Press, 1921).

[2] See Donald Guthrie, *The Pastoral Epistles and the Mind of Paul* (London: Tyndale Press, 1956), 6–16. For more recent statistical analyses, see D. A. Carson and Douglas J. Moo, *An Introduction to the New Testament*, 2nd ed. (Grand Rapids: Zondervan, 2005), 555–61.

Rom 16:1). The fact that senior leaders in the church are called both elders (Titus 1:5–7) and overseers (1 Tim 3:1) in the Pastorals suggests that these offices are not yet formalized throughout the church. (c) Finally, a perspective on the gospel as a legacy to be guarded is not surprising in light of Paul's circumstances. A shift from innovation toward preservation is natural as Paul sees the end of his life drawing near and the need to pass the torch to the next generation.

The strongest support for the authenticity of the Pastorals are Paul's personal comments, such as his request for Timothy to bring the cloak that he left in Troas with Carpus (2 Tim 4:12) and the comment that he left Trophimus sick at Miletus (4:20). These do not fit well with the view that this is a testament to honor Paul rather than a forgery intended to deceive. Furthermore, self-denigrating remarks like "I am the worst of [sinners]" (1 Tim 1:15) are unlikely to have been introduced by a later admirer. As pastoral counsel to these two close disciples, the Pastorals work well. As pseudonymous letters meant to celebrate or clarify the apostle's legacy, they are less easy to explain.

Recipients

Timothy

According to Luke's account in Acts, Timothy was a native of Lystra, the product of a mixed marriage between a Greek father and a Jewish mother (Acts 16:1). Paul may have led him to Christ on his visit to Lystra during his first missionary journey (Acts 14:8–20). When Paul passed through Lystra on his second journey, he was so impressed with Timothy that he took him along. In light of Timothy's Jewish heritage, Paul had him circumcised so as not to cause offense among the Jews in that area (Acts 16:1–3). Timothy became Paul's closest disciple (Phil 2:20–22) and was with him for much of his subsequent ministry: in Macedonia and Achaia on Paul's second journey (Acts 17:14, 15; 18:5); in Ephesus, Macedonia, and Achaia on his third journey (Acts 19:22); on his return trip to Jerusalem after the third journey (20:4); and during Paul's first Roman imprisonment (Phil 1:1; Col 1:1; Phlm 1). Paul mentions Timothy as coauthor of six letters (1 Thess 1:1; 2 Thess 1:1; 2 Cor 1:1; Phil 1:1; Col 1:1; Phlm 1), and he is with Paul during the writing of two others (Rom 16:21; 1 Cor 4:17). Timothy had rich pastoral gifts (Phil 2:19–24) but may have been somewhat timid and reserved by nature. When Paul sends Timothy to Corinth, he warns the Corinthians not to mistreat him (1 Cor 16:10–11). And in the Pastorals, Paul repeatedly spurs him on to a greater sense of authority and to greater action (1 Tim 1:3; 4:11; 5:7; 6:2; 2 Tim 1:6–7; 3:14; 4:2, 5).

Titus

Though we know less about Titus than Timothy (he is not mentioned in Acts), there are a number of things we can discern from Paul's letters: (1) He was likely a convert of Paul's, since Paul refers to him as "my true son" (Titus 1:4). (2) He was a Gentile. In Gal 2:1–3 Paul uses the fact that Titus was accepted as a true believer by the Jerusalem apostles to show that uncircumcised Gentiles are saved by faith. (3) He must have been quite mature spiritually and a very trusted associate. Paul sent Titus to represent him in Corinth during some of Paul's most challenging trials with the church there (2 Cor 2:13; 7:6–7, 13–15; 8:6, 16–17; 8:23; 12:18). His maturity is further seen in the fact that Paul left him in charge at Crete, a difficult area of ministry (Titus 1:4). According to 2 Tim 4:10, Titus later worked in the Roman province of Dalmatia, a region northeast of Italy.

Occasion

If the Pastoral Epistles were written by Paul, they were likely written after the imprisonment described at the end of Acts.[3] Paul's accusers from Jerusalem (Acts 24:1) probably did not take the long and arduous journey to Rome to press charges against him, and so his case was dismissed. Sometime after his release, Paul visited Ephesus and left Timothy there (1 Tim 1:3) to supervise the church and combat false teaching. Paul wrote the letter we call 1 Timothy, probably from Macedonia (1 Tim 1:3), to encourage and instruct Timothy in his ministry. Paul also visited the island of Crete with Titus and left him there to "to set right what was left undone and . . . to appoint elders in every town" (Titus 1:5). He then went on to Nicopolis in Achaia (3:12). Perhaps either from Macedonia or Nicopolis, he wrote the letter we call Titus to encourage and instruct his disciple.

Sometime after writing 1 Timothy and Titus, Paul visited Troas (2 Tim 4:13), where he was arrested again and taken to Rome. His arrest may have been part of the persecution of Christians instigated by the emperor Nero. Paul wrote 2 Timothy from

---

[3] See, for example, William C. Mounce, *Pastoral Epistles*, WBC (Nashville: Thomas Nelson, 2000), xlviii–lxix; George W. Knight, *The Pastoral Epistles: A Commentary on the Greek Text*, NIGTC (Grand Rapids: Eerdmans, 1992), 15–20. For the alternative view that they were written earlier, during the period of Acts, see Peter W. L. Walker, "Revisiting the Pastoral Epistles. Part I," *EuroJTh* 21 (2012): 4–16; Walker, "Revisiting the Pastoral Epistles. Part II," *EuroJTh* 21 (2012): 120–32.

Rome sometime around 64–67 CE. This was Paul's last letter. Church tradition tells us that soon afterward he was beheaded on the Ostian Way, west of Rome.

This route is speculative and based on incidental references in the Pastorals. Some believe that during one of these later journeys, Paul also visited Spain, since in his letter to the Romans he mentions his plans to do so (Rom 15:24).[4]

1 Timothy

Probably written from Macedonia to Timothy in Ephesus ca. 62–65 CE

Outline

I. Greeting (1:1–2)
II. Paul's Charge to Timothy: Teach the Truth and Oppose False Teachers (1:3–20)
III. Instructions Concerning Worship and Leadership in the Church (2:1–3:16)
IV. Opposing False Teachers and Pursuing Godliness (4:1–16)
V. Guidance for Various Groups in the Church (5:1–6:2)
VI. Final Warnings and Conclusion (6:3–21)

Message

First Timothy was written to help Timothy in his oversight of the church in Ephesus. Paul encourages and instructs Timothy on the issues of opposing false teachers (1:3–20; 4:1–16; 6:3–5), properly conducting worship in the church (2:9–15), appointing leaders (3:1–16), relationships within the church (widows, 5:3–16; elders, 5:17–25; masters and slaves, 6:1, 2), and the dangers of materialism (6:6–10).

Interpretive Overview

Greeting (1:1–2)

Paul identifies himself as "an apostle of Jesus Christ" and writes to Timothy, "my true son in the faith." For Christians, spiritual family relationships are even more authentic than physical ones.

---

[4] 1 Clement 5:7 says that Paul journeyed to the outer limits of the West, which could perhaps refer to Spain.

Paul's Charge to Timothy: Teach the Truth and Oppose False Teachers (1:3–20)

Paul begins by reminding Timothy of the charge that he gave him. This was to instruct the church and oppose false teachers, who were prioritizing Jewish myths, genealogies, and certain principles of the OT law instead of faith in Christ and love for others. While the law was a good gift from God, it was never meant to be a means of righteousness, but rather to convict of sin. This reality may be seen in Paul's own life. Although he was a self-righteous and arrogant persecutor of the church, God saved him by his grace. Timothy should therefore continue to fight the good fight of faith and so affirm the prophecies that were made about him when he was called to serve God. This will set him apart from false teachers like Hymenaeus and Alexander, whose faith has been shipwrecked (cf. 2 Tim 2:17–18; 4:14).

Instructions Concerning Worship and Leadership in the Church (2:1–3:16)

Paul turns next to propriety in worship, beginning with the priority of prayer. Prayers should be made for everyone, including secular leaders, since God desires all people to be saved. Men should pray and worship in a spirit of unity, without arguing with one another. Women should dress modestly and without showing off their wealth. Women should also be respectful and quiet in worship services (see sidebar 12.1: Can Women Teach Men in the Church?).

SIDEBAR 12.1: CAN WOMEN TEACH MEN IN THE CHURCH?[5]

Paul's statement in 1 Tim 2:12, "I do not permit a woman to teach or to assume authority over a man" (NIV), has been the topic of enormous controversy. "Egalitarians" claim that Paul is referring here to a specific cultural and religious situation in Ephesus and does not intend for this command to apply for all time. They point to passages like Gal 3:28, where Paul says, "There is no Jew or Greek, slave or free, male and female; since you are all one in Christ Jesus."

---

[5] For a balanced discussion of this disputed issue, see J. R. Beck, ed., *Two Views on Women in Ministry* (Grand Rapids: Zondervan, 2005).

"Complementarians," by contrast, claim that this command and others like it in the NT apply to the church of all time. They point to Paul's appeal to the order of creation in verse 13.[6]

Chapter 3 continues the theme of church order by focusing on qualifications for leaders in the church. Paul first deals with the qualifications for overseers (or "bishops"; Greek: *episkopoi*) (3:1–7). This office is likely the same as "elder" (see Titus 1:6–9, where the terms seem to be parallel). Paul stresses that what is seen on the outside—personal behavior, family relationships, reputation in the community, and so on—should reflect godly character on the inside. Next come qualifications for the office of deacon. This appears to be a more administrative and supportive office than overseer/elder, but still requires godly character and lifestyle. It is debated whether the "women" of v. 11 refer to female deacons or to the wives of deacons. In either case, they, too, must be people of faith, good character, and self-control.

Opposing False Teachers and Pursuing Godliness (4:1–16)

Paul next responds to some specific claims and actions of the false teachers, which he attributes to demonic influence (4:1–2). The first is a kind of false asceticism that claims godliness is achieved by rejecting certain good things that God has created, such as sexual relations in marriage or certain foods (4:3–5). The second is obsession with Jewish myths that have nothing to do with the practice of godliness (4:6–10). Paul encourages Timothy to boldly preach the truth and to set an example for other believers in his words and actions (4:11–16).

Guidance for Various Groups in the Church (5:1–6:2)

Paul next turns to relationships within the church. He encourages Timothy to show respect toward people of all ages (5:1–2). Then he turns to the specific issue of widows, who were among the most vulnerable members of Greco-Roman society. Families should take care of their own family members, especially the widows. Younger widows should be encouraged to remarry so as not to become a financial burden to the

[6] Publisher's note: As a confessional publisher, B&H Academic holds to the complementarian position outlined in the Baptist Faith & Message 2000.

church. Yet the church should support older widows who are truly in need (5:3–16). Elders, who are good leaders should be given special honor, especially those who take on the burden of preaching and teaching. Elders who sin should be disciplined, but only if the accusations against them are valid and supported by two or three witnesses (5:17–25). As elsewhere, Paul encourages slaves to be submissive to their masters (6:1–2; see sidebar 11.1: Why Does Paul Not Condemn Slavery?).

Final Warnings and Conclusion (6:3–21)

In his concluding instructions, Paul again warns against false teaching, arrogance, and dissension (6:3–5, 20–21). He encourages Timothy to be content in his circumstances, avoiding the dangers of greed and the seductive power of money (6:6–10, 17–19). Timothy should pursue spiritual riches, such as "righteousness, godliness, faith, love, endurance, and gentleness" (6:11). He must fight the good fight and stay true to the faith in preparation for Christ's glorious return. He must guard the rich deposit of faith that has been entrusted to him (6:11–16, 20).

Titus

Probably written from Nicopolis to Titus in Crete ca. 62–65 CE

Outline

I. Greeting (1:1–4)
II. Guidance for Various Groups in the Church (1:5–2:15)
III. Instructions for Living in State and Society (3:1–11)
IV. Conclusion (3:12–15)

Message

Titus shares many characteristics with 1 Timothy. Both relate to combating heresy, teaching sound doctrine, and appointing church leaders, as well as to relationships within the church. The closely related passages of 1 Tim 3:1–13 and Titus 1:6–9 provide qualifications for leaders. Two major themes run through this letter. First, Paul stresses the teaching of sound doctrine and warns against those who would distort the truth. Second, the letter emphasizes the importance of good works and the conduct of various groups within the church.

Interpretive Overview

Greeting (1:1–4)

Paul introduces himself as a servant (or "slave") of God and an apostle of Jesus Christ. As such, his mission is to call God's chosen people to faith and knowledge of the truth, which leads to godliness and the assured hope of eternal life (1:1–3). He is writing to Titus, whom—like Timothy (1 Tim 1:2; cf. 2 Tim 1:2)—he calls "my true son" in the faith. He gives his traditional greeting, "Grace to you and peace" from God the Father and Christ Jesus our Savior. This title, "Savior," is Paul's favorite in this letter, appearing six times and applied to both the Father and the Son (1:3, 4; 2:10, 13; 3:4, 6). It occurs four other times in the Pastorals (1 Tim 1:1; 2:3; 4:10; 2 Tim 1:10) and only twice elsewhere in Paul's letters (Eph 5:23; Phil 3:20).

Guidance for Various Groups in the Church (1:5–2:15)

Paul says that he left Titus in Crete to appoint elders in the churches of various towns. As in 1 Tim 3:1–7, he provides a list of qualifications, focusing on godly character and behavior, and the ability to teach sound doctrine. This last is essential in Crete, since there are rebellious teachers present who are distorting the truth and disturbing whole households. Paul blames this in part on the low moral character of Cretans, citing a Cretan prophet who said that "Cretans are always liars, evil beasts, lazy gluttons"![7] This testimony is true, Paul says. As in 1 Timothy, these opponents appear to be Judaizers ("of the circumcision party"; 1:10), who are teaching an ascetic legalism and are obsessed with debates about Jewish myths and genealogies (1:10, 14–17; 3:9) and are themselves motivated by greed (1:11).

Paul continues with instructions for teaching various age groups within the church (2:1–8). The older people should be an example of faith, love, and self-discipline for the younger, and Titus himself should be an example for all. Wives should love and submit to their husbands and slaves should respect and submit to their masters. Living in this peaceable manner is essential for the spread of the gospel in this interim period, the "present age": "while we wait for the blessed hope, the appearing of the glory of our great God and Savior, Jesus Christ. He gave himself for us to redeem us from all lawlessness and cleanse for himself a people for his own possession, eager to do good works" (Titus 2:13–14).

---

[7] Probably citing the fifth- or sixty-century BCE philosopher Epimenides. See Towner, *Letters to Timothy and Titus*, 700–701.

Instructions for Living in State and Society (3:1–11)

From relationships within the church, Paul turns to societal relationships in general. He encourages Titus to teach submission to rulers and authorities. Believers should live in a countercultural manner by doing good works, slandering no one, and showing kindness and gentleness to others (3:1–3). This reflects the kindness and love of God, our Savior, who saved us. This was not on the basis of anything we have done, but according to his mercy which he revealed in Jesus Christ and in the Holy Spirit he has given (3:4–8). Paul concludes this section by returning to a warning against false teachers and those who are divisive within the church (3:9–11).

Conclusion (3:12–15)

Paul concludes the letter with personal instructions (3:12–13), a final call for good works (3:14), greetings, and a benediction (3:15). When Paul sends Artemis or Tychicus as Titus's replacement,[8] Titus should come to Paul in Nicopolis, where he is spending the winter. He also encourages Titus to aid and support two men on their journeys, Zenas the lawyer and Apollos.[9] Apollos is probably the gifted preacher and apologist mentioned in both Acts and Paul's letters (Acts 18:24–28; 19:1; 1 Cor 1:12; 3:4–6, 22; 16:12). The two are probably mentioned here because they are traveling missionaries, coming to preach in Crete. Such missionaries were supported by the hospitality given by local Christians (see 3 John 5–10).

2 Timothy

Written from prison in Rome ca. 64–67 CE

Outline

I. Greeting (1:1–2)
II. Thanksgiving and Charge to Faithfulness (1:3–18)
III. Renewed Charge to Strength and Endurance (2:1–13)

---

[8] See Acts 20:4; Eph 6:21; Col 4:7; 2 Tim 4:12.

[9] The Greek term for "lawyer" (*nomikos*) here may mean a Greco-Roman barrister, or it may mean a Jewish scribe/expert in the law (cf. Luke 10:25), who in this case has come to follow Christ.

IV. Warning Against False Teachers (2:14–3:17)
V. Final Charge to Timothy (4:1–22)

Message

Second Timothy represents a passing of the torch. In a cold and dingy dungeon in Rome, Paul is well aware that his time on earth is drawing to a close. Deeply missing his friends, he encourages Timothy to come and visit him. Meanwhile, he calls on Timothy to carry on the ministry that the Lord had given him with faithfulness and endurance. The letter is a combat manual for spiritual warfare. Paul exhorts Timothy as a good soldier of Jesus Christ to use the spiritual weapon of the Word of God to overcome all obstacles to the spread of the gospel. He appeals to him to "guard the good deposit" that was entrusted to him (1:14), to preserve, protect, and pass on the message of salvation.

Interpretive Overview

Greeting (1:1–2)

In this second letter to Timothy, Paul identifies himself as an apostle of Christ Jesus by God's will "for the sake of the promise of life in Christ Jesus." The promise of life—abundant life in the present and eternal life in the future—is particularly compelling to someone who is facing impending death. Whereas in the previous letter he addressed Timothy as "my true son in the faith," now he refers to him as "my dearly loved son." Paul's emotions are on his sleeve in this intimate letter.

Thanksgiving and Charge to Faithfulness (1:3–18)

After a greeting of "grace, mercy, and peace," more emotions are evident as Paul remembers the joys and sorrows he and Timothy have experienced (1:3–4). He thanks God for the spiritual heritage Timothy received through his grandmother Lois and mother, Eunice (1:5; cf. Acts 16:1). On the basis of this heritage, Paul encourages Timothy to reignite the spiritual gifts and the passion he received when Paul first commissioned him. Timothy need not be ashamed of the gospel message or its humble messengers like Paul. Despite the derision and suffering that so often accompany Christian service, Timothy can preach boldly and without fear, because this "shameful" gospel has the power to abolish death and bring life and immortality (1:8–12).

In light of this confidence, Paul calls on Timothy to preserve and pass on the gospel message that was entrusted to him. He provides examples of some who are and who are not doing this. Those in the province of Asia, including Phygelus and Hermogenes, had deserted him. But Onesiphorus, at great personal cost, had supported him (1:15–18).

Renewed Charge to Strength and Endurance (2:1–13)

A new charge begins here, as Paul encourages Timothy to "be strong in the grace that is in Christ Jesus" and to pass on this faith to others. As Paul trained his replacement in Timothy and others, so Timothy should carry on this discipling ministry (2:1–2). Using three metaphors—a soldier, an athlete, and a farmer—Paul encourages Timothy to steadfast devotion, discipline, and hard work (2:3–7). A steadfast focus on Christ will enable him to endure all things in this life and so to reign with Christ in the next (2:8–13).

Warning Against False Teachers (2:14–3:17)

Paul next turns to the dangers of false teaching. He first addresses those who engage in divisive and destructive arguments and word battles. These arguments are of no value and lead to the ruin of those who practice them. Timothy needs to combat such disputes by being "a worker who doesn't need to be ashamed, correctly teaching the word of truth" (2:15). Paul names two offenders, Hymenaeus (mentioned in 1 Tim 1:20) and Philetus. Their error was in claiming that the resurrection had already taken place (2:14–18). This may refer to a proto-gnostic teaching that denied a bodily resurrection, replacing it with a spiritual resurrection in the present (cf. 1 Cor 15:12–19; see Ancient Connections 10.1). In any case, Paul seems most concerned that this teaching is causing divisiveness and destroying faith. The antidote is to purify oneself from anything dishonorable (2:20–21), to flee youthful passions, and to pursue righteousness, faith, love, and peace (2:22–24). In this way, they will escape the trap of the devil, who is using these divisive people to do his will (2:25–26).

Timothy should not be surprised by the presence of these false teachers, since Scripture predicts that "hard times will come in the last days" (3:1). Paul provides a list of almost twenty vices that will be characteristic of this period. He singles out in particular some who "worm their way into households and deceive gullible women overwhelmed by sins" (3:6). This was evidently a problem at Ephesus and one of the ways false teachers were influencing the community. Paul compares these false teachers to

Jannes and Jambres, the traditional names of the Egyptian magicians who opposed Moses and were eventually unmasked as frauds (see Ancient Connections 12.1).

To avoid such errors, Paul tells Timothy to follow Paul's own example of teaching, conduct, purpose, faith, patience, love, and endurance. This includes the persecution and suffering he endured from the early days of the Gentile mission in Antioch, Iconium, and Lystra (cf. Acts 13–14). Such suffering should not come as a surprise, since "all who want to live a godly life in Christ Jesus will be persecuted" (3:12). Timothy will endure if he keeps himself rooted in the truths of Scripture, which he has learned since infancy. Such training is successful, since all Scripture is inspired by God and is profitable for spiritual growth and correction (3:14–17). (See Old Testament Connections at the end of this chapter.)

ANCIENT CONNECTIONS 12.1: WHO WERE JANNES AND JAMBRES?

Readers who know the Old Testament account of the Exodus might be surprised to learn in 2 Tim 3:7–8 that the Egyptian magicians who resisted Moses were named "Jannes and Jambres." While the account in Exodus speaks of Pharaoh's magicians, these opponents are not named (Exod 7:11, 22; 8:7, 18, 19; 9:11). Various later Jewish and Christian traditions, however, identify them as Jannes (or Hebrew *Yoḥanah*) and Jambres (sometimes "Mambres"), and a whole body of stories and legends arose around their exploits and ultimate demise. Most traditions identify them as brothers and magicians who were in league with the devil in opposition to Moses. Their schemes failed, however, and they were struck with disease.[10]

The earliest record of the tradition appears in the Damascus Document, from about 100 BCE. It reads, "For in earlier times Moses and Aaron arose with the help of the Prince of Lights, while Belial raised up Yoḥanah and his brother" (CD 5, 17b–19). The most detailed description of the brothers appears in an apocryphal work known as *Jannes and Jambres*, likely composed sometime from the first through the third centuries CE.[11]

---

[10] See Albert Pietersma, "Jannes and Jambres," in *ABD* 3:638–40. In another version of the story, coming from the pagan writer Numenius (second c. CE) and reported by the early church historian Eusebius, Jannes and Jambres were able to undo even the greatest of the plagues brought against Egypt (Eusebius, *Praeparatio evangelica* 9.8).

[11] For the text and description, see A. Pietersma and R. T. Lutz, "Jannes and Jambres," in *OTP* 2:427–42.

Final Charge to Timothy (4:1–22)

Paul's final words to Timothy are truly inspiring. He charges him to "preach the word; be ready in season and out of season; rebuke, correct, and encourage with great patience and teaching" (4:2). Though people will increasingly reject the truth, Paul calls on Timothy to remain faithful to the end, just as Paul has. He has fought the good fight, finished the race, and kept the faith (4:7).

In a series of final instructions, Paul urges Timothy to come and visit. He mentions some who have deserted him and others who were pursuing ministries elsewhere. Only Luke remains with him. He asks Timothy to bring Mark, who is now a useful partner in ministry. This is almost certainly John Mark, who had deserted Paul and Barnabas on their first missionary journey (Acts 13:13; 15:36–40). Mark has obviously redeemed himself in Paul's eyes and proven himself faithful in ministry.[12] Paul then warns Timothy about Alexander the coppersmith, who did Paul great harm, and speaks sorrowfully about those who deserted him at his first trial. His faith, however, remains in the Lord, who has always stood by him and will ultimately bring him into the eternal safety of his heavenly kingdom (4:14–18). Paul concludes with greetings from friends and ministry partners and a final benediction (4:19–22).

Old Testament Connections

Perhaps the most important connection to the Hebrew Scriptures found in the Pastoral Epistles is not a citation from the OT,[13] but the paradigmatic statement on the inspiration and authority of Scripture found in 2 Tim 3:16–17. The statement comes in the context of Paul's discussion of the important role the Scriptures have played in Timothy's spiritual development. In contrast to the false teachers, Timothy is well grounded in the truth because he has been taught by reliable teachers and because "from infancy you have known the sacred Scriptures, which are able to give you wisdom for salvation through faith in Christ Jesus" (3:15). This leads to a description of the nature and function of Scripture: "All Scripture is

---

[12] Further evidence of John Mark's restoration is his ministry with Peter in Rome (1 Pet 5:13) and his likely authorship of the Second Gospel. See M. L. Strauss, *Mark*, ZECNT (Grand Rapids: Zondervan, 2014), 28–32.

[13] For a survey of the distinctive use of the OT in the Pastorals, see P. H. Towner, "Timothy and Titus, Letters to," in *DNTUOT*, 852; Towner, "1–2 Timothy and Titus," in *CNTUOT*, 891–918, and the bibliography cited there.

God-breathed and is useful for teaching, rebuking, correcting and training in righteousness, so that the servant of God may be thoroughly equipped for every good work" (2 Tim 3:16–17 NIV).

The term translated here as "God-breathed" is the adjective *theopneustos*. This seems to be the earliest appearance of this word in Greek literature, so its meaning must be determined from its context and its etymology, combining *theos* (god/God) with *pneustos* (related to breath, wind, blowing), hence "inspired by God" (most versions) or "God-breathed" (NIV). The sense is that God is the ultimate agent behind the message of Scripture.

(1) Some have claimed that *theopneustos* is an attributive adjective modifying "Scripture," rather than a predicate adjective, so the sentence should be translated, "All Scripture *that is God-breathed* is profitable . . ."). This would limit inspiration to only part of Scripture. This reading is unlikely for several reasons: (a) The two adjectives, *theopneustos* and *ōphelimos* ("God-breathed and profitable"), make the best sense when read in parallel, rather than the first being attributive and the second predicate. (b) The idea of the partial inspiration of Scripture is alien to the context, where Paul is affirming the powerful impact Scripture as a whole has had on Timothy's Jewish upbringing.

(2) Others point out that this passage concerns the inspiration of the Old Testament, not the New Testament. This is technically true. "Scripture" (*graphē*) here certainly refers to the OT, since the NT canon was not yet established. Yet the inclusion of the NT books as similarly inspired Scripture was a natural and nearly inevitable development. The events of the life, death, and resurrection of Jesus and the expansion of the church were viewed by the early Christians as *the continuation of the OT story and the fulfillment of its covenants, promises and prophecies*. This accounts for the nearly immediate and universal recognition that the teachings of Jesus recorded in the four Gospels and the writings of the apostles were authoritative and inspired. This development can be seen in seminal form in passages like 2 Pet 3:15–16, where Paul's letters are identified as "Scripture," and in 1 Tim 5:18, where "Scripture says" apparently refers to both an OT text (Deut 25:4) and a saying of Jesus (Luke 10:7).[14] Paul clearly sees both his preaching and his writings as carrying prophetic authority as the word of God for the people of God (1 Thess 2:13; 1 Cor 7:40; 11:2; 2 Cor 13:10; 1 Thess 5:27; 2 Thess 3:6; Col 4:16).

---

[14] Mounce, *Pastoral Epistles*, 568.

Gospel Connections

The Pastoral Epistles contain five statements that are introduced with the formula, "this saying is trustworthy" (*pistos ho logos*; 1 Tim 1:15–17; 3:1; 4:9; 2 Tim 2:11; Titus 3:8).[15] This formula likely means that this is a creedal statement that the author has introduced at this point. In the same way that Christians today write songs, hymns, and poems about their faith, so the early Christians expressed their beliefs in similar ways. These songs or poems were subsequently picked up and quoted by others. A number of these hymn-like constructions appear in the New Testament, including the Prologue to John's Gospel (John 1:1–18); the *Carmen Christi*, or great "Hymn to Christ" in Phil 2:5–11; the Christological hymn/poem of Col 1:15–20; and perhaps others (Rom 1:3–4; Heb 1:1–3; 1 Pet 2:21–25). In some cases, the author of the book or letter may have composed the song or poem themselves. In others, they were likely quoting a well-known hymn. It is not surprising that five of these kinds of creedal statements appear in the Pastoral Epistles, since in these letters Paul places such a high value on the preservation and passing down of the treasured truths of the Christian message.

Life Connections

"Discipleship" means training and passing leadership on to others. Jesus established the model of discipleship when "he appointed twelve, whom he also named apostles, to be with him, to send them out to preach, and to have authority to drive out demons" (Mark 3:14–15). Jesus trained these disciples by living as an example for them and then sending them out to replicate his ministry.

No letter of Paul illustrates the principles of discipleship better than 2 Timothy. Paul has taught and trained Timothy. He has sent him out on challenging tasks and then supported and encouraged him in those tasks. Now, he is passing the torch of leadership and training on to him. Second Timothy 2:2 is often viewed as a paradigmatic statement on discipleship: "And the things you have heard me say in the presence of many witnesses entrust to reliable people who will also be qualified to teach others" (NIV). Timothy is to take teaching and training that Paul has modeled for him and to entrust it to others, who will then pass it on to still others.

---

[15] Two of these add "and worthy of full acceptance" (1 Tim 1:15; 4:9). On their background and content, see G. W. Knight, *The Faithful Sayings in the Pastoral Letters* (Kampen: Kok, 1968); R. A. Campbell, "Identifying the Faithful Sayings in the Pastoral Epistles," *JSNT* 54 (1994), 73–86; Towner, *Letters to Timothy*, 143–54; I. H. Marshall, *The Pastoral Epistles: A Critical and Exegetical Commentary*, ICC (Edinburgh: T&T Clark, 2004), 326–30; Mounce, *Pastoral Epistles*, 48–49.

This principle of a disciple-making ministry confirms that the most important role of any Christian leader is to train their replacement, to equip and empower others to carry on after them. Sadly, Christian leadership is often about building one's own personal kingdom and then hanging on to power as long as possible. Instead, it should be about preparing others, and empowering them to build not their own kingdom, but the kingdom of God.

Interactive Questions

1. What are the major challenges to Pauline authorship of the Pastoral Epistles? How do those defending Pauline authorship respond to these?

2. What do we know about Timothy from the book of Acts and the letters of Paul?

3. What is the occasion of 1 Timothy? (Where is Timothy? Where is Paul and why is he writing to Timothy?)

4. What is the nature of false teaching that Paul addresses in 1 Timothy?

5. What do we know about Titus from the letters of Paul?

6. What is the occasion of Titus? (Where is Titus? Where is Paul and why is he writing to Titus?)

7. What does Paul say about the character of the people of Crete and how does this create challenges for Titus?

8. What is the occasion of 2 Timothy? (Where is Timothy? Where is Paul and why is he writing to him?)

9. Why does Paul place so much emphasis on the preservation of sound doctrine in the Pastoral Epistles?

10. What does 2 Tim 3:16–17 teach about the inspiration and authority of the Bible?

11. How might reading the Pastoral Epistles benefit Christians today?

Study Resources

Belleville, Linda. "1 Timothy," in *1 Timothy, 2 Timothy, Titus, Hebrews*. Cornerstone Biblical Commentary. Carol Stream, IL: Tyndale House, 2009.

Fee, Gordon D. *1 and 2 Timothy, Titus*. NIBC. Peabody, MA: Hendrickson, 1995.

Johnson, Luke Timothy. *The First and Second Letters to Timothy*. Anchor Bible. New York: Doubleday, 2001.

———. *Letters to Paul's Delegates*. NT in Context. Valley Forge, PA: Trinity Press International, 1996.

Knight, George W. *The Pastoral Epistles: A Commentary on the Greek Text*. NIGTC. Grand Rapids: Eerdmans, 1992.

Marshall, I. Howard. *The Pastoral Epistles: A Critical and Exegetical Commentary*. ICC. Edinburgh: T&T Clark, 2004.

Mounce, William C. *Pastoral Epistles*. WBC. Nashville: Thomas Nelson, 2000.

Padilla, Osvaldo. *The Pastoral Epistles: An Introduction and Commentary*. TNTC. Downers Grove, IL: IVP Academic, 2022.

Pao, David. *1 Timothy, 2 Timothy and Titus*. BECS. Leiden: Brill, 2023.

Spencer, Aída Besançon. *1 Timothy*. NCCS. Eugene, OR: Cascade Books, 2013.

———. *2 Timothy and Titus*. NCCS. Eugene, OR: Cascade Books, 2014.

Towner, Philip. *The Letters to Timothy and Titus*. NICNT. Grand Rapids: Eerdmans, 2006.

Yarbrough, Robert W. *The Letters to Timothy and Titus*. PNTC. Grand Rapids: Eerdmans, 2018.

SUBJECT INDEX

F

G

R

V

W

Z

SCRIPTURE INDEX

2 Corinthians

Galatians

Ephesians

Philippians

Colossians

1 Thessalonians

2 Thessalonians

1 Timothy

2 Timothy